Harbour City

Nanaimo in Transition, 1920–1967

Harbour City

Nanaimo in Transition, 1920–1967

Jan Peterson

VICTORIA • VANCOUVER • CALGARY

Copyright © 2006 Jan Peterson

All rights reserved. No part of this publication may be reproduced, stored in a retrieval system, or transmitted in any form or by any means—electronic, mechanical, audio recording, or otherwise—without the written permission of the publisher or a photocopying licence from Access Copyright, Toronto, Canada.

Heritage House Publishing Company Ltd.
#108 – 17665 66A Avenue
Surrey, BC V3S 2A7
www.heritagehouse.ca

Library and Archives Canada Cataloguing in Publication

Peterson, Jan, 1937-
Harbour city: Nanaimo in transition, 1920-1967 / Jan Peterson.

Includes bibliographical references and index.

ISBN-13: 978-1-894974-20-2
ISBN-10: 1-894974-20-4

1. Nanaimo (B.C.)—History—20th century. I. Title.

FC3849.N35P472 2006 971.1'2 C2006-904153-9

Edited by Ursula Vaira
Book design and layout by Darlene Nickull
Cover design by Frances Hunter
Front cover: *Princess Marguerite* at the CPR wharf, Cameron island, Nanaimo, painted by marine artist Michael Dean.
Back cover: Photo of the Great National Land Building by the author. The Nanaimo Coat of Arms, designed by city engineer Arthur Leynard, was officially registered by the College of Arms in England on September 28, 1951. Reproduced with permission.

Printed in Canada

Heritage House acknowledges the financial support for its publishing program from the Government of Canada through the Book Publishing Industry Development Program (BPIDP), Canada Council for the Arts, and the province of British Columbia through the British Columbia Arts Council and the Book Publishing Tax Credit.

Contents

Acknowledgements 7

Introduction 9

Chapter One: The Roaring Twenties 11

Chapter Two: Lawmakers, Rum-Runners, and Game Poachers 22

Chapter Three: Mining Communities and Mine Safety 29

Chapter Four: Making a Difference 37

Chapter Five: Building a Future 49

Chapter Six: Changes in Education 59

Chapter Seven: Fire and Brimstone 66

Chapter Eight: The Emergence of the CCF 79

Chapter Nine: The Depression Years 86

Chapter Ten: Doctors and Their Clinics 97

Chapter Eleven: The Depression Ends 102

Chapter Twelve: The Harbour, Wharves, and Ferries 110

Chapter Thirteen: The Second World War: Defending Freedom 118

Chapter Fourteen: Peace with a Price 132

Chapter Fifteen: The Postwar Period 140

Chapter Sixteen: A Growing Forest Industry 153

Chapter Seventeen: Mayors and Aldermen, 1920–1967 163

Chapter Eighteen: The Fabulous Fifties 170

Chapter Nineteen: The Sixties 188

Chapter Twenty: The Future Secured, History Preserved 197

Epilogue 204

Appendix I 206

Appendix II 207

Appendix III 210

Appendix IV 211

Appendix V 212

Endnotes 213

Bibliography 226

Index 232

Photo Credits 238

Acknowledgements

I would like to acknowledge the help received from the Nanaimo Community Archives and the volunteers who work there. Archives manager Christine Meutzner and assistant Dawn Arnot were especially helpful, as were volunteers Jill Stannard, Daphne Paterson, Shirley Bateman, and Anne Royle. Christine and Daphne also scrutinized the manuscript. I also thank the Nanaimo Historical Society, the Nanaimo District Museum, and the Vancouver Island Regional Library. Among the many individuals and organizations that helped along the way are Gordon Miller, Parker Williams, Albert Dunn, Rollie Rose, Robert and Lionel Beevor-Potts, Joe and Olive Annau, the Nanaimo Golf Club, Denise Wood of the Nanaimo Curling Club, and Parks, Recreation and Culture staff.

I also thank editor Ursula Vaira whose skill brought the manuscript to publication. Heritage House gets a big thank you for publishing this trilogy about Nanaimo, and for its dedication to authors of regional history.

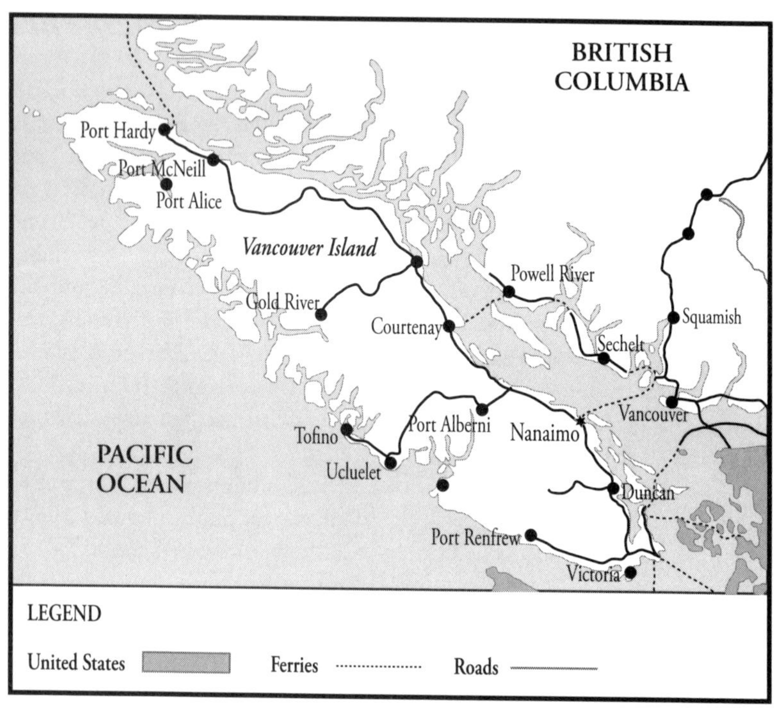
BRITISH
COLUMBIA
Port Hardy
Port McNeill
Port Alice
Vancouver Island
Gold River
Powell River
Courtenay
Squamish
Sechelt
Vancouver
Port Alberni
Nanaimo
Tofino
Ucluelet
PACIFIC
OCEAN
Duncan
Port Renfrew
Victoria
LEGEND
United States
Ferries
Roads

Introduction

Nanaimo is situated in Central Vancouver Island on the west coast of Canada. Since its birth in 1852, the town known for its coal-mining resources was officially named Colevilletown before being named Nanaimo, but nicknames were added to the mix, including Newcastle of the Pacific Coast, Black Diamond City, and Hub City. These names only indicate the city's history, not a search for identity. Today it is known as the Harbour City, drawing attention to the importance of its harbour sheltered by Newcastle, Protection, and Gabriola islands. The city nestles between the mountains and the sea. To the west is Mount Benson, and to the east are the Strait of Georgia and the snow-capped mountains of the mainland. Over the years this beautiful historic city has witnessed and been part of the growth of Vancouver Island.

The rich coal was first mined by the Hudson's Bay Company, then later by the Vancouver Coal Mining and Land Company of Great Britain; it helped support the fledgling colony of Vancouver Island until it became part of the province of British Columbia. In 1903 the Western Fuel Company purchased the company, then sold it in 1928 to Canadian Collieries (Dunsmuir) Ltd., which operated it until the end of the Depression.

The city and the early mines were first located along the shoreline. Later as the mines expanded, seeking to tap into the three prominent coal seams, the Douglas, the Newcastle, and the Wellington, new communities such as Cassidy, Cedar, Extension, Ladysmith, Lantzville and Nanoose were developed. The markets for coal were the United States, Central America, Hawaii, Alaska, and Asia. The population of Nanaimo in 1921 was 6,304. Only another 441 people were added to the census by 1931.

As fuel oil replaced coal, forestry became the city's main economic engine. The building of the pulp mill Harmac in 1950 and the development of the seaport brought increased employment opportunities for workers in the declining mining industry.

Harbour City traces the development of the city of Nanaimo and the people who made it happen. Interwoven in the story are the lives of ordinary people who achieved success in various fields such as music, science, sports and politics. The Roaring 20s, the Depression years, another world war, and the following boom times are all absorbed into this wide-brush portrait of historical Nanaimo.

Chapter One

The Roaring Twenties

The Sounds of Nanaimo

The rhythm of the day in Nanaimo was set by mine whistles and by the chimes of "Big Frank," the Dominion Post Office clock. Time passed with unbroken regularity—morning, noon, and night whistles sounded as men streamed back and forth to work. Bells and whistles also rang out in celebration of New Year's Eve and other happy occasions. The mournful whistle of the CPR's E & N Railway passenger and freight trains as they approached each crossing added to the cacophony of sounds.

Ship horns, foghorns, and ferry engines broke the silence of an early morning or late evening. Western Fuel Company miners digging deep under the harbour and under Protection Island and Northumberland channels regulated their day to the throb of ship's engines passing overhead. They set their clocks by the whistle of the CPR *Princess Patricia* as she left for Vancouver. Women listened for the five o'clock pit steam horn to tell them the shift was over and their husbands, sons, or brothers would be home soon. Their workday began at 7:00 a.m. and ended at 5:00 p.m., except for when work finished at 1:00 p.m.[1]

The harbour and the mud flats of the Nanaimo River also had their share of noisemakers. Gulls squawked overhead when an eagle entered their space; crows and starlings competed with them for food and space, and the magnificent blue heron gave its eerie, almost prehistoric, cry as it came to rest along the shoreline. In the fall, flocks of geese and ducks flying in formation as they prepared for another migration added to the sights and sounds. Everything in the sky and in the water was on the move!

The first airplane, the *Pathfinder II*, touched down in Nanaimo on August 4, 1919. The strange noise brought residents rushing from their homes and looking to the sky. The plane had left Victoria that morning, travelling at 80 miles per hour, carrying the first airmail on Vancouver Island by special arrangement with the postal authorities. This new form of transportation had proved itself in the First World War; now it began to play an increasingly important role in the movement of goods and services in the province. There was no radio communication, so pilots took along pigeons to send messages back to base in case of a forced landing or other emergency.[2] Ten years later service clubs such as the Rotary, Gyro, and Kiwanis advocated that a progressive city like Nanaimo should have airmail service to Vancouver. The first Vancouver Airport was established at Lulu Island, Richmond, in 1929, then moved to Sea Island. Nanaimo had to wait for another world war before it got its own airstrip.

The automobile, first a curiosity, became a status symbol for the wealthy. It was already in use in Nanaimo before the First World War. The first automobile came via the Malahat from Victoria in 1906. Robert Hutchison drove it with passenger Walter Thompson, who was then the operator of a horse-drawn stagecoach running between Nanaimo and Alberni. The car was a 1906 single-cylinder eight-horsepower. Oldsmobile, and it made the trip to Nanaimo in four hours and 30 minutes. Residents turned out en masse to see their first horseless buggy. Hutchison wanted to prove to Thompson that cars were really as practical for use on the stage route. He didn't make the sale.[3] A year later, three Nanaimo men, Dr. J.H. Hogle, George Fletcher, and Guy Burnham, each bought into this futuristic form of transportation by buying their own automobiles.

The first annual licence fee was set in 1903 at $36. In 1907, 175 vehicles were registered in the province.[4] The Victoria Automobile Club was founded in 1906 for motoring enthusiasts to help each other when their vehicles broke down. This was the beginning of the British Columbia Automobile Association (BCAA). By 1915, the BCAA had its own newsletter, and by 1936, membership included emergency roadside service with free towing.

By 1920, mass production and declining prices made cars more widely available for transportation and for recreation. There were 18,000 car licences in the province, and a decade later this number had increased to 100,000. The car was here to stay, and the horses that had once provided such stalwart service were put out to pasture. More cars also meant improved roads. The Island Highway now stretched from Victoria to Campbell River.

The trip over the Malahat was still a difficult one for those early roadsters, for by the time they reached the summit after the long gruelling drive, thirsty radiators almost ended the trip. A roadside spring provided the remedy. In 1925, at the north end of the Malahat Drive, where horses once drank from a wooden trough, the Nanaimo Rotary Club and the Victoria Rotary Club joined forces to provide a new concrete trough and watering fountain for cars. The official dedication ceremony was held on April 28, 1925. Later guests enjoyed dinner at the Tzouhalem Hotel in Duncan. The headlines on that date read: "Big Rotary Party to Open Malahat Drinking Fountain."[5] It is interesting that the Victoria Rotarians travelling by car used the Mill Bay ferry to get to their destination, avoiding the Malahat altogether.

Cars drove on the left side of the road in the early '20s. Premier John Oliver anticipated a road to California and decided British Columbians would conform to American rules. William Rae, Government Inspector of Equipment, gave the official notice of the change at a meeting of the Vancouver Automobile Rule of the Road Committee in October 1921. At precisely 6:00 a.m. on January 1, 1922, drivers switched from left to right.[6] The change applied at first to the Lower Mainland and Vancouver Island. Eventually the entire province changed sides.

An auto mechanic school opened in Nanaimo on March 20, 1921. The Hemphill Auto and Tractor School taught drivers how to repair cars, tractors, trucks, and gasoline engines. The school had branches across Canada and in the U.S. Advertisements stated, "Those who only know their car from a catalogue can take a course at this school and learn to know and talk the good points of their car."[7]

In 1921 a good used Ford Touring 1918 model sold for $500, a 1918 Chevrolet Touring car for $750, and a Saxon Light "Six" car could be purchased at Weeks Motors Ltd. for $1,000.[8]

Some time passed before people became accustomed to automobile traffic. Even in 1925, there were still a number of people injured while crossing streets at intersections. "There is a need to educate pedestrians," advised Chief of Police John Shirras in his annual report to city council.[9] He suggested a signal light with a large red globe could alert drivers to drive slowly. He identified the dangerous spots at Bastion and Commercial, Wallace and Albert, and by the Dominion Post Office.

William E. Morrissey applied to the city to install a gasoline pump and a 15-gallon storage tank at Selby Street, and George A. Rosewall wanted to install one on Comox Road.[10]

All That Jazz

The '20s were marked by an explosion of music and dance. Radio was introduced after the war. The first legislation governing transmission was passed in 1913, and by 1920 the first radio program in Canada was broadcast from Montreal. Soon there were a number of private stations established around the country. Most carried U.S. programs. The first three radio stations in B.C. were licensed in 1922 and were all owned by newspapers such as the *Vancouver Sun*, *The Province*, and the *World*. Most operated only a few hours a day. It wasn't until the late '20s that Earle Kelly, a *Province* reporter, pioneered news broadcasts.

The first radio station in Nanaimo was CFDC; it went on the air in 1923. The call letters were thought to mean Canada Frequency-Direct Current. The radio station was an experiment of Arthur "Sparks" Holstead and William Hanlon. The two transmitter towers, 65 feet high, were built of wooden laths. Their power supply came from a 500-volt wet cell battery with an output of 10 watts.

The two men worked from a studio in a building owned by Holstead and located behind another of his businesses, Willard Service Station & Auto Electricians, at Wallace and Fitzwilliam streets, the location today of New York Pizza. Here he sold Willard storage batteries, RCA radio sets, cord tires, and automobile electrical equipment; he also provided service.[11] The service station had facilities for truckers and teamsters to wash up after their travels—the first truck stop on Vancouver Island. The radio station was more a hobby than a paying proposition.

Holstead and Hanlon were soon surprised to learn that their radio signal and call letters were being picked up as far away as eastern Canada, the United States, and New Zealand. Meanwhile, people living in Nanaimo and Chase River had difficulty picking up the signal on their crystal sets. The

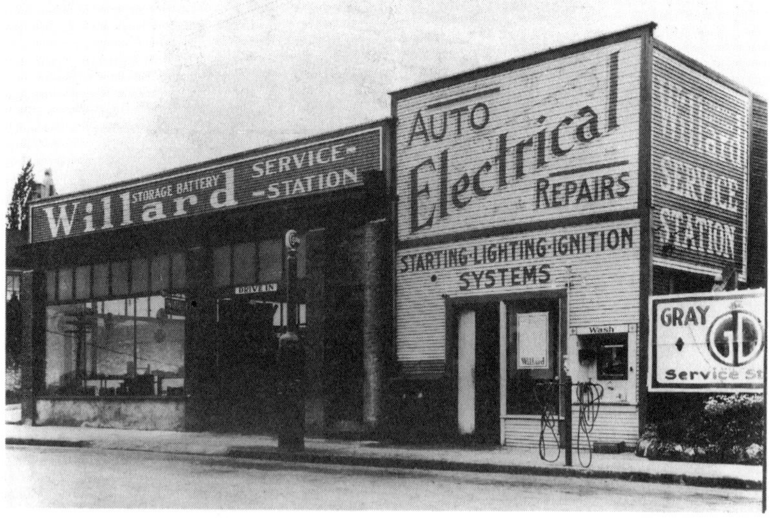

The Willard Street Service Station, at the corner of Wallace and Fitzwilliam streets, was the site of the first radio broadcast in Nanaimo. The station had facilities for truckers and teamsters to wash up, so it was also the first truck stop on Vancouver Island. The radio station was more a hobby than a paying proposition for owner Arthur "Sparks" Holstead.

popular "experiment" soon drew the attention of authorities. One day there was a knock at the studio door—it was the licence inspector from Victoria. They were ordered to "cease and desist."[12]

In 1926, Holstead married Robina Godfrey, and before long the transmitter, assessors, and other items, minus the poles, were packed up in suitcases and on their way with the young couple to Vancouver. Holstead went on the air, but the federal government's broadcasting regulatory agency objected and ordered him off. Petitions demanded the station's return, and finally, with the consent of authorities, Hosltead returned to broadcasting on April 1, 1928. The call letters CFDC were changed to CKWX, a popular radio station still going strong today in Vancouver. Arthur (Sparks) Holstead died in 1971 at age 81.

Judge Stanley Wardill remembered the first time he heard radio "at Doug Manson's house around 1928. I can remember sitting with the earphones saying, 'I can hear Vancouver. I can hear Vancouver.' It was tremendous."[13]

The Canadian Broadcasting Corporation (CBC) was formed in 1936. Nellie McClung was on the first Board of Governors of the corporation. In 1937, almost 60 percent of all Canadians received CBC radio. She said:

> Radio has got to be good, or else it will prove a loss to us. In past days the families would spend the evening reading, or singing around the organ or attending singing classes. Now families sit around the radio and radio must be as good a substitute for the old days. Radio can be a golden shuttle welding the people of Canada together.[14]

An early broadcast about Nanaimo was heard over CBC radio on November 21, 1937, when Bruce A. McKelvie, a Victoria reporter, and B.C. historian E.V. Young presented a program entitled "Within These Walls." The program told the story of the historic Bastion.[15]

In the '20s, local dance halls jumped to jazz music, and the Charleston became the dance craze. "Up on your heels, down on your toes ... " began instructions for dancing the Charleston. The dance cut across age lines; middle-aged ballroom dancers were doing it in 4/4 time, and those who usually loathed exertion stood perfectly still while criss-crossing their hands back and forth across their knees.

Up and down the Island, young people were kicking up their heels and indulging in what seemed like a frenzy of rebellion against the standards and values of their parents and grandparents. According to some this was a youth revolt and a sign of serious moral crisis. The new styles of dress and dance were singled out as the chief culprits, and this new type of music was too much for some. The flapper dress, with its drop waist and its pleated or fringed skirt, became popular.

In 1921, a delegation of citizens approached city council asking that something be done about jazzing at local dances. A few aldermen at first suggested it was something the police should look into, then opted to have the Police Commission instruct its officers to see that dances were conducted in a "fitting and proper manner."[16]

This prompted a letter to the editor of the *Nanaimo Free Press*:

> Dear Sir:
>
> I notice in your report of Monday night's Council meeting an item asking the Mayor to rid the city of rats, dogs and jazz dancing. I think the parties that started the holler about jazz dancing really meant the "shimmie" as the fox trot and one-step are always called jazz dances, and if you take these off your programme, what do you have left? If the public could see these dances (the fox trot and one-step) danced correct, they would really enjoy them. Therefore, it is up to the parties running dances to see all dances are danced correct. This will give no cause for complaint from either party concerned.
>
> What it takes to stop jazz dancing (not the shimmie):
>
> 1st. The party giving dances must not have fox trots or one-steps on their programmes.
>
> 2nd. If fox trots and one-steps on said programme, stop musicians from playing jazz music, which in all cases is the cause of jazz dancing.
>
> 3rd. In order to stop musicians from playing jazz music you will have to stop music companies from publishing same, which is an impossibility.
>
> 'Tis folly to have jazz dances on your programme and expect not to have jazz dancing. Remember jazz dancing is not the "shimmie." Thanking you for valuable space in your paper. Signed A. Musician.[17]

Whether it was a shimmie (shimmy), a fox trot, or a one-step, Nanaimo residents continued to kick up their heels in total abandonment. As for the eradication of rats, the heaps of rubbish in the ravine would be a breeding ground for the obnoxious rodents for some years to come.

G.A. Fletcher Music Co. Ltd. on Commercial Street placed large advertisements for the "New Columbia Dance Records" by such famous orchestras as Art Hickman's, Paul Biesse's, and Ted Lewis and The Happy Six. "They are sure to tickle your fancy and get your feet to tapping."[18] The list of hits included "Ain't We Got Fun," a foxtrot, "Think of Me Little Daddy," a one-step, and "Peggy O'Neil," a waltz.

Local bands that kept the feet tapping during this time included Bennie's Orchestra, Jensen's Band, Sam Rogers' Ramblers' Orchestra, Bob Thompson's Vagabond Orchestra, and Pimlott's Orchestra; they played in dance halls in Granby and Lantzville, in McGarrigle's Hall in Northfield, and in Nanaimo's Oddfellows Hall and the Elite Hall. Most were five-piece bands; admission was usually $1 for gents and 50 cents for ladies.

There were dance halls all around Nanaimo, and jazz music was a tide the Police Commission could not hope to stem. At their next board meeting they dealt with complaints about jazz dancing and lotteries. "No action was taken in regard to either."[19]

In the late '30s, police were again called in to stop the "nickel dances" held on Sunday nights around the district. There were two dance halls that drew carloads of young people from Nanaimo; one was near Ladysmith, the other at Departure Bay. According to authorities each contravened the Lord's Day Act. One dance for the price of a nickel dropped into a machine and young people could dance the night away.[20] This was an early version of the jukebox.

Music teacher Andrew Dunsmore offered piano and organ lessons from his studio on Commercial Street, and was also the organist and choirmaster at the Methodist Church.

Should you require private dance lessons, then Miss L. Rouvier's Dancing Academy on Prideaux Street was the place to go. Andrew Dunsmore offered piano and organ lessons from his studio on Commercial Street, and R. Robertson gave violin lessons at his studio on Prideaux Street.

Andrew Dunsmore was also the organist and choirmaster at the Methodist Church. In 1927 he suggested having an Upper Island Musical Festival, an event in which music teachers could send their students for adjudication in various musical disciplines. The Rotary Club supported the idea and sponsored the first festival in 1928. The festival drew 150 entries; in 1978, there were over 1,000.

The first honorary president was MLA George S. Pearson, with Dunsmore as president, Norman Carter as treasurer, and R.T. Covenay as secretary. Dunsmore remained as president from 1928 to 1935.

After 77 years of competition, the festival continues to attract musical students from Vancouver Island communities such as Port Alberni, Parksville, Qualicum, and Nanaimo. Andrew Dunsmore died in 1955 at age 63; his musical legacy lives on in the festival he initiated.

Nanaimo City Services

New technology had greatly improved the quality of life and city services. Residents now had telephone, electric light, and sewer connections. The Nanaimo Electric Light, Power and Heating Company contract was renewed for another five years in 1919 at a cost of $50 per year for arc lights and $16 per year for incandescent lamps. Under a provision of the Unemployment Relief Act, unemployed workers completed the sewer system in the '30s at a cost of $100,000.[21] One major stumbling block for city services was the lack of an adequate water supply.

The water situation, or lack of it, was something the Medical Health Officer, Dr. W.F. Drysdale, often complained about to city council:

> The Water Works was woefully insufficient and last summer saw the usual shortage only a little accentuated. For this condition there is not a particle of excuse as there is a plentiful supply at the South Forks only waiting to be piped in, and no very great engineering difficulties in the way either.[22]

Since 1910 the Colliery Dams had supplied the city's water. Dr. Drysdale wanted the present reservoirs fenced off "so that not even a cat could crawl through" and he wanted the caretaker's homes placed somewhere outside the fence. The water supply problem was finally alleviated when the South Fork Dam was completed in the 1930s.

Dr. Drysdale also complained about the city's treatment of garbage—and oh, that ravine!

> Probably no other city in Canada the size and importance of Nanaimo is so poorly supplied in respect to the collection and disposal of garbage as Nanaimo. Practically the only dumping ground is in the Ravine in the heart of the city where everyone can get a good look at it in all its dangerous and disgusting ugliness.

> Many times have the inspector and myself gone down into it and paddled around in the dirty mess there, and then brought in recommendations. But it is still the same old dirty Ravine with its millions of flies and its brigades of rats, both of which, when their food supply runs low, leave it to invade the adjacent houses, carrying their disease and filth with them.[23]

The doctor reasoned that if an incinerator were installed then everything could be burned and only clean ashes dumped in the ravine.

By 1930, Mr. J. Griffiths had taken on the onerous task of collecting garbage, but the task became too much for him. The city then purchased his equipment for $4,500 and took over the plant. Homeowners were charged an annual fee of $4, rooming houses $6, and hotels and boarding houses $8.

Dr. Drysdale also saw the need for an isolation hospital. In 1922 there were 462 patients that required quarantine. The year began with an epidemic of scarlet fever followed by a few cases of smallpox, then a severe epidemic of measles and a few cases of diphtheria. The situation was so critical that schools were closed for several weeks and other restrictions enforced.

Dr. Drysdale, who had practised in Nanaimo since 1894 when he first assisted Dr. R.E. McKechnie, was born in Lanark County, Ontario, and was educated at McGill University. In 1909, he married Catherine (Kate) Allen, from Puget Sound, Washington, known in the community as an excellent singer. Both husband and wife sang in St. Andrew's Presbyterian Church choir for 25 years. The Drysdales had one daughter.[24]

The doctor had endeared himself to the community with his dedicated service during the Spanish influenza epidemic in 1918 and 1919. During his practice in Nanaimo and district he attended the births of 10,747 babies.

In 1919, the city improved postal service by providing letter carrier service. The service boundaries were Townsite Road to the north, Robin Street to the south, Pine Street to the west, and the waterfront to the east. Six letter carriers delivered mail twice a day to 2,700 residents. The carriers were Harold Walbank, William John, James Broadbent, John Hacker, William Ince, and Edgar Snowden; William McMullen was a relief carrier.[25] Adam H. Horne was postmaster, having taken over in 1890 from William Earl, who had operated the post office from his store. Horne was the son of pioneer storekeeper and explorer Adam Grant Horne.

Parks and Recreation

The Parks and Recreation Board, a committee of city council, now managed the Athletic Club, which had housed many sporting clubs over the years. By 1920, the old wooden building showed signs of wear; it had become dilapidated and its foundations needed repair. The building, which began life as a courthouse and jail, had witnessed a few troubling events during the 1912–1914 Big Strike and it had come to the aid of the medical profession as an emergency hospital during the Spanish influenza epidemic. The Basketball Association still used the gym, and schools used the building extensively for recreation programming. The city allocated money in 1920 to renovate the upper floor for a public library.

In 1922, the Nanaimo Board of School Trustees built the Franklyn Street Gymnasium adjacent to the John Shaw High School. Peter Maffeo, a sports enthusiast, headed up the campaign to raise funds that involved many service clubs, including the Gyro and Rotary Clubs. As well, schoolchildren contributed 10 cents a week to the project—the money was collected in the schools.[26]

The Central Sports Ground opened in 1924; with its convenient stadium seating, it became the home for soccer, baseball, lacrosse, school sports, and other celebrations. This is now the location of Port Place, formerly Harbour Park Mall. The Nanaimo Lawn Bowling Club was once located adjacent to the sports ground. The club officially opened on July 21, 1923, with Coal Company representatives George Bowen and John Hunt officiating. R.C. Barrie was the first president and remained so until 1933.[27] One summer the grass of the Bowling Green turned yellow, and people smelled sulphur fumes. Those miners who bowled knew that internal combustion had occurred below the surface of the fill, which had lain dormant for years. Fortunately the fire never ate through to the surface to bring disaster to the tennis court, greens, and sports field.[28] The facilities were leased to the club for $1 a year. The club relocated to Bowen Park when that facility was developed in 1967.

Deverill Square, or Haliburton Street Park, later Haliburton Street Gyro Park, was improved for sporting activities. A wire screen was erected to protect properties on the south side of the playing field. The park consisted of a soccer field, a playground, and a wading pool for children. In 1920, the city granted Millstream Park the grand sum of $362 to cut trails, burn underbrush, and prepare a campground for tourists.

The Parks and Recreation Board maintained Townsite Beach, located at Rosehill Street and Newcastle Avenue, near the present-day Nanaimo Yacht Club. The committee chairman complained to council about how difficult it was to keep the beach in good condition as "there is a certain class of boys who make it their business to destroy and mutilate."[29]

A second bathing beach became available to residents of the south end of the city in 1922 thanks to the Snuneymuxw who gave permission for the use of a beach on their No. 1 Reserve, provided a caretaker would be on site. Prior to this agreement, the beach had been used without permission, and some rowdies had damaged property and caused disturbances. The Western Fuel Company cleared a portion of the beach, and two bathing houses were built on the property. This beach became known locally as Indian Beach, or South End bathing beach. The Nanaimo Rotary Club took over the supervision of both bathing beaches as one of its earliest projects. In 1926, the city paid $100 to the Snuneymuxw for the use of beach.[30]

The Rotary Club of Nanaimo No. 589 formed on April 30, 1920, and held its first meeting in the Windsor Hotel, on Church Street. George Sharratt Pearson was elected president; he served for two years. The inaugural board members included vice-president Harvey Murphy, secretary James Galbraith, treasurer Oliver Eby, sergeant-at-arms Fred Jepson, and directors Dr. G.B. Brown, R.H. Ormond, and Thomas Cunningham.[31]

There were early attempts to establish golf during the First World War when a large tract of land was purchased for a golf course. This was later abandoned because it proved too expensive to clear and develop, but golfing enthusiasts did not give up. After the war, on April 20, 1920, a group of golfers established the Nanaimo Golf Links Limited. The first Board of Directors included E.H. Bird, John W. Coburn, J.H. Doyle, Arthur Leighton, Harvey Murphy, Dr. P.E. Margeson, W.R. Mitchell, Noel McFarlane, and C.J. Trawford.[32] John Coburn, owner of the New Ladysmith Lumber Company, served as first president from 1920 to 1925. Oliver Eby succeeded him from 1926 to 1929.

The club developed a nine-hole course on 86 acres of land leased from Western Fuel Company at Wakesiah Avenue, Jingle Pot Road, and Comox Road (now Bowen Road). Club members put a lot of sweat equity into clearing the course, which had been designed by A.G. Meakin. Fifty-three shareholders paid $100 each and were expected to buy another share.[33]

The club limited memberships to 250. Tourists also played golf—Bird did a little promotion by quoting CPR statistics showing that from January 1 to August 31, 1921, 1,338 motor cars crossed from Vancouver to Nanaimo compared to 1,053 the previous year. He added, "Most tourists carry golf bags."[34]

In 1923, the club purchased another one-and-a-half acres for a clubhouse on Wakesiah Avenue, but it took another year to build. Meanwhile, the Quarterway Hotel served as clubhouse. Members would shoot a few holes, then break for a cool one before returning to finish the course.

The club struggled to survive during the Depression and the Second World War. Canadian Collieries, which had purchased Western Fuel Company, helped by reducing the lease payments by half. It was not until 1946 that the club was able to purchase the land. During the war years there were three presidents: J. Malpass, H. Eakins, and R. Burton.[35]

Chapter Two

Lawmakers, Rum-Runners, and Game Poachers

Nanaimo police felt additional pressure as the population increased and new regulations governing the use of alcohol and drugs were introduced. The Narcotic and Drug Act was new legislation that, according to the new chief of police John Shirras, applied "mostly to the Chinese."[1] Police regularly raided Chinatown in their search for opium. Shirras became chief in 1921 following the death of Jacob Neen who had served in that position since 1912.

Shirras had been wounded in the First World War. On his return home in 1918, he took charge of policing the North Island until he was hired as assistant collector in the Nanaimo Provincial Assessor's Office. Originally from Scotland, he came to Canada with a background in law enforcement from Aberdeen, Kincardine, and Lanarkshire. Shirras served as Chief of Police until the Provincial Police took over in 1926.

In the early '20s, drug trafficking was causing "considerable excitement" across the country. Nanaimo police, however, appeared not to be alarmed over this "terrible habit," for there were few drug addicts in the city. Shirras was only concerned about gambling, but that too he considered a Chinese pastime.

The Alcohol Prohibition Act, enacted in 1917, was amended in June 1920. The original act banned the use of beer, wine, and whisky. Returning vets were not happy coming home to a "dry" province. Saloons managed to survive by selling near beer, an experiment by the brewers of B.C. to produce a palatable substitute for the original article. Only doctors had the power to decide who could or could not have alcohol. Meanwhile, provincial government coffers grew from the monthly sales of more than $150,000 worth of liquor camouflaged as medicine. Local MLA James H. Hawthornthwaite publicly rebuked Prohibition, claiming it was a big failure:

> Prohibition has not decreased the percentage of crimes. The Nanaimo people had to open their jail after Prohibition came into effect. As far as B.C. is concerned [Prohibition] is an absolute farce. 90 percent of the near-beer dealers are selling intoxicating beer. There is not a single town where one cannot get intoxicated. Blind pigs are operated, Chinese opium joints open, and drugs peddled to all regardless to whom sold.[2]

Shirras reported that Prohibition gave police "considerable work and worry trying to keep down illegal liquor traffic."[3] Their search for stills, often located in the forest, was ongoing. In 1921 there were 40 convictions under the act.

Three years later the beer-by-the-glass plebiscite approved the sale of beer by the glass in licensed premises. Before long, most of the hotels in the Nanaimo district had liquor licences. The provincial government established liquor outlets in the Government Agent's offices at Cranbrook, Nelson, and Prince Rupert, plus two official stores in Victoria and Nanaimo. They became known as "John Oliver's drugstores" as they were extremely profitable and brought increased revenue for the province.

British Columbia had its problems dealing with liquor laws and with the Temperance Movement, but in the U.S., congress had bowed to a campaign by suffragettes, church groups, politicians, and others, and had outlawed liquor completely. In 1920, the Volstead Act put the entire U.S. under Prohibition.

On Vancouver Island and elsewhere along the Pacific Coast, there were more than a few willing and eager entrepreneurs who seized the lucrative opportunity to come to the rescue of the "alcohol impoverished" nation south of the border. Anyone with a boat could make a few dollars, and there were a million places to hide the booze in trees in bays along the B.C. coastline. The Dominion government took full advantage of the situation by creating a $20-per-case export duty on liquor cleared to American ports. Later a general tax of $10 per gallon was applied to all liquor exported from Canada. This was not a deterrent for rum-runners who easily absorbed the taxes into their cost of doing business.

Rum-running, unlike tax evasion, was not illegal in Canada. The Pacific Coast came alive with all sorts of vessels loaded with contraband liquor transporting their precious cargo to thirsty customers in Washington State and California. Customs officials did their best to stem the flow, but in many cases, it was a losing battle. Almost every island in the Strait of Georgia became a way station for smugglers at one time or another. The smuggling operations shipped not only moonshine, but also more exotic forms of contraband such as opium.

The legends of this extraordinary time in B.C. history remain—some true, some improbable, some products of fantasy. There is the story about the term "six pack," which supposedly originated in Victoria during the rum-running era. A man named Swede Peterson, a crew member of the steamer *Emma Alexander*, would sew six bottles of Scotch into burlap while aboard ship. Once in a U.S. port, Peterson slipped the "six pack" through a porthole to eager thirsty Americans waiting patiently below in a dinghy.

A distilling plant on Texada Island produced quantities of whisky before the Royal Canadian Mounted Police (RCMP) shut it down. In Ladysmith, ships coming into the harbour were welcomed by "relations" on the wharf waiting to come aboard with suitcases loaded with gifts. When B.C. had Prohibition, the same relations waited with light suitcases, and were seen staggering off the ship with heavy cases full of "gifts."[4] The police tracked down stills, found caches under chicken houses or in pigsties, some buried in dirt cellars or lashed to booms meant to be towed to the 12-mile limit, where fast launches from the U.S. waited to cut the cases loose and race back to American waters.

The old lighthouse tender SS *Quadra*, which had collided with the CPR steamer *Charmer* at the entrance to Nanaimo Harbour in 1917, became a rum-runner. After the collision, the ship had been salvaged and made an ore carrier running between the Britannia Mines on Howe Sound and Tacoma; then it was sold in 1924 to Consolidated Exporters Limited and became part of the rum fleet. The latter company was a discreet rum-running co-operative of distillers and distributors from Vancouver and Victoria. Loaded with liquor and cleared for Mexico, the *Quadra* lay off the coast of San Francisco until fast motor boats arrived to off-load her precious cargo. Each load made huge profits for those in the rum trade.

The U.S. Coast Guard seized the *Quadra* on her last jaunt in 1924, and for four months she and her crew remained in the San Francisco harbour awaiting trial. The crew received full wages during their wait. The trial began on March 10, 1925, but finding an unbiased jury was difficult. It came down to one point: was the *Quadra* in or out of the 12-mile limit when seized? When the geographical position was finally decided, the jury had no trouble finding all had conspired to breach the Prohibition laws of the U.S. Consolidated Exporters Limited was fined $10,000, and members of the crew received various jail sentences. But the quibbling continued over the fate of the ship, until the *Quadra* gave the final answer—she sank at her moorings in San Francisco and had to be scrapped. One crew member, devastated at her sinking, complained, "She took with her the seven cases of whisky that I had hidden away."[5]

Rum-running ended on December 5, 1933, when President Franklin Roosevelt repealed Prohibition.

New Provincial Police Force

Since 1894, the city's Board of Police Commissioners had administered a small local municipal police force. The RCMP stationed two members, Sergeant W.G. Binning and Sergeant W.J. Moorehead, in Nanaimo. The Nanaimo detachment was closed in 1924 and did not reopen until August 15, 1950.

In the legislative session of 1925, amendments were made to the Police and Prison Regulation Act that allowed the British Columbia Provincial Police (BCPP) to contract their services with municipalities. The BCPP were highly regarded, and there was also a financial incentive to change; no longer would the city alone have to shoulder the cost of policing. In 1926 Nanaimo joined North Cowichan, Courtenay, Prince Rupert, Coquitlam, and Port Coquitlam in opting for the new system. Of the 43 communities that went provincial, none returned to local policing.[6]

In 1950, provincial and federal governments agreed the RCMP would handle the policing of B.C. outside of those municipalities such as Vancouver and Victoria which had their own forces.[7] Many members of the BCPP were taken into the RCMP, and Sergeant C.C. Jacklin took charge of the Nanaimo Detachment. The Adirin Building on Fitzwilliam Street served as quarters until the new Nanaimo City Police Building was opened on August 1, 1956, on Prideaux Street. In 1966 an addition to this building was completed; the Nanaimo Detachment had 25 members at this time.[8]

Charles and Lionel Beevor-Potts

Police magistrates who presided over the local court served as another arm of the law. From 1902 to 1985 six men filled this position in Nanaimo: E.M. Yarwood (1902–1910), J.H. Simpson (1911–1915), Charles Herbert Beevor-Potts (1916–1944), Lionel Beevor-Potts (1945–1964), E.W. Winch (1965–1967), and S.H. (Stan) Wardill (1968–1985).

The father-son Beevor-Potts duo of lawyers marked up 48 years of service to Nanaimo. City records reveal that Charles H. Beevor-Potts was paid $100 a month in 1919, an increase of $25 a month from the year before.[9] He was the magistrate who, in 1928, presided over the trial of Brother XII, the leader of a religious cult who was accused of bilking his followers out of thousands of dollars. His most common sentence was $30 or 30 days.

Charles came to Nanaimo from Buckinghamshire, England, in the 1880s with his wife, Gertrude. The couple had five children: three boys and two girls. Family members remember him as a tall, good-looking man who always smoked a pipe.[10]

The unusual name Beevor-Potts dates back to the family's English history, from an ancestor named Sir Thomas Beevor, of Yorkshire. Gertrude's family name was Potts, and so the two names were combined.

Son Lionel was born in Nanaimo on May 31, 1894. He attended school in Nanaimo before furthering his education at the University School in Victoria. He was studying law with his father when the First World War erupted. He enlisted in the 7th Battalion 1st B.C. regiment and in 1914 attended the Royal Military College at Sandhurst, England. During his military service he was awarded the Military Cross for gallantry in France while serving with the South Wales Borderers as a second lieutenant.[11]

As a young man, Lionel enjoyed sports such as swimming, diving, rugby, riding, soccer, badminton, and tennis; he also liked to go trout fishing and was a keen gardener. Between wars he practised law in Nanaimo. Then in 1939 he again enlisted, joining the Canadian Scottish Regiment, until the Royal Canadian Air Force (RCAF) accepted him in 1941. He served as a flying control officer at various stations across Canada, including Port Hardy, where he helped rescue eight men from a crashed transport plane. For this heroic deed he was made a Member of the Order of the British Empire. In 1945 he succeeded his father as magistrate in Nanaimo.

Lionel was known for his no-nonsense approach to juvenile delinquency. In 1954, he ordered one youth who appeared before him to get a haircut before he would hear the case. He then fined the youth, whom he called a "punk," $100 for possessing a knuckle-duster.[12]

Lionel was an active member of the Gyro Club, the Fraternal Order of Eagles, and the Royal Canadian Legion. Following retirement, he and wife Helen took a year's vacation before settling down in Osoyoos. He died at 72 years of age and was buried in Nanaimo.

Frank Greenfield, Game Warden

There was another arm of the law, the game warden, perhaps not quite as visible as the police officer, but equally as important to the conservation of wildlife.

Franklin (Frank) Harris Greenfield started as game warden in 1929 and was a dedicated conservationist until his retirement in 1967. Up to 1955, he held the record for catching the most poachers and pit-lampers throughout B.C.[13]

Frank was the eldest of two sons born to Herbert and Elizabeth Greenfield. Herbert, originally from England, was a successful farmer and was the driving force behind the United Farmers of Alberta. He was premier of Alberta from 1921 to 1925.

Frank and his wife, Marian (Min), were married in Edmonton and moved to Victoria in 1926, where he worked for the Eaton's department store. The next year he worked at the Pheasant Farm in Saanich, an outdoor job he enjoyed. The government-run farm raised pheasants that were released on Vancouver Island and the Lower Mainland. This position led to him join the BCPP, where he was in charge of distributing the birds. In 1929 he became game warden in charge of Central Vancouver Island.

He and Min settled in Nanaimo, first buying a house at Comox Road and Fraser Street. Unfortunately they were unaware of the flourishing red-light district then present in their area. This was not exactly the environment in which they wished to raise their children. Before long they moved to another home at Milton and Wentworth. They had two sons and two daughters.

The hunters and fishermen in the district soon got to know Frank. He was a very diligent game warden and regularly posted warnings in the *Nanaimo Daily Free Press*. This was particularly important during the Depression years when unemployed workers took more liberties finding food to feed their hungry families.

> Notice: No shooting allowed on Newcastle Island. Deer must be tagged as soon as the hunter begins to carry them. Hunters can only have a two-day bag limit of birds at one time. Frank Greenfield, game warden.[14]

Frank used his discretion during the Depression years. Author Joe Garner knew him well. He wrote, "It was not unusual for some needy family to hear a heavy thump on the porch after dark. When they went to investigate, there would be meat and groceries in a box or bag. By the time the door opened, Frank made sure he was out of sight."[15]

Frank joined the Nanaimo Fish and Game Club in 1929. The group had formed in 1905 soon after the Canadian Pacific Railway purchased the E & N and began encouraging hunters and fishermen to use the railway. When rumours started that the land grant might become an American hunting ground, local hunters got mad and took action.

> They set up shop outside the Royal Bank on payday of March 17, 1905, collecting a dollar per person from each interested individual who wanted to stop the American hunters. This was the money that started the Nanaimo and District Fish and Game Protective Association.[16]

The Nanaimo Association celebrated its 100th anniversary on March 17, 2005. With Vancouver Island being a fishing and hunting paradise, it was not unusual for hunters to play fast and loose with the hunting or fishing laws. More than likely Frank Greenfield or Jim Dewar, the predator patrol officer with his cougar hounds, were there to catch the culprit with an illegal catch. Such was the case when two hunting companions were caught red-handed:

> We did things in those days we weren't supposed to. One time we were out hunting for blue grouse with our German shorthaired pointer. Jack got his gun out when the dog stopped and pointed. Jack fired and the dead bird crashed to the ground. Suddenly we heard a vehicle coming. Jack picked up the grouse and threw it into the bushes. Frank Greenfield asked if we had caught anything. "No," we replied. Then the dog broke point, ran into the bushes and brought out the grouse. We were caught.[17]

In 1942 Jim Dewar moved to Port Alberni, where he was appointed game warden and predator control officer.

Local and visiting hunters and fishermen usually met at Johnson's Hardware, where they could buy Dominion ammunition, get the latest sportsman information, or see the latest trophy of deer horns hung in the store window. The store was founded in 1920 by Ray Colcough and sold in 1940 to Ernie Johnson. The store gained a reputation for outstanding sales in ammunition and was named the "Biggest Little Store in Canada in the sale of Dominion Ammunition."[18] Over the years Johnson's Hardware became a much-loved destination for the home handyman, hunter, and fisherman.

Chapter Three

Mining Communities and Mine Safety

District Coal Production

Before the First World War, coal mining accounted for almost half of all mining employment in the province. The province's coal reserves seemed inexhaustible and figured prominently in economic forecasts through the next two decades. Nanaimo relied heavily on the coal industry for its economic stability. In the heyday of mining, steamships waiting to load coal dotted Nanaimo Harbour. At one time this harbour had more shipping than any other port in B.C.

By 1923 the annual coal production here was 1,298,445 tons and the number of employees working in the mines was 3,400. This production figure was one the mines could not sustain; as the use of coal began to decline with oil becoming the fuel of choice, so too did the number of workers.

The year 1923 would forever be the record production year for Nanaimo. By 1930 the amount of coal being produced was reduced to 744,876 tons and the number of employees to 2,158. In 1945 only 432 employees remained, producing 271,865 tons. In 1960, 14 miners produced 2,357 tons.[1]

Nanaimo's largest mine, the Esplanade No. 1 and Protection Mine, owned and operated by Western Fuel Corporation of Canada, Ltd., held the record in B.C. for the total amount of coal produced from a single underground mine. From the start of production in December 1883 to its closure in October in 1938, the total output was 18,000,000 tons.[2] Canadian Collieries (Dunsmuir) Ltd. purchased it in 1928 and continued to operate it under the old name until Weldwood of Canada Ltd. purchased it in 1965. By that time the company had left Nanaimo and moved its headquarters to Union Bay. Canadian Collieries eventually got into the oil business in Alberta, and changed its name to Canadian Collieries Resources Ltd.

The Depression years finalized the fate of the mining industry. The closing of the Western Fuel Company's Esplanade No. 1 Pit on October 5, 1938, was not unexpected. It had been generally known that the end was in sight. Still, it was a sad day for Nanaimo when its most productive mine closed for good. Miners who thought they would have jobs for life suddenly realized the jobs were gone forever. The tough exteriors of hard-working miners softened as the grim reality sank in. Coal piled up in Central Sports Grounds in readiness should an order come in. Depending on the size of the order, there might be two or three days' work a month. Within a year, Western Fuel Company closed all its mines in the Nanaimo region including its Reserve mine, south of Nanaimo, which reopened briefly in 1934, providing work for a few unemployed men. However, a fire in December 1939 sealed its fate.

The Extension mines closed in 1929. Hundreds of men lost their jobs. The well-worn railway tracks to Ladysmith were torn up and the docks and bunkers dismantled. Ladysmith was hard hit by the closures, but a new economy slowly made headway in the region. The Comox Logging Company began logging in the area in 1935 and located its workshops and offices in Ladysmith. Many of the Nanaimo and Extension miners found work in the forest industry.

Granby Colliery

Several small communities emerged during the mining industry period. At Cassidy, south of Nanaimo, near the present-day airport, the Granby Consolidated Mining, Smelting and Power Company entered the coal industry to supply coke for its smelter at Anyox in northern B.C. At the peak of production in 1922, 300,000 tons of coal had been mined and 450 men employed. But the seam proved unpredictable, with gas explosions, or blowouts, happening frequently. The mine gained a reputation as "the slaughterhouse." The company halted production in 1932, and in 1936 the town was put up for sale.[3]

Despite the danger, there was no shortage of miners wanting to work, for the mine paid high wages and offered comfortable modern housing for their families. There were also showers for the miners coming off a shift, something no other mine in the district had. The company spared no expense in developing the town. Situated near Haslam Creek Bridge, the 100-acre settlement was almost idyllic, with connections to electricity, sewer, and water. A two-storey 80-room California-style boarding house for single men is still remembered today. Each room had similar services and had access to a balcony that surrounded the 14,000-square-foot building. About 200 families lived in Granby Village. Married employees could buy company-built bungalows for between $2,500 and $7,000. There was a grocery store, a theatre, a recreation hall, a well-used sports field, and paved streets which were lined with trees and shrubs.

Lantzville-Nanoose Wellington Collieries

Another community developed north of Nanaimo, at Nanoose Bay, where William Jack first discovered coal in 1907. John Grant purchased the mine in 1916 and renamed it Grant's mine. He sold it on March 8, 1920, to the Nanoose Wellington Coal Company, whose headquarters were in Seattle. The company president was Louis Williams, and the general manager was Frank H. Lantz, from Seattle. The Minister of Mines at this time estimated the value of the plant at $200,000. The mine had a first-aid station, a mine rescue station, and an ice plant.

At the peak of production, 300 miners processed the coal at a rate of 500 tons per day from the 4,700 acres. Employees were transported by private jitney from Nanaimo or from Northfield. This was a small bus, open on both sides, with little shelter from the elements. The return fare was 25 cents a day from Nanaimo. Miners' daily wages averaged from $6 for skilled labour to $8 for supervision and clerical staff. Fifteen Chinese employees received $4.50 per day.

The small mining village became known as Lantzville, recognizing the contribution made by the Seattle general manager. Over the course of two years, 40 houses were constructed on the hillside overlooking the bay, all with modern plumbing. Miners liked the new accommodations. A new school

At Lantzville Colliery's peak of production, 300 miners processed coal at a rate of 500 tons per day. Lantzville was named after the mine's general manager, Frank H. Lantz.

This GMC "Char-a-Banc" jitney bus was used to transport miners in 1922.

was opened in 1921, and a recreation hall constructed the same year on the Island Highway, on the western outskirts of the village. Mrs. Vansickle, a well-known resident of the area, managed the hall. The village grocery store offered more than just food and produce. In the back room a few gamblers could settle a debt or lose a day's wage. The social life was considerably improved after the Lantzville Hotel opened in 1925, providing room and board for single miners and, between beers, some friendly interaction among them. For additional shopping or entertainment, most relied on the jitney to take them back and forth to Nanaimo.

After the company suffered financial problems, Canadian Collieries Ltd. purchased the mine in 1926. By this time, the mine operated only part-time. All the miners were paid off and the mine declared closed in 1928. A total of 538,303 tons of coal had been mined during its lifetime. It reopened for a short time during the early days of the Depression in 1931 when J. Michek & Associates mined small amounts of coal.

The Morden Mine Provincial Park

The Morden Mine site, in the Cranberry District south of Nanaimo, was declared a provincial park in 1972, and some dedicated volunteers are working hard to make this a showcase for the area's once thriving mining industry. Today this is all that remains of the coal industry in the Nanaimo region.

This mine had a short life. Pacific Coast Collieries opened it in 1912. Coal was shipped along a private company railway to Boat Harbour, in the Cedar District. The mine was described as the most modern, unique in the province and absolutely fireproof. A tipple and header were built of concrete to ensure the mine would be fireproof and have longevity. Five hundred cubic yards of concrete were used in its construction; the mine also had electricity.

In 1920, more money, an estimated $3 million, was poured into the operation and more development was done underground. During that year, cottages and boarding houses from the South Wellington mine were moved to the Morden Mine site. Even the large water tank was dismantled, then rebuilt at Morden to improve the water supply system to the boilers. The mine employed 280. The original slope, abandoned four years before, was reopened and cleared, and the ventilation improved.

When the provincial mining inspector detected volatile gas, he ordered the mine closed until improvements could be made. In 1921 the company declared bankruptcy.

In 1930, the Canadian Coal and Iron Company reopened the flooded mine, pumped out the water, and retimbered several hundred feet of the main tunnel, but cave-ins forced the company to abandon the mine.

St. John Ambulance Association

Safety was a major concern in the early mines. Management always hired a mine doctor, and miners recognized the value and necessity of having first-aid training. Labour unions were also concerned, and before long each mine in Nanaimo had a mine rescue team.

Under manager Samuel Robins, the Vancouver Coal Company, forerunner to the Western Fuel Company (WFC), purchased the first ambulance in 1900. George Yarrow was one of the first miners to be trained in first aid in Nanaimo, although he had some training before he emigrated to Nova Scotia in 1887, from Durham, England. Two years later he settled in Nanaimo as miner and fireboss. First-aid classes started in 1904 under the tutelage of Dr. Oswald Grey Ingham, who had just arrived in the community. A year later Yarrow won a gold medal for proficiency in a class of approximately 30, which included most of the WFC officials. Yarrow was placed in charge of the company's first Mine Rescue Station.[4]

At a November 2, 1911, meeting, the decision was made to affiliate with the St. John Ambulance Association and create a Nanaimo Branch.[5] The Order of St. John came to Canada in 1884; its origin dates back to the Christian Crusade. The first classes were held in schoolrooms until WFC provided a headquarters at the St. John Ambulance Hall on Esplanade, the location of the present stevedore office. WFC mine manager Harry N. Freeman was president of the branch at this time. He and R.B. Fulton actively represented Nanaimo on the B.C. Council of the association from 1915.

In 1915 Yarrow earned a government certificate and a second-year certificate with St. John Ambulance. WFC had 61 men fully trained in mine rescue; 20 held government certificates and another 13 held St. John Ambulance certificates. Yarrow planned to train 16 men a month.[6]

During the Spanish influenza epidemic, the WFC first-aid workers provided valuable service to the community. James N. Jemson and Yarrow transported sick patients from Chase River to the hospital, while other miners helped out in the emergency hospital.

The Ministry of Mines Report of 1920 noted the Mine Rescue Station in Nanaimo was under the supervision of J.D. Stewart, "who conducts it in a practical and educational way. Mine rescue practices are performed with approved Gibbs and Paul breathing apparatus."[7] Stewart was widely known for his experience in the Klondike when Soapy Smith and his Skagway gang robbed him.

On October 17, 1921, elections were held for a WFC mine doctor. There were 33 applications for the position; however, most were eliminated—only six made it to the ballot. The voting results were as follows: Dr. Ingham, Nanaimo, 90; Dr. Hall, Vancouver, 75; Dr. Lane, Nanaimo, 72; Dr. McIntyre, Nanaimo, 65; Dr. Moore, Victoria, 61; Dr. Wilks, Nanaimo, 53.[8] Dr. Ingham was clearly the winner in this unusual election.

This same year the WFC "miner's first-aid team" under Captain Barton won the Coderre Cup and the Montizambert Cup; the latter was awarded to the winner of the Canadian championship. Barton's team repeated the double win in 1921. The team included Barton, George Carson, David Stobbart, Charles Nichols, J. Brown, and R. Shields. The Cumberland team under Captain A.J. Taylor came in second. Dr. Brydon-Jack, of Vancouver, the provincial president of the St. John Ambulance Association, made the presentations at an award ceremony in the Oddfellows Hall.[9]

MP William Sloan presented gold medals, designed and made by Mr. Forcimmer of Nanaimo, on behalf of the Ministry of Mines. An editorial in the *Nanaimo Free Press* praised the team and noted that police, civilian, railway, and mining teams from all across Canada had competed for the honour won by Nanaimo.

A local team led by Charles Wharton and Seiriol Williams won the Canadian Junior Championship in 1921. This was the beginning of Seiriol Williams' medical career. The Wharton family came to Nanaimo in 1907 from Staffordshire, England. His father worked in the Protection Mine. Charles attended Harewood School and then worked for 28 years in the mine maintenance shop. In 1927, Wharton's team, which included his father and two brothers, Len and Sid, and his brother-in-law, George Cottle, placed second in the Canadian Mine Competition.

Charles Wharton joined the St. John Ambulance in 1918. He served as class secretary from 1928 to 1936, covering an area between Parksville and Ladysmith, and as president from 1936 to 1968. During the Depression, he

The Western Fuel Company Mine Rescue Team of 1922 was a winning combination in first-aid competition.

taught first aid at two work camps for the unemployed at Englishman River Falls. "The men slept in tents, were given camp rations and 25 cents per week for personal needs."[10] Wharton loved the falls: "Englishman River Falls in the winter time is [a] beautiful, beautiful sight. Because [of] the spray, it just steams up and then it gets frozen. Frozen sprays on the trees—what a beautiful site [*sic*]." Wharton also conducted first-aid classes in Qualicum; Seiriol Williams joined him in these classes after he became a doctor. When Wharton retired, he was named Honorary President.

WFC had a way of inducing young miners to take first-aid classes. The company held dances every Saturday night in the Oddfellows Hall, where Jensen's or Doug Manson's Orchestra provided the music. Admittance was by ticket only, and one way of getting tickets was to attend the class, "so we always had a good attendance at the first-aid class because the kids wanted to go to the dance. It was a good way to get them started."[11] The miners taking the training course were paid $2.50 for every two hours and were provided with a shirt and overalls.[12] In one of the first classes Wharton attended with his father in September 1918, there were over 200 class members registered.[13]

First-aid tests were held in the old cricket field, now Robins Park. Over the years many local doctors donated their time as lecturers and examiners. They included Dr. J.H. Hogle, Dr. R. O'Brien, Dr. O.G. Ingham,

Dr. W.F. Drysdale, Dr. T.J. McPhee, Dr. G.A.B. Hall, Dr. Earl Hall, Dr. A.E. Manson, Dr. Hannington, and Dr. Larry Giovando. The doctors took turns giving a presentation at Sunday morning lectures. Charles Wharton praised Dr. Carman Browne who for 32 years gave two-hour lectures: "Never once did he say no when asked."[14]

Miners Join the UMWA

In the dying days of the Depression, the coal companies on Vancouver Island finally recognized the United Mine Workers of America (UMWA) union. In 1937, over 2,000 miners were members of the UMWA, about 50 percent of the workforce. From the time of the Big Strike, 1912–1914, it had taken over two decades for an agreement to be signed between the union and management. The agreement went into effect on June 15, 1937. By January 1938, labour on Vancouver Island was 100 percent organized. For the first time there were paid holidays, rest breaks for lunch, a pension plan—and dignity in the workforce. During the Second World War the right to strike was taken away; the danger of working underground continued as before.

Although safety precautions had improved greatly in the Nanaimo district, which was once considered the most dangerous in the province, accidents still happened. The Minister of Mines Report continued to record them. One such accident happened on June 11, 1937, when three men drowned and two were saved at the Beban Mine in Extension. Water burst into the face of the tunnel at the 400-foot level from the old Extension slope, trapping the men. Frank Beban had opened the small mine in 1935, tapping into the coal left behind when the Extension mine was closed. This small mine produced only 40 tons of coal a day, but during the Depression it provided a small income for a few men.

On this day there were 10 men working. When John Senini heard a rumble, he rushed to investigate and found a wall of water rushing up the main slope towards him. The water took the men by surprise; five men rode the crest of the water to safety, while others fought for their lives against its force before being swept away. John Senini, of Extension, and Louis Tognela, an Italian war veteran from Five Acres, were saved. The dead included Nelson Shepherd, his nephew Joseph Shepherd, and Joseph Carr, all from Nanaimo. The five who managed to escape were Alex Webster, Tony Senini, brother of John, Joe Wilson, mine foreman, Lorne Perry, and Joe Foster.[15]

The establishment of St. John Ambulance with its teams of first-aid workers greatly improved survival rates for miners.

Chapter Four

Making a Difference

In life there are people who make a difference in the world; whether for their talent, politics, knowledge, or determination, they are remembered for improving the life of the community.

William Sloan

William Sloan was one of Nanaimo's most popular provincial members of parliament. As Minister of Mines he was relentless in looking for ways to improve the safety of men working underground, and as Provincial Secretary he was an early and constant advocate for the old-age pension, for improved health and hospital facilities, and for mental institutions.[1]

Sloan was born September 19, 1867, at Wingham, Ontario, and was educated in the public schools and college at Seaforth, Ontario. When William was still a boy, his father, Dr. R.J. Sloan, took a position in Shanghai. After graduation, William joined him in the Orient, where he remained for several years working in a clerical position within the customs department. Here he formed opinions and acquired knowledge of Asian customs and character that he later applied in his efforts to restrict immigration into B.C.

For a number of years he lived in Vancouver before moving to Nanaimo to join in a business venture, Sloan and Scott, a partnership that lasted five years. He married Flora McGregor, a daughter of the pioneer mining family. The couple had one son, Gordon, who became a Chief Justice of the province. In 1916, several years after the death of Flora, he married Catherine McDougall, a marriage that produced two children, William and Barbara Jean.

Sloan was also a Klondiker and his stake on Eldorado Creek proved the fabulous richness of the creek that led to the Klondike Gold Rush. He sold his claim and returned home to Nanaimo, richer by far perhaps than those prospectors who stayed behind.

He was defeated in his first entry into politics in 1900 as a candidate for Vancouver district, now known as the Nanaimo federal riding. Four years later he was acclaimed in the Comox-Atlin riding, and again in 1908, but in this election he gave up his seat to William Templeman, a minister in Prime Minister Sir Wilfred Laurier's cabinet. During his time as a federal minister, Sloan urged the Dominion government to do a thorough survey of the fishing grounds of B.C.[2] He also supported the Reverend George Taylor in his efforts to establish the Pacific Biological Station at Departure Bay.

Sloan next ran provincially in 1916 as a Liberal candidate in Nanaimo. In this election, the Liberals swept the province and Premier Brewster appointed him Minister of Mines, a position he held for 12 years through the governments of Premiers John Oliver and John Duncan MacLean. In this portfolio, he waged war against mine operators and worked continually to improve the safety of miners.

There were two political parties in the province at that time, the Liberals and the Conservatives, although for one brief period there were three socialist members elected from Nanaimo and Newcastle who managed to sway legislation: Parker Williams, James Hurst Hawthornthwaite, and Jack Place. Like today's voters, most seemed to favour the two-system form of government for it gave a simple choice—you are either for us or against us!

Mary Ellen Smith

Mary Ellen Smith was Canada's first female cabinet minister, but in Nanaimo she was just Mary Ellen, the wife of MP Ralph Smith. For a decade, between 1918 and 1928, she spearheaded social reform in British Columbia. Women were granted the right to vote in 1917, the year her husband Ralph died. She ran in a by-election as an independent and was elected to fill his Vancouver seat.

Ralph Smith had represented Nanaimo federally from 1900 to 1911 until he and Mary Ellen left the community to join their sons already living in Vancouver. Like William Sloan, the Smiths also supported the establishment of the Pacific Biological Station at Departure Bay. Mary Ellen was there for the official opening in 1908.

In Vancouver, Ralph ran unsuccessfully for the provincial Liberals in 1912, but four years later he topped the polls in the Harlan Carey Brewster Liberal government. The victory for the provincial Liberals was something the Smiths could celebrate and Ralph became the new Minister of Finance.

Mary Ellen was born October 11, 1861, in Gunnislake, Cornwall, England, but claimed Tavistock, Devon, as her ancestral home. She was the only daughter of Mary Ann and Richard Jackson Spear, a mining family from the village of Framlington, near Newcastle-on-Tyne. She and her brother were educated at schools in Northumberland where she became an elementary schoolteacher. Music was always part of her life; she was gifted with a beautiful voice, and she sang at various music events. She also enjoyed drama, a skill that may have helped in her public life. At family gatherings she and her brother were encouraged to listen and take part in discussions, and later she developed a life-long interest in current affairs. Those interests were compatible with those of a young miner she met and soon married, becoming the second wife of Ralph Smith, whose first wife had died when their daughter was born. Mary Ellen and Ralph had three sons.

When Ralph's health began to deteriorate, they decided to come to Canada, hoping the climate would be beneficial. Nanaimo seemed like a natural location for a young miner to settle. Ralph became involved in the turbulent fledgling trade union movement before entering politics.

Ralph Smith and mine owner James Dunsmuir did not agree on most things. In a speech he delivered in the Nanaimo Opera House, he offered this observation of the Dunsmuir colliery: "As workingmen they ought to draw a distinction between corporations that were bad and corporations that were worse."[3] Smith charged that "the throats of the people of the province had been grasped by a corporation that was prepared to throttle them without mercy."

Mary Ellen fully supported her husband in his political career while she became involved in community life. She was elected vice-president of the inaugural Women's Auxiliary to Nanaimo Hospital in 1900, and was elected president in three subsequent years.

The Smiths lived in Nanaimo for 22 years; when they left in 1911 they were recognized for their service to the community. The Nanaimo Laurier Liberal Ladies League hosted a farewell reception for Mary Ellen and presented her with a salad bowl. After paying tribute to her years of service to social, religious, and political organizations, they closed the evening by singing "For She's a Jolly Good Fellow."[4]

Women welcomed Mary Ellen Smith's entry into the provincial legislature after Ralph's death. Provincial male counterparts had different views on gender equality. Some believed a woman's place was in the home, not in the legislature. However, members put any misgivings they may have had aside and welcomed "Mrs. Ralph" into the chamber for the first time. They gave her a rousing ovation and presented her with flowers.

Her maiden speech was delivered on March 11, 1918; she said she was not there with a chip on her shoulder or sword in her hand but with a willingness to meet on equal ground as a representative of the people.

> I like to think that the honourable members of this house welcome a woman into their midst, and I extend to all of you the olive branch of

> peace. Not only did I come to ask for legislation in the best interests of the women and children but also legislation for the protection of the best interests of all people of this province.[5]

In 1920 Mary Ellen ran as a Liberal and won by a large majority. She suggested to Premier Oliver that he make her a cabinet minister. He pacified her by offering the speaker's chair, a position she declined. He then appointed her the first female cabinet minister in the British Empire, but she was a minister without portfolio. Being left out of the decision-making did not appeal to her, so after a few months she quit and began fighting for women's issues, mothers' pensions, and other important social reforms from outside caucus. She was re-elected in 1924, defeating millionaire General Alexander McRae, leader of the newly formed Provincial Party, and she stayed in government until the Liberals were swept from power in 1928.

The first bill she introduced was the Female Minimum Wage Bill. The industry wage for women aged 18 and over was fixed at $12.75 per week. The bill passed but had little power, as no actual minimum was set for any occupation, only provisions made for an inquiry into each case. Mary Ellen followed this up with a push for mothers' pensions. A commission was established in the fall of 1919 to investigate mothers' pensions, public funding for nurses, and maternity benefits. The final report recommended an allowance of $42.50 per month for a widow with one child under 16, and $7.50 per month for each additional child. There was no provision for unwed mothers, and she made a special plea for them. When the bill came up for second reading, she spoke in its support:

> Mr. Speaker, there are no illegitimate children. It may be there are ... people who will contend there are illegitimate parents, but in God's name, do not let us brand the child.[6]

The Mothers' Pension Act of 1920, known later as Mothers' Allowances, came up again in 1924, and once again Mary Ellen spoke in its defence. She said the act had benefited 950 women and 2,500 children. Then she took aim at municipalities; she felt they should take some responsibility for the relief of poverty within their borders. She cited one municipality where a mother and six children outside the limits of the act had been allowed only $20 a month. The Workmen's Compensation Board (WCB) administered the act, which eventually was absorbed into the general welfare system in 1958.

The WCB also administered the Old Age Pension Act that was enacted in 1927. This legislation was a Dominion government responsibility, but it had a rough ride through parliament; it was even defeated by the Senate before being reintroduced and finally passed. Mary Ellen commented on the Senate being an "old man's home":

> Why the senate should reject the Bill is more than I can understand. The senate should be the last body to do any such thing, as the senators themselves are living in a luxurious old man's home, drawing down the handsome stipend of $4,000 a year.[7]

The provinces paid 75 percent of the cost of the Old Age Pension while the Dominion government covered the remaining 25 percent. Richer provinces like B.C. entered the plan, but it was difficult for the poorer ones although they did contribute through taxation to the Dominion portion. Eventually the burden of cost sharing was changed to a 50-50 basis.

In the summer of 1923, Mary Ellen embarked on a tour of England as a representative of the Dominion's Immigration Department to promote Canada to potential immigrants. The placard on her touring car read "Canada Needs You." Throughout her tour mayors, clubs, and civic officials feted her. She visited over 100 cities, towns, and villages, and her message was always the same: "If you are able to work hard and want work, you may safely look to Canada as a land of promise, promise coupled with fulfillment."[8] The tour established her as an international figure, but it was her work in pushing for social reform that earned her a place in B.C. history.

Mary Ellen suffered a stroke on April 22, 1933, and never regained consciousness. The *Nanaimo Free Press* of May 3, 1933, reported her passing, stating that as president of the B.C. Liberal Party she had presided over the party's convention the previous fall "like a firm mother."

Nanaimo named Mary Ellen Drive in her honour.

Audrey Alexandra Brown

Audrey Alexandra Brown was the city's only nationally recognized poet. Despite ill health and rejection letters from publishers, she managed to rise above it all and become a celebrity.

She was born in Nanaimo on October 29, 1904. Her father, Joseph, was a respected watchmaker in town. He followed the trade of his father, a former native of Gloucestershire, England. Her grandparents came to Nanaimo in 1862. Her mother was born in London. Audrey was the niece of W.E. Rumming of Rummings Bottling Works in Nanaimo. She was an only daughter and fifth in a family of eight children. From an early age she loved books; she was a voracious reader and loved to write letters, a hobby that often taxed her eyesight. Before the age of 10 she had a personal library of 87 books.

At the age of eight, she entered school as a day pupil in St. Ann's Convent in Nanaimo, a period she often referred to as one of the happiest times of her life. She continued in the public school system until she reached the junior fourth grade level; then a debilitating rheumatic illness afflicted her for three years.

Audrey wrote her first poem at the age of six. Throughout her life she took great delight in collecting words, often repeating them to herself, she said, "for the sake of feeling their beauty on my tongue."[9] Her poem simply titled "Nanaimo" was written to mark the jubilee anniversary of the city's incorporation, and was recited by Jackie Cooper at a civic banquet. The poem is dated May 1934. The first and second verses read:

Here the sun found her once and finds her still,
Lovely between the mountain and the sea—
And here returns the gold April bee
Among her blossomed streets to drink his fill,
And through her chestnut-branch trembles the show,
And all her lilies break in silver bud and flower.

The sea is at her feet, the dreaming sea
That loves her, and the mountain keeps her rest;
She has a spell to charm the fevered breast
And make the heart forget mortality—
This was her ancient art, and now as then
She lays her fragile net about the souls of men.[10]

At 19 she sold one of her poems to *The Christian Guardian*. A year later, another sold. About this time she read a speech that said literary aspirants should never be disheartened by rejection slips, for some of the best work ever written had been rejected more than once. She decided that if the very finest work was rejected, then her own efforts had no chance at all, and so she stopped aggressively pursuing magazines and decided to write just for pleasure. It was a good stance to take, for if there is no pleasure in the creation, it is unlikely to draw public attention.

In 1927, after suffering another attack of rheumatism, Audrey was unable to walk. During recuperation she remained cheerful and managed to keep her sense of humour. She contributed verses to the *Nanaimo Herald*, and it was there that Dr. and Mrs. Wilbert Amie Clemens recognized her talent. Dr. Clemens was a scientist working at the Pacific Biological Station at Departure Bay. They sent copies of her poems to their friends. In this way "Diana" and "The Reed," written a year before, reached Professor Pelham Edgar, head of the English Department at Victoria University in Toronto, in the spring of 1928. He immediately recognized her gift and got in touch with her and became her literary godfather. With his help her career as a poet took off.

In 1932, she was presented with a life membership in the Women's Canadian Club at a meeting of the Nanaimo branch held in the Hotel Malaspina. President of the club, Mrs. G. Bell Brown, said Nanaimo was very fortunate in having "a native daughter a poetess known from coast to coast." This was the highest honour the club could bestow on anyone.

At a meeting of the Canadian Authors Association in Montreal, Professor Edgar read one of Audrey's poems from an unpublished manuscript. "Laodamia," he said, was one of the most beautiful, decorative narrative poems to have come out of America. Audrey was not present to hear the praise, but she would have been proud of his comments.

At the end of the glimmering street—
Pale in the summer twilight, leading away
To the wine-red heart of the day—
There is a place untrodden by human feet,
A little knoll of ancient enduring trees,
Veiled in a delicate mist of meadow-sweet,
Haunted of bees.

Time has forgotten this place: the years have spared
One pleasance—this—for the year's return of Spring,
Lest it should come some desolate day, and find
Nanaimo unprepared
For its sweet wild miracles sown to the rain and wind,
Its buds for the deaf, its song of birds for the blind—
Lest it find no place of rest from its wandering,
And so take wing.[11]

Through the professor's efforts, *A Dryad in Nanaimo*, a collection of 20 of her best poems, was published in 1931.

During the Christmas season of 1938 Audrey returned to St. Ann's Convent to recite her work before the school that had given her such happy memories.

Prime Minister Robert Borden once sent her a cheque to buy a typewriter, and Her Majesty Queen Mary received a specially bound edition of one of her four books.

Audrey Alexandra Brown was made a member of the Order of Canada in 1967. She lived to the grand age of 93, passing on September 20, 1998, in Victoria.[12]

Men and Women of Science

The Reverend George W. Taylor's efforts to establish the Pacific Biological Station (PBS) at Departure Bay received wide support from Nanaimo residents and from politicians such as William Sloan and Ralph and Mary Ellen Smith. Since those early years, PBS has played a major role in adding to the scientific knowledge of fish in the province's rivers, lakes, and oceans and has attracted scientists and researchers from around the world. From a modest beginning of one building, the station has grown into a first-class research complex.

The original station consisted of a one-room museum and workroom, a storeroom, an office, a darkroom for photography, and a dining room. Upstairs were four rooms to accommodate visiting scientists; the caretaker and the resident scientist had separate houses. The museum housed Reverend Taylor's scientific library and zoological collections. Visitors were welcome on Thursdays. Nanaimo residents took advantage of the opening to come and picnic on the grounds.

Following the death of Reverend Taylor in 1912, Dr. C. McLean Fraser, a graduate of the University of Toronto, took over as director. He continued research on the diversity of animals in the sea. He was the only year-round employee and remained director until 1924. During his tenure, the station got water for the first time from a nearby creek and purchased a 40-foot gasoline launch, the *Ordonez*, for marine research. Fraser was appointed head of the Department of Zoology at the new University of British Columbia (UBC) in 1920; this reduced the time he was able to spend at the station. For 40 years, until his death in 1946, Fraser studied hydroids (jellyfish and sea anemones).

Dr. and Mrs. Wilbert Amie Clemens arrived in 1924. Dr. Clemens had been reluctant to accept the appointment until he talked to a young student who had worked a summer at the station under Fraser. Dr. Russell Earle Foerster (1940–49) recalled their meeting:

> [K]nowing that I had come from there, he [Clemens] was of course interested and quite keen on finding out what I thought of the job, the place, and so forth. He thought that the coastal area was populated mainly by Indians, and that the conditions were rather unsatisfactory. I quickly assured him, quite the contrary, and I thought it was a wonderful opportunity for a young biologist to come out and start in a new field. I did not realize at that time that I would be working for him for many, many years."[13]

Clemens turned out to be the perfect combination of scientist and administrator, for the station grew under his guidance, and scientific staff increased. He had been totally ignorant of the fauna of the Pacific coast, a situation he quickly rectified, eventually co-authoring and publishing with

G. Van Wilby *The Fishes of the Pacific Coast of Canada*, a book that became the standard reference work from California to Alaska.

Dr. John Hart joined the staff in 1929; he came to assist Dr. H.C. Williamson with his studies on pilchards and herring. These were Hart's impressions:

> I arrived in Nanaimo on July 1, 1929. This happened to correspond with the day that they opened the new resident building. I can just imagine how glad Mrs. Clemens, who was acting as housekeeper, was to see a new and unexpected face show up at that time. Mrs. Clemens acted as supervisor of staff... an arrangement that started then and continued for several years, as long as the residence stayed open, or as long as Mrs. Clemens was there. She was a very considerate and thoughtful woman. Lucy Smith Clemens was a Ph. D. in her own right and worked to some extent with her husband on some of the papers. But she was particularly dutiful as a wife and mother, and she didn't have much time left for research.
>
> There were two dining rooms. Most of the year only one was used, and the Clemenses sat as a family at one end of the table and the rest of us sat around. It was run as a family affair. Quite a few of us stayed in the residence after marriage, mainly because we were doing a lot of fieldwork, and it seemed economically impossible to maintain decent homes in Nanaimo and to do the fieldwork. Most of us were away from Nanaimo for four to eight months of the year. As long as you gave warning, you were not charged for meals that you did not eat. The meals and the service were good.[14]

The Clemenses had worked closely with volunteer workers at the station, but the Depression years and subsequent curtailment of funding brought an end to the volunteer worker program in 1934. Volunteers had previously received travelling expenses and room and board. The government also reduced staff wages by 10 percent, as it had for all government employees across the country. No one complained—everyone compared his or her situation to those of jobless friends. Dr. Clemens resigned in 1940 to succeed Fraser as head of the Department of Zoology at UBC.

Two dedicated volunteers who lived close to the station divided their time between their garden and the study of polychaetes (marine worms). Cyril J. Berkeley and his wife, Edith, moved to Departure Bay in 1919, where they purchased the house previously owned by the Reverend Taylor. Cyril was from London, England, and Edith from South Africa; both were educated in London. He specialized in chemistry, she in zoology. They

This group photo was taken at the Pacific Biological Station in 1929 on the occasion of the official opening of the residence building. Since those early years, PBS has attracted scientists and researchers from around the world. See Appendix IV for the individuals' names.

married in 1902 when Cyril was appointed government bacteriologist in the state of Bihar, India. They came to B.C. in 1914 and farmed for three years near Vernon; then for two years afterwards they both taught at the new UBC.

From the time the Berkeleys made contact with the station in 1917, they nurtured an extensive garden, planted rare species, and cultivated irises and rhododendrons, even developing a few new ones. Cyril was assistant curator during 1920 and 1921 and afterwards worked as a volunteer. Edith carried on the research that she had begun 20 years before. She discovered that the classification of the species found on the coast was in chaos and undertook to reorganize it. For 12 years she worked alone, then Cyril joined her. Between 1923 and 1962 they authored 40 publications. They discovered many new species and recorded new distributions.

Dr. William Edwin (Bill) Ricker recalled the Berkeleys and the relaxed atmosphere at the station:

> In those days the station still had a foreshore that went dry at any really low tide, exposing a clam bed with two or three kinds of starfish scattered about, the curious egg collars of the moon-shell, and rocks for small crabs, blennies and clingfish. Underneath the

> dock you could see yellow shiners and white seaperch, rock cod, schools of young herring and salmon, pulsating jellyfishes, and sometimes the awkward contractions of a *Melibe*, a sea slug trying to become a medusa.
>
> Punctually every afternoon Mr. and Mrs. Berkeley would come down for a swim to be joined by some of the visitors. However, it was better fun to dive off the dock at night, when your body would be surrounded by great clouds of phosphorescence caused by *Noctiluca* and comb-jellies. One year Cliff Carl arrived at the station with a new accordion, on which he played and we sang in the residence living room after dinner.[15]

Dr. John Patrick Tully joined the staff in 1931. He came from Manitoba and was educated as an oceanographer, but had never seen the ocean. Oceanographer Neal Carter, who had researched the inlets along the coast, described Tully's first encounter with the ocean:

> He lived in Winnipeg and had never seen salt water, and he had a wooden leg. I felt a little reticent about employing him because in oceanographic work you have to be on a boat in rough weather when the decks are wet and slippery, and I wondered how his wooden leg would behave. He assured me that it wouldn't be any trouble.
>
> He arrived when I happened to be away on the boat on a week's cruise. When we came chugging up the dock at the station on Friday afternoon, here was this individual whom I had never seen before walking down to meet the boat in a resplendent yachtsman's uniform, complete with brass buttons. He figured he had to have a uniform if he was going to work on a boat, not knowing that we didn't go for uniforms. When the boat docked, I had on a dirty old sweater and was carrying some of the bottles of seawater ashore. He asked where Dr. Carter was. The skipper of the boat pointed to me and said, "That's Dr. Carter." Tully's face fell. I never saw the uniform again.[16]

Tully was assigned to investigate the Alberni Canal when forest company Bloedel, Stewart & Welch proposed constructing a pulp mill in Port Alberni. The Department of Fisheries asked the board to investigate. Henry Vollmers, with his new trolling boat, was hired for the project, and the fish hold was fitted up for a laboratory. Tully and Vollmers lived and worked on the boat accumulating and analyzing a mass of data. Later in the project, they used the PBS vessel *A.P. Knight.*

Tully decided he needed a model of the upper end of the Canal to confirm his conclusions regarding water movements. This was made using plaster of Paris, buckets, pulleys, hoses, parts of alarm clocks, and an electric fan. The six-by-four-foot model was complete with tides, river flow, and winds. Tully's study predicted the dispersion pattern of the pulp mill effluents, and measures were taken to reduce damage to the fisheries. The pulp mill was built in 1946/47.

During the war, Tully joined the navy and did hydroacoustic work. He was elected a Fellow of the Royal Society of Canada and awarded the Monaco Commemorative Medal for his work in oceanography.

Dr. Bill Ricker joined PBS in 1931 as scientific assistant to Dr. Foerster. He left in 1939 to take the position of professor of zoology at Indiana University, returning 11 years later as publication editor. He held this post from 1950 to 1962. In 1966 he was named chief scientist, a title he held until his retirement in 1973.

Ricker was born at Waterdown, Ontario, in 1908, and graduated from the University of Toronto, obtaining a Ph.D. in 1936. He is best known for his "green books," guides to the calculation and interpretation of the vital statistics of fish populations, which were updated in 1948, 1958, and 1975. During his tenure in Indiana, he learned Russian to read the pioneering treatise of Professor F.I. Baranov. One of his major contributions as editor was to translate into English more than 170 published Russian research papers and make these available in a Fisheries Research Board Translation Series.[17]

The credits awarded to Dr. Ricker are long: He was a Fellow of the Royal Society of Canada and was awarded its Flavelle Medal in 1970. The Wildlife Society gave him a citation in 1959 for the best research paper in fisheries. The Professional Institute of the Public Service of Canada presented him with its gold medal "for outstanding achievement in the field of pure and applied science." The University of Manitoba conferred an honorary Doctorate of Science on him in 1970, and Dalhousie University made him a Doctor of Laws in 1974 and he was awarded an Honourary Doctor of Science at the University of Guelph in 1996.

Ricker's associates considered him to be an excellent fishery biologist and a modest man with a generous spirit. He was an amateur authority on Native people. On early alphabets, he was a walking directory—and he also played the bull fiddle. He earned the respect of scientists around the world.

These are only a few of the men and women of science who contributed to our knowledge of the ocean and marine life and who left a legacy with the Pacific Biological Station in Nanaimo. Reverend Taylor would indeed be pleased with its progress and his part in it.

Chapter Five

Building a Future

As the city prospered during the '20s, it saw the establishment of a new library and the building of a new hospital and hotel. While the business community had no trouble raising money to build the hotel, it struggled to finance the new hospital. The cloud of the postwar depression had lifted and a building boom had started.

The Canadian Pacific Railway (CPR) built a new railway station in 1920, replacing the old building that had served the E & N Railway since 1886. The B.C. Telephone Exchange on Bastion Street received a face lift, and the Hall Block and the Parkin Block were added to Commercial Street.

Nanaimo Public Library

The second floor of the Athletic Club became the city's new library in 1920. The original library, which had started with great fanfare in 1864 with the opening of the Nanaimo Literary Institute at Bastion and Skinner streets, was plagued with financial problems. It struggled to survive until 1886, when a bylaw authorized the city to purchase the building for use as a city hall.

The first public libraries act, called the Free Libraries Act, which passed in 1891 allowing the formation of municipal libraries by passage of a bylaw, gave no incentive or financial aid to small communities. It was not until the British Columbia Public Libraries Act passed in April 1919 that the newly formed Nanaimo Public Library Association organized a public library. The association received moral and financial support from the Imperial Order of Daughters of the Empire (IODE).[1]

Thirty-three residents signed the application for a charter; by August it had arrived along with best wishes from Dr. Helen Stewart, the Librarian of the Victoria Public Library and acting secretary for the Libraries Commission. She expressed hope that "together a service could be developed to the satisfaction of all concerned" and congratulated the group "on being pioneers in this matter."[2]

Under the act the Nanaimo library could withdraw from the Victoria Library up to 2,000 books a year, but it was suggested that perhaps it should start with only 500 volumes. These books were changed four times a year at a cost of approximately $270 per year. Members could order special books; a weekly express service covered up to 20 books a week. The additional cost for this service was $25 to $40 a year. The Nanaimo Library Association decided that the library should include reference and children's sections. The success of the library depended on users willing to pay a subscription fee.

The Library Association was enthusiastic despite receiving little cooperation from city council, which held the purse strings. After much lobbying, the city finally agreed to pay $175, and with donations of materials and volunteer labour, the Nanaimo Public Library officially opened on February 5, 1920. Mayor Henry McKenzie praised the efforts of the IODE Bastion Chapter for their "most persistent effort," and added, "City Council had only done what it had been forced to do."[3]

Following the opening comments made by Mayor McKenzie, University of British Columbia librarian Dr. John Riddington offered his congratulations. He said, "City Council has been placed somewhat in the position of the man mentioned in the Bible who said that while he feared not God and feared not man, yet he had yielded because of the importunities of the women."[4] Dr. Helen Stewart, also present, promised assistance and wished Nanaimo success.

The IODE raised over $500 by organizing a tag day and sponsoring a visiting theatrical play from UBC. Library costs for the first year were $682. The next year City Council granted $225. With that plus the IODE fundraising and the $1 subscription fee, the library seemed to be off to a good start, but it still required volunteers to stock and staff the facility. In 1921 when the Victoria Public Library could no longer increase the number of books loaned, Nanaimo began its own permanent collection.

The library hired a manager in 1922, but later that year funds ran out; the city no longer offered financial support. Then another influenza epidemic surfaced; membership fell off, books were not returned, and fees owed to Victoria on overdue books piled up. A city library bylaw that could have helped the situation was defeated. The library board responded:

> We look enviously on the appropriation of the smaller B.C. mining city of Nelson which supports its library with city funds to the extent of $2,500 per year. We trust that our 1922 council will not cut down the amount which we intend to ask for. They need to give us a whole lot more encouragement than they have done so far.[5]

The closure of the library seemed inevitable. Once again volunteers rose to the occasion. The efforts of the three chapters of the IODE, the Native Sons Society, the Native Daughters Society, the Local Council of Women, and other clubs resulted in a permanent library consulting board. It decided to charge borrowers $1 for a reader's card. Children still got in free.

City Council gave its support following the success of a 1923 bylaw and appointed members to the Nanaimo Municipal Library Board. The first chairman was Joseph Randle. Edward Cavalsky followed him in 1925, and he brought stability to the organization by remaining on the board for 10 years. The priority was to hire a trained librarian with the limited funds available. The first two apprentices appointed by the Victoria Library were Phyllis Knowles and Hero Calvert.[6]

As the library grew, the need for a larger space became paramount. In 1924, the library moved to a former lumber store at Wallace and Fraser streets. The 1926 library board report noted that there were 2,340 adults and 683 juveniles using the service, and that the rent had been increased from $240 to $300. The city now felt it was "well worthwhile for the city to purchase the site."[7] It purchased the building in 1927 with the understanding that the money would be paid back from the library appropriation over a period of time. The space gained the unfortunate reputation of being the worst library building in the province. The staff, forced to wear fur boots and coats in winter to keep warm, dubbed it "the hole" or "the dungeon," and it was a never-ending battle for volunteers trying to maintain the building and its leaky roof.

The board's selection of books did not always meet the approval of some members in the community. On April 2, 1925, Father Heyman, of the Roman Catholic Church, requested that Dickens' *A Child's History of England* and *Pictures from Italy* be excluded because they were anti-Catholic. The latter was not in the library, and the former was dutifully removed from the children's selection.

For years volunteers saw the library through many difficult times until 1936, when the Vancouver Island Union Library was inaugurated. The Union Library was on the lower floor of the Municipal Library building, but it had its own entrance on Fraser Street. A new library facility was built in 1955 on Strickland Street.

The Hotel Malaspina

There were already a number of hotels within Nanaimo catering to local and Island trade, but most had been built before the turn of the century. The Occidental, the Commercial, the Globe, the Lotus, and the Old Flag Inn were names that had survived from an earlier time; the Windsor became the Plaza after renovations in 1924. Most of these establishments served liquor.

It had been years since anyone had built a new hotel, and some businessmen decided there was a need for a new "modern hotel" that would fulfill a civic need and serve as a social centre. Such a hotel would make Nanaimo a "favourite stopping place for the better class of travelling people" and attract the American tourists in the 51 cars that used the Island Highway each summer.[8] After all, Nanaimo was now considered the "Hub City" on Vancouver Island because of its central location and access to transportation to the mainland.

In 1926 a group of local businessmen decided to do something about the situation; they included Frank S. Cunliffe, E.H. Bird, Oliver Eby, John W. Coburn, and Robert H. Ormond. For a year they studied "the hotel situation" and proved that the need was real and that it could be a success. They presented their idea to the Board of Trade, which endorsed the scheme but decided to take "no action." The group then formed Nanaimo Community Hotel Limited, and its Hotel Executive Committee brought forth a plan of action including estimates of the cost. They concluded $220,000 could finance the entire project, with $95,000 of that mortgaged. They chose a hotel site adjoining the Dominion Post Office overlooking the harbour.

On the Executive Committee were chairman and lawyer Frank S. Cunliffe; vice-chairman John Charles Dakin, a merchant on Commercial Street; secretary J.D. Galloway; and 26 directors. The list of directors included the who's who of Nanaimo business: John W. Coburn, owner of the New Ladysmith Lumber Company (the old Nanaimo Sawmill); Frederick A. Busby, former mayor and manager of butchers Burns & Co; pharmacist A.C. Van Houten; Oliver Eby, manager of a clothing store; and Pete Maffeo, owner of the Davenport Ice and Ice Cream Plant. Others who added their names to the list were Dr. T.J. McPhee, Frank A. Hanna, and John M. Rudd, as well as car dealership owners Norman T. Corfield and Thos. H. Weeks.

A Citizens' Sales Organization was formed to seek funding for the hotel and to recruit assistance from an American company, Hockenbury Systems Inc., which specialized in financing community hotels. They managed to raise $125,000 through the sale of $100 shares.[9]

Large advertisements appeared in the *Nanaimo Free Press* promoting the sale of shares beginning March 25, 1926. These promotions stated the hotel would be available for concerts and banquets. Most important, it would be "modern"—this meant it would have elevators and telephones, and it would attract the right type of clientele. To further distinguish it from other establishments in town, there would be no liquor permitted in the hotel. The Temperance movement remained strong both in Nanaimo and in the province, and the U.S. was in the midst of Prohibition.

The ad slogans were designed to appeal to the civic-minded individual: "Invest in Nanaimo"; "A Safe Investment, and a Civic Duty"; or "Forward or Backward? It Is Up to Us Citizens of Nanaimo."[10] Every ad included

This view of the Hotel Malaspina is from the harbour. The hotel opened July 30, 1927, and a new wing was added in 1940.

the names of the executive and directors. Within 10 days the financial goal had been reached.

Architects G.L. Thorton Sharp and Charles J. Thompson of Vancouver, who had designed the original block of UBC, were chosen to design the hotel. Ryan Contracting Ltd. of Vancouver built the seven-storey hotel in a simple classical style, with 86 rooms, a banquet hall with dance floor, business lobby, Palm Room, and Ladies' and Men's retiring rooms—and it had elevators and telephones. A community contest decided on the name "Hotel Malaspina" after the famous Malaspina Gallery, situated on Gabriola Island, opposite Nanaimo Harbour.[11] The hotel was officially opened on July 30, 1927, with a community banquet and dance.[12] The first manager was Fred J. Fall.[13]

For the next two decades the Hotel Malaspina was a top attraction in downtown Nanaimo. The official program of the Upper Island Musical Festival held in April 1937 included an advertisement for the hotel, then being managed by Thomas Stevenson. The ad prominently asked for "Expert White Help Only. Unquestionably the best meals in town are served in our beautiful dining room. Properly cooked and smartly served. Club Breakfasts from 35 cents; luncheons 50 cents; afternoon teas 35 cents, and dinners from 65 cents."[14] Prejudice against Asian people, Native people, and people of colour staying in the hotel continued throughout the '40s and '50s.

In 1938 three artists created murals for the hotel dining room, depicting historical events from the time of the arrival of the Spanish explorers in 1791. The artists were Orville Fisher, Paul Goranson, and

Edward John Hughes. The men had formed a partnership in a commercial art firm. Together they created several mural projects, including one at the B.C. Pavilion at the 1938 San Francisco World's Fair. Hughes was from Nanaimo; he had studied at the Vancouver School of Decorative and Applied Arts, now known as the Emily Carr Institute of Art & Design. During the Second World War he became a war artist. Fisher was also from the same school and joined Hughes after graduation. He too became a war artist.

In the late 1940s, a new wing was added to the hotel, creating another 35 rooms. A new ballroom was added to this wing in 1953, with access through the old dining room. After the Second World War, Mr. and Mrs. Russell Annett took over the management, bringing with them a wealth of experience gained from having owned three other hotels. When the Annetts took over, engineer George Pimlott had worked at the hotel for 25 years; A. Dustin, was assistant manager.[15]

Ray Knight bought the hotel in 1954 and immediately began major renovations. He added a new parking lot and a B.C. Airlines dock. Knight hoped that soon there would be scheduled flights to the mainland.[16] In 1958 the Wedgewood Coffee Shop operated from the ground floor of the hotel. When Knight retired in 1962, he sold the hotel to Elgin Investments Limited of Vancouver; the new manager was Walter Shepherd, former manager of the Tzouhalem Hotel in Duncan. Shepherd planned to develop a marina on the hotel's waterfront property.[17]

During the 1980s the hotel changed ownership several times, and in 1984 it closed as a hotel and became a training facility for the hospitality industry. In 1985 it was used for emergency housing for Social Assistance recipients. A year later the building closed for good.[18]

The Hotel Malaspina played an important role in the life of the community. The building was once a proud part of Nanaimo's heritage. Soon the derelict building will once again hum with activity as its role is changed from hospitality to housing.

Building a New Hospital

The Franklyn Street hospital that opened in 1883 had served the community well, but as the population increased in the early '20s, it became necessary to put all talk aside and seriously consider building a new hospital. The need had already been evident during the Spanish influenza epidemic a decade before when the old Athletic Hall was seconded as an emergency hospital for overflow patients.

With the future of medical care in the community at heart, a board of directors was established in 1924. Charles McCallum presided over the board. Other members were vice-president L.A. Dodd, Drs. George B. Brown and G.A.B. Hall, Frederick A. Busby, A. Rowan, and John Shaw, with John W. Coburn serving as chairman of the finance committee. The building committee included George S. Pearson and H.L. Good.[19]

Several community groups had recognized the need for a new hospital and had been quietly fundraising for the project. The Nanaimo Hospital Auxiliary met with the board on several occasions. The group's minute book recorded, "Little progress appeared to be made." It decided it would not turn its money over to the board "until such time as the New Hospital Building is an assured fact and the cornerstone laid, and also that the Auxiliary approve of the plans."[20]

The board of directors held a special meeting on October 17, 1924, with architect Mr. A.E. Henderson of Vancouver. He had designed the building in the form of the Tau, or Greek cross. The board approved the design and had copies sent to the Department of Provincial Public Works and others, including the Hospital Auxiliary, who invited the superintendent of the Victoria Jubilee Hospital to come to Nanaimo to look the plans over and make suggestions. Her suggestions were duly passed on to the board. By February 1925, the plans had changed—the number of beds had been reduced from 75 to 62. After approval from the provincial government, the call for tenders went out. The site chosen for the new hospital was the same as the old, on Machleary Street.

> From the windows and wide verandahs there is an inspiring view of the Gulf of Georgia, with its many evergreen islands, still in the distance the snow-capped mountains on the mainland form a background to delight the artistic sense and give an incentive to renewed life and action.[21]

Finance committee chairman John Coburn presented his report and submitted an idea to raise money. His plan was for the city to hire Ward Systems Company, of Chicago, Illinois, to put on a six-week fundraising drive in the city and district.

The successful tender was received in April from Luney Bros. for $107,650. Since the board had only enough money to erect the walls and the roof, the contract allowed for a delay in construction. Luney Bros. was also encouraged to use local labour.

Lieutenant-Governor W.C. Nicholson laid the cornerstone for the new hospital on August 20, 1925. A 54-man guard of honour attended from HMS *Capetown*—the ship happened to be in port at the time, and the Silver Cornet Band played several musical selections. Present at the historic event were two former mayors, Mark Bate and John Hilbert; both had been members of the first hospital board in 1883. Also present was local MLA William Sloan,

The Nanaimo (Malaspina) Hospital, opened in 1928, was a triumph for the community. An extension was built in 1942.

now Provincial Secretary and responsible for hospitals.[22] A month later, the Hospital Auxiliary felt confident enough to hand over $18,000.

During discussions over the new hospital in 1925, Dr. Hall suggested changing the system of nursing. Instead of nurses in training, he wanted trained nurses. The Training School for Nurses had been in existence since 1906. A committee of Dr. Hall, Dr. McPhee, and Mrs. King was appointed to consider his suggestion.[23] One year later the School for Nurses closed. About this time the Public Health Nursing Council of Nanaimo was formed.[24]

Meanwhile, the old Franklyn Street hospital had deteriorated to such an extent it had to be closed on May 31, 1927, before the new one was finished. Until the new hospital opened, patients were transferred to the Ladysmith and Victoria hospitals. For some time the new hospital structure lay dormant awaiting much needed money, and that was slow to materialize until a group of residents known as the "Lottery Committee" took on the task. They raised $25,000, and the provincial government gave a special grant of $15,000 to enable the building project to continue.

When Lieutenant-Governor Randolph Bruce opened the new hospital on October 10, 1928, it was a triumph for the community. Tributes were paid to MLA William Sloan and to architect A.E. Henderson, who both died before the building was completed.

The first baby born in the new hospital was Trixie Irene Chilton, on October 13, 1928. The Native Daughters of B.C. Post No. 2 presented a silver cup to the child.[25]

Within a year the hospital managed to reduce its debt from $9,000 to $4,000. Financial difficulties continued to plague it for some time, but all who had contributed to the facility were proud of what had been accomplished.

The Passing of an Era

Three respected pioneers, Mark Bate, John Hilbert, and William Sloan, had been present at the laying of the cornerstone for the new hospital. All three had worked hard for the community. Bate and Hilbert had served on the old Franklyn Street hospital board, and Sloan had worked federally and provincially for Nanaimo constituents. The hospital event may have been their last public function together.

John Hilbert, 81, originally from England, died on July 24, 1926.[26] He had served the community well as businessman, alderman, mayor, magistrate, and hospital board member. Hilbert was a pattern maker by trade who began making household furniture. Later he built the Methodist Church in North Wellington and the Crace Street schoolhouse and several homes. He expanded his business into manufacturing caskets.

In 1927 Mark Bate, the city's first mayor, now the grand age of 90, expressed his desire to visit his hometown of Birmingham, England. He received his doctor's permission for the trip, provided someone in his family travelled with him, so he took along his daughter and son. Bate had last visited there in 1901 when he brought back his new bride, Hannah Harrison. His previous wife Sarah had died in 1897 after their 38-year marriage.

Bate died unexpectedly while on vacation in Birmingham. His son Mark, in Nanaimo, was informed by cable. Bate's remains were returned to Nanaimo for burial. Bate left three sons: Mark Bate, of Nanaimo; Thomas Bate, Kerrisdale; Augustus (Gussie) Bate, Los Angeles; and five daughters: Mrs. Alport, South Africa; Sally, wife of W.J. Goepel, Victoria; Lucy, wife of Monty Davys, Kaslo; Mrs. Heathcote, California; and Elizabeth, wife of James Hawthornthwaite, Nanaimo.[27]

Flags in Nanaimo were lowered to half-mast as the city acknowledged the passing of its first mayor. Funeral services began at the Bate home with the Reverend Stephenson and members of council in attendance. The pallbearers who carried the casket from the home to the hearse were aldermen Cavalsky, Barsby, Rennie, Ironside, Smith, and Hart. The Silver Cornet Band led the cortège along Prideaux Street to Victoria Road, to Victoria Crescent, Commercial Street, and along Comox Road to the cemetery. Police, fire department, city workmen, and members of the Masonic Order attended. The honorary pallbearers were Mayor Frederick Busby and five former mayors: Victor B. Harrison, Senator Albert E. Planta, Thomas Hodgson, John Shaw, and William Manson.[28]

Mark Bate had seen the town transformed from a small mining village when he arrived in 1857 to a major city in the province. Bate was also a prolific writer who recorded much of the early history of the community, describing its people, places, and social events. Even after he retired in 1913 he stayed committed to public service. He once wrote:

> I know I gave my best service when in office, always endeavoured to do my duty effectively. The feeling that you are doing all that is expected of you in a public capacity is very gratifying, a pleasure is given to the individual in such a circumstance, which cannot be paid for in gold.[29]

MLA William Sloan never saw the hospital he had worked so hard for. He died on March 1, 1928, in St. Joseph's Hospital in Victoria, just seven months before the official opening. He was 61. His death came suddenly following a stroke suffered while attending the theatre in Victoria. He had been ill for several months and had been relieved of his Provincial Secretary portfolio weeks before. The popular member from Nanaimo is remembered as a man who worked hard for his constituency.

Another man of importance to the workings of the city died on December 24, 1925. Samuel Gough had served as city clerk since July 19, 1880. He was only 5 years old when he came with his parents Edwin and Elizabeth Gough aboard the Hudson's Bay Company ship the *Princess Royal* in 1854. Samuel spent 17 years in the mines before becoming city clerk. In his 45-year record of service, he was secretary of the Board of School Trustees from 1893 to 1925, and treasurer and charter member of the Independent Order of Good Templars from 1892 to 1925. Shortly before his death, the Native Sons of British Columbia, Post No. 3, Nanaimo, awarded Gough their appreciation medal.

Six former mayors attended Gough's funeral: Mark Bate, Frederick Busby, Thomas Hodgson, William Manson, Albert Planta, and John Shaw. The Silver Cornet Band followed by uniformed police and fire department staff led the funeral procession.[30]

Gough's death brought about the reorganization of city hall staff. The City appointed Harold Hackwood, a First World War veteran, the new city clerk, assessor, and comptroller at $180 per month; T.D. James as treasurer and accountant at $150 per month; and E. Hiram Gough as tax collector for $150 per month.[31] Hiram Gough, the son of Samuel, was tax collector for 41 years, retiring in 1951. He also worked for the city water works department and was secretary of Nanaimo School Board.[32]

Chapter Six

Changes in Education

School District 68

Education in Nanaimo had come a long way since 1852 when the first teacher, Charles Alfred Bayley, taught the children of the Hudson's Bay Company "labouring class." The city has one of the longest records of continuous education in the province. Nanaimo School District is one of the oldest, having been established in 1865. By 1912 there were schools at Brechin, North Cedar, Chase River, Harewood, Nanaimo City (Central), North Ward, South Ward, Middle Ward, and Quennell. Forty teachers taught 1,826 students, and their salaries were between $70 and $90 per month.[1] Lantzville opened in 1921, North Cedar and Brechin in 1927, and the Bay School (Departure Bay) in 1929.

Mr. A.S. Towell introduced the junior high-school system in 1929. At that time the high school moved to the Quennell School, and the Junior High occupied the former Central High School building. This school was renamed the John Shaw High School. The former high-school building on Wentworth Street became an elementary school and was renamed the Thomas Hodgson School. No new schools were built during the Great Depression and the years of the Second World War.

In the '20s and '30s, the lack of employment kept children in school longer. Schooling was particularly difficult for Native children, who experienced segregation for the first half of the century when they attended residential schools run by the churches. It was not until 1951 that the Indian Act allowed reserve children to attend public schools.

In 1945, Dr. Maxwell Cameron completed a report recommending the province be divided into 74 new school districts, reduced from the 650 that then existed. Cameron was a professor of education at UBC. Inspector

Claude Campbell, who was responsible for the Central Vancouver Island area, planned and guided the consolidation of the districts in the region.

School District No. 68 was established to administer all schools in the area—Harewood, Brechin, Mountain, Gabriola Island, Cedar, Extension, South Wellington, Chase River, Waterloo, and Lantzville. The board had nine members, four elected by Nanaimo taxpayers and five elected by rural taxpayers; each member was elected for a two-year term. Under this new system, rural taxpayers paid for education on the same basis as city taxpayers: "Equality of opportunity for equality of payment."[2] The Cameron Report previewed the outcome from the pupil's standpoint:

> [A] larger school unit tends to produce better results. Better graduation results. Classes become large enough to prove interesting. Socialization rather than isolation marks the education of the child. Transportation can be furnished when schools are centralized, thus promoting better attendance and less exposure to bad weather conditions, providing more safety than when walking on the highways, and providing more constant control by responsible adults. Fewer classroom teachers are required for regular academic work.[3]

The report claimed the new system would end the professional isolation, loneliness, and stagnation in which the one-room teacher too often found herself, and would result in better salaries, housing, and working equipment.

In September 1945 School District 68 Board of Trustees met to consider a report by its building committee, headed by trustee A.W. Bradfield. The board already had proposals before Victoria for three primary schools costing $50,000 each on plans prepared by architect Thomas McArravy. Victoria recognized Nanaimo's need for new schools and decided the government would provide grants of 20 percent for elementary schools and 40 percent for junior-senior schools.[4]

The first new school built after the war was the Pauline Haarer School in 1948 on the site of the old North Ward School on Campbell Street. The new Nanaimo District Senior High School, later called the Nanaimo District Secondary School (NDSS), was built in 1952 on Wakesiah Avenue, on the former Camp Nanaimo grounds. It had a registration of 475 pupils and 25 teachers. At that time the NDSS was considered one of the most modern schools in the province, with classes in carpentry, machine shop, boat building, foods, clothing, typing, and bookkeeping, as well as academic courses. The former John Shaw High School continued as a junior high until John Barsby, Woodlands, Wellington, and Cedar junior high schools were built. John Shaw was demolished and Quennell became an elementary school.

The North Ward School's Division 2 Class of March, 1937, is shown here. The school was later replaced with the Pauline Haarer School.

In 1967, the district employed 300 teachers and enrolled 8,000 students in 26 elementary schools, 3 junior secondary schools, and 1 senior secondary school. Twelve kindergartens were incorporated into elementary schools.[5]

Pauline Haarer

After spending 46 years teaching in Nanaimo, Pauline Haarer had an elementary school named in her honour. Pauline was born in Somersville, California. She came to Canada with her widowed 46-year-old mother, Mary, and two sisters—Julia, 12, and Isabella (Isabel), 8—and brother Fred, 15. Another sister, Helena, was born in Canada.

Pauline began teaching at age 15 in the Girls' School that opened in 1878 under principal Margaret Planta. Pauline's salary for the first month was a $50 gold piece, which she dutifully dropped into her mother's apron pocket when she got home. Her mother was happy and probably relieved, for she exclaimed, "Now my little girl can help me."[6]

Pauline was the family's only wage earner until her brother got a job as a waiter and her sister Isabel began teaching. Isabel taught in the South School on Gabriola Island in 1903 and at the South Wellington School.[7]

After the war Nanaimo teemed with children—14 in just one block. The overcrowding situation was remedied by Miss Laura Campbell, who operated a private kindergarten in the tall brown house at the corner of Wentworth and Milton streets. Her kindergarten was held in high esteem and always had a waiting list. Campbell accommodated the school by adding a grade one class and this took care of the overflow for those who could afford the tuition of $7 a month.

In 1948 the sod was turned for the Pauline Haarer Primary School on Campbell Street—the first new school to be built since 1914. The official opening was held before a large crowd of parents, pupils, and invited guests that included minister of education the Honorable R.T. Straith and his deputy, Colonel Fairey. Local MLA George Pearson was unable to attend. Fairey spoke of the two wars and the Depression that had precluded any new schools being built. He said it was about time Nanaimo had new educational institutions. Straith paid tribute to Pauline Haarer, who had given so much to the community: "Her most enduring recognition lay in the hearts of the people she had so faithfully served."[8] Pauline Haarer signed the school register. Dudy Norris, the youngest pupil in the new school, gave the elderly schoolteacher a corsage and a basket of red and white chrysanthemums.

The first principal of the new school was Tommy Bennett. The first teachers were Minnie Stewart, Vickie Rogers, Miss A. Kenyon, and Miss Mercer. Classes in the school were large; Miss Mercer felt lucky if she had only 40 pupils. In the second year, Miss Rogers' class was so large that the children who lived on the border were told to report to another school. To help the janitor keep the tile floors clean, children were asked to keep a pair of slippers in school, and those who had not yet mastered the art of tying shoelaces wore penny loafers.[9]

Other Schooling Opportunities

The Sprott-Shaw Business College was founded as a service to young men and women going into the business world. Mr. Perry administered the first school and managed it until it was taken over by Sprott-Shaw in 1912 under the management of Mr. J.H. Beatty. Hannah McLean succeeded him for a year and was followed by Norman Carter.

The college offered commercial, stenographic, secretarial, civil service, and preparatory courses. It offered evening classes for those unable to attend during the day, and courses in elementary education for those who had neglected their early schooling and now wanted to remedy their situation.[10] The college was still operating in 2005.

Two private schools in the city were not included in School District 68; they were St. Ann's Convent and Boarding School and St. George's On-The-Hill Boys' School. Until 1935 St. Ann's offered instruction from grades one to eight. In September of that year a three-year commercial high-school course began, with the first class graduating in June 1938. The course was designed to prepare students for a practical and purposeful career. The school also taught domestic science.[11] St. Ann's Business School registered the first class of 28 students in 1941.

St. Ann's Convent, on Wallace Street, continued to serve the community from 1877 to 1966, despite suffering two major fires.

The school seems to have been plagued by fire; it was destroyed in 1910, then rebuilt. In 1955 another fire caused extensive damage.

In 1962 the high school was closed to increase facilities for primary and elementary grades. The staff included four sisters and three lay teachers with one part-time physical education teacher. The 1961/62 registration was 203 children, 87 boys and 116 girls. The Business School registered 37 young men and women.[12] When St. Ann's Convent closed in 1966, its pupils were absorbed into the public school system.

St. George's On-The-Hill Boys' School was located in the area known as Nob Hill, at Hecate and Prideaux, in one of the most prominent houses, built before the turn of the century for Judge Eli Harrison and later used by Dr. J.H. Hogle. The grand and gracious home once provided accommodation for the doctor's female patients—in the early days there were no beds for female patients in the hospital. After the First World War the house was transformed into the school.

The private boys' school catered to pupils from 7 to 15 years and offered both residential and day school. School advertisements promised "A sound preparation for the Universities or for a Professional or Business career."[13] The school also offered Boy Scout and Wolf Cub training, summer camp, and bodybuilding exercises.

The curriculum emphasized resourcefulness and confidence in mathematics, languages, and "the usual English subjects." Art instruction was used to develop a sense of beauty and refinement. The school's crest was proudly featured on the school caps worn by the boys, well-recognized in town. The school motto, *Credo quod habes et habes*, means "Believe that you have it, and you do."

The 26-room school had hot water heating. The halls and rooms had high ceilings and a wide, central staircase. The dining room looked out over the city towards Protection and Gabriola islands and the Strait of Georgia. Each dormitory room accommodated three or four beds. The boys did their preparation in the lounge on the first landing. The original drawing room was converted into a chapel, and parents and friends were encouraged to attend. Another building on the grounds was used for drill practices, gymnastics, and "the noisier games."

Headmaster Mr. P. Chapman, with his acknowledged academic credentials, was a talented musician and master of 45 members of the St. George's Troop and Pack of Cubs.

Nanaimo's First Boy Scouts

In 1911 there were 21 Boy Scout troops in B.C.; Nanaimo district had 3 troops with 116 boys enrolled. The district included Ladysmith, Wellington, and the outlying areas of the city. This same year, Lt. Col. Hall and Chief Commissioner Beerbohm, from England, visited the city to inspect the local Scouts. The boys lined up in front of the Dominion Post Office building to demonstrate their skills at signalling and their first-aid abilities.[14]

Credit for the formation of the movement in the city went to C.L. Brigade and Mr. Rowlands; the latter taught at the Chinese School and had previously been in charge of the Victoria Troop. Scoutmasters were Mr. J. Hunt, the manager of Western Fuel Company, and Mr. J.M. Thomson, newly arrived from England. Three city troops were formed under Mr. S.M. Skinner of the Presbyterian Church and Mr. S.M. Bradfield of the Methodist Church, and Mr. S.M. Thomson of St. Paul's.

The First World War intervened, and the Boy Scouts disappeared from the streets of Nanaimo. Some scouts made the supreme sacrifice, while others returned home and became Scoutmasters. The Nanaimo Troop was reinstated under the headmaster of St. George's Boys' School, Mr. P. Chapman. Within three weeks of his arrival, he had a troop of 12 boys, most of whom had been connected with the earlier troop. In 1922 the headquarters for the Boy Scout movement was at St. George's School. The first Nanaimo St. George's Troop and Pack grew steadily until it numbered 40 boys by 1924.

Under Chapman's supervision, the boys hiked, swam, did cross-country runs, and played football. The Scouts and Cubs had their own banners donated by Senator Albert E. Planta and MLA William Sloan.[15] Summer camps were held at Departure Bay, on the hill behind the Pacific Biological Station. Another was held in Parksville with 29 Scouts and Cubs living in tents for 30 days. In 1930, a Scout hall was built on Comox Road on the Gyro Playground.

The Girl Guides and Brownies were equally successful, and by the 40s there was a long waiting list for young people interested in joining the movement.

Chapter Seven

Fire and Brimstone

Church Union Controversy

St. Andrew's Presbyterian Church amalgamated with Methodist and Congregational churches in 1925 to form the United Church of Canada. In Nanaimo, however, this union did not come as easily for the Presbyterian as it did for the Methodist and Congregational churches. St. Andrew's held out for a year that was full of "intense, bitter infighting that before long, spread far beyond its own congregation."[1]

One-third of all Presbyterian churches across Canada decided to remain part of the Presbyterian Church of Canada. Those who voted against the union started new congregations elsewhere. However, St. Andrew's Presbyterian Church in Nanaimo did not give in so easily. The church took its case before the Presbytery Synod and General Assembly—it reached civil court, the B.C. Legislature, and finally the Supreme Court of British Columbia. The dominant force behind the dissent was the Reverend David Lister, minister at St. Andrew's.

Reverend Lister joined St. Andrew's congregation in 1921. Born in Fifeshire, Scotland, he came from a very strict Scottish Presbyterian background and was not easily swayed by the new movement. During the union debate, the church had 13 elders, 8 of whom favoured union and strongly defended their position; the other 5 decided not to join. The church held many meetings and allowed all to express their opinions pro or con.

A voters list was drawn up from the Church Roll, which contained all the names of regular church members. Clerk of Session, Mr. J.W. Murray, and Reverend Lister noticed that a number of names had pencilled marks beside them; these were members who had missed communion a number of times. The two men decided they were therefore not members in good standing and should not be allowed to vote. It was an arbitrary decision which perhaps should have been debated with the Church Session.

The controversial vote was taken on January 19, 1925, with 115 voting for union and 125 against. It seemed St. Andrew's would remain Presbyterian. However, two days later, 98 members met for a special meeting, including those not allowed to vote. They strongly protested the voting procedure and informed the Presbytery in Victoria, claiming the vote was either illegal or invalid and that Reverend Lister should not have decided who could or could not vote. Meanwhile, the eight elders in favour of union stopped attending St. Andrew's and began attending the Wallace Street Methodist Church that had already decided to become "united." The St. Andrew's congregation was bitterly divided; soon other members began attending the Methodist Church.

Reverend Lister openly defended his views from the pulpit and attacked the pro-union position. More members stayed away from his services. One Sunday when all the pro-union elders were absent, he decided they were no longer members in good standing and the congregation should elect new ones immediately after the service. Of course the nine new elders were all against union. A new Clerk of Session was appointed to replace the absent Mr. Murray.

The other eight pro-union elders were asked to resign but they refused, opting to await a decision from the Presbytery regarding the voting procedures. The Clerk of the Presbytery favoured union but did not want to see the Nanaimo congregation so divided. After a special meeting the eight elders were reinstated. The church now had 22 elders with a majority of anti-union members. It was a small victory for Reverend Lister.

Most congregations throughout the province settled down and moved on. Not so Nanaimo! St. Andrew's pro-union forces continued to petition the Presbytery in Victoria on the issue of the Church Roll and who had not been allowed to vote. Reverend Lister turned a deaf ear to all charges against him. The debate now went to the Clerk of the Synod. A Committee of the Whole tried to decide how to handle Nanaimo. Finally the Synod ruled the vote had been illegal. The Presbytery objected; it petitioned the General Assembly to have the decision overruled. Now the matter lay at the feet of the national Presbyterian Church in Toronto, and time was running out. The official opening of the new United Church of Canada was scheduled for June 1925.

Back in Nanaimo, only a few members continued to attend St. Andrew's. They were united in their belief to stay Presbyterian. The pro-union members now attended the Wallace Street Methodist Church. The General Assembly upheld the decision of Synod that the vote was illegal and unconstitutional. Reverend Lister had had no right to deprive members of their voting privileges.

On Communion Sunday elders found the church vessels were missing. The pro-union elders had taken them to the Methodist Church. St. Andrew's elders had to borrow from St. Paul's Anglican Church.

The National General Council of the United Church of Canada was duly proclaimed, but Nanaimo St. Andrew's Presbyterians clung to their church at Fitzwilliam and Wesley streets. A lawyer for the United Church was appointed to take the matter to civil court. The Supreme Court of British Columbia ruled the voters list had not been accurate—all members should have been allowed to vote. This judgement had far-reaching consequences. According to a provincial act passed at the time, all church congregations were obligated to vote on the church union before June 10, 1925. Any church that had not voted by then automatically entered into union by default. St. Andrew's congregation entered the United Church despite the majority of its members being opposed, and St. Andrew's Church became the property of the United Church of Canada.

The church keys were taken from Reverend Lister, and the Presbyterians were left without a home while the United Church had two. It was finally decided that the United Church should keep St. Andrew's and the Presbyterians would have the old Wallace Street Methodist Church, which by this time was old and rundown. It was demolished in 1929. The Presbyterians continued to worship in a rented community hall until they built their own church at Franklyn and Wesley streets. Reverend Lister left Nanaimo to serve a new congregation in Kerrisdale, a district of Vancouver. He was invited back for the laying of the cornerstone for the new church on July 19, 1930. He said he missed a number of "kent" faces, then read a poem, a portion of which follows, his Scottish voice coming out loud and clear:

Come ane an' a', lift up yer voice,
Rejoice, Nanaimo friends, rejoice;
Give thanks to God, extol His Word,
And praise and magnify the Lord.
For noo has dawned the day at last,
When, trials and tribulations past,
Abune the murky, misty mirk,
We gaze upon a rising kirk,
The magic words hae weel been said,
The Cornerstone at last is laid.[2]

Fire Destroys Church and Businesses

While the St. Andrew's Presbyterian Church congregation faced a crisis of conscience, St. Paul's Anglican Church expanded services to include missionary work in Cedar and Five Acres (Harewood). After the First

World War, Canon S. Ryall managed to pay off debt and back taxes, and by 1923 repairs to the church were completed. He and his wife were championship tennis players and frequently entertained in the well-kept rectory grounds. On September 5, 1927, Canon Ryall accepted the position of Rector at St. Luke's Cedar Hill Church, in Victoria. Canon Harry V. Hitchcox replaced him.

St. Paul's was dealt a terrible blow on Saturday, July 19, 1930, when fire destroyed a good portion of Nanaimo's business sector bounded by Front, Chapel, Church, Commercial, and Skinner streets. Six business blocks and one residence were totally destroyed, including the church and its institute (hall); others were partially damaged. The rectory received some damage but escaped total destruction.

The fire was first discovered during the early morning hours in Shaw's 40-year-old condemned IXL Stables on Skinner Street. It quickly spread to the home of Horace Johnson, then destroyed the IXL, Garage and Storage Rooms, Pontiac Sales, Tom Weeks & Sons Garage and Service Station, the Wilson Block, and the small home of J.C. McGregor. The Nanaimo Free Press Block received damage, as did Tom Weeks & Sons display rooms and offices adjoining the Canadian Bank of Commerce. The IXL building had been used by Weeks as storage for 34 second-hand cars, and the basement, rented to Mr. Adirim, a local junk dealer, had been filled with second-hand goods, including 2,500 old tires, wool, and other items.[3]

The flames jumped Chapel Street and started on St. Paul's Church and its institute and rectory. For a time it seemed that Fire Chief John Parkin and his firefighters had it under control in the Wilson Block, the location of Gilbert Holt's billiard and pool rooms and Frank Doran's barber shop, but flames found their way into vacant upper stories of the building. St. Paul's was one of the oldest churches in the city, having been founded in 1859. The present church had been built in 1906, the institute in 1925. The three-storey brick Wilson Block was built in 1892 by Walter Wilson.

The Fire Warden Committee had alerted the city in February to the dangerous condition of the IXL building, but as the city had no regular building inspector, the committee recommended that two local contractors be hired to examine the building.[4] The warning came too late.

The estimated loss to businesses was $100,000, and another $30,000 for the church and hall. St. Paul's lost almost everything but was insured for $20,000. Canon Hitchcox urged his congregation to focus on rebuilding. He noted:

> This is a very serious blow to our work and it remains to be seen whether it will unite our people as never before, or simply accentuate their differences. If these people are of the right stuff they will accept

> the challenge and will rebuild in a manner that will symbolize their faith and courage.[5]

A new city bylaw demanded that future buildings have fireproof construction; for St. Paul's this meant an increased cost for a community that was beginning to feel the repercussions of the Great Depression. Canon Hitchcox pleaded with Anglicans outside the district: "Our people are sadly impoverished owing to the greatly decreased coal trade, few pits are working, and these only two or three days a week."[6]

Architect J.C.M. Keith, who designed Victoria's Christ Church Cathedral, was hired to design a new church, but his first set of plans were too expensive. Keith modified his plans to suit church officials and these were accepted. The contract for the new church and hall was awarded to a local company, Turley Brothers, for $23,296. During construction, church services were held in the rectory, in the Bijou Theatre on Commercial Street, and in the Capitol Theatre. The cornerstone was laid August 24, 1931, and the first service was held in the new church on January 3, 1932.

Although the Canadian Bank of Commerce on Church Street suffered about $100,000 damage, it still came out a winner. Known today as the Great National Land Building, it escaped the flames because of its brick and terra cotta construction, and it was partly covered by insurance. Several staff members lived inside the building. R.E. Avery described the fire in *The Caduceus*, the bank newsletter:

> At about 3:30 a.m. on 19th July our staff were awakened by the siren just outside the bank. They didn't wait to hear the bell, for smoke and flame were simply pouring over the building, so with very commendable speed they unreeled our fire hose and dashed out through the trapdoor in the roof. At once [staff] had a fine stream of water saturating the tar and gravel, and running down over the cornice.
>
> The heat was terrific. Our boys stuck it well, and did excellent work not only with the hose but [also] in spotting further outbreaks. By 6 o'clock ten buildings had been destroyed and the new paint from our metal cornice lay in small piles on the sidewalk, seven big plate glass windows were cracked in all directions, and five plate fan-lights, beside ten other windows of staff quarters.
>
> Had the building been of wood, nothing could have saved it. Business opened as usual at 9:30 a.m. and we are making the most of the opportunity to push Safety Deposit Boxes, pointing with just pride at our scarred building, which enabled the firemen to confine the blaze to this section of the town.[7]

Mr. Avery also described how the fire alarm system worked. The city was divided into numbered fire zones. When an alarm was raised, a bell rang out the number of that particular fire zone. The bank was in zone 32. When the electronic sirens started screaming, they drowned out the noise of the bell, leaving one to guess where the fire was. "This is extremely annoying especially to the volunteer firemen, who may be needed in the event of a really big blaze to augment the regular staff of four."[8]

All telephone and electrical wiring was burned early so it was impossible to warn those living outside the bank.

Another fire on January 10, 1937, in the commercial district had losses estimated at $55,000; it injured three firemen: Albert Dunn, Jim Anthony, and William Gordon. According to the annual fire report, 21 firemen responded to the fire. Fire Chief John Parkin suffered pneumonia and died February 25, 1937.[9]

This fire began on a Sunday morning shortly before 7:00 a.m. in the Williams Block, in the basement of Powers, Doyle & Berry men's wear store, jewellers Harding & Aird, Gray Brothers, and Mrs. Meeks Tea Room. The stores were fully involved when the alarm was turned in. Firemen tried desperately to confine the flames to the two buildings, but it was impossible.[10]

The fire next spread north to the shoe repair shop of E. Ranger and totally gutted his entire stock; then it travelled south to Finette's Ladies' Wear. Pete Brennen's barbershop next caught fire, but by this time most of the contents had been cleared by friends. Volunteers succeeded in helping James Gray remove most of his stock of cigars, fruit, and candy, though his shop suffered water and smoke damage. The tenants in three apartments above the stores lost everything—one woman managed to save her fur coat.

Firemen Dunn and Gordon were directing the fire hose from the verandah, which extended along the front of the two-storey building. Suddenly the verandah collapsed. The firemen fell about 30 feet; then all the debris fell on top of them. Jim Anthony was also injured, though he was working the fire on the other side of the street where the Fish Store, Walls & Bradshaw, and Stearman Drug Store were located. All three men were treated at the hospital.[11]

Nanaimo Fire Chiefs: "We Strive to Save"

John Parkin

Nanaimo's longest-serving fire chief was John Parkin; he held the post from 1897 to 1937. He joined the Black Diamond Fire Company in 1889; it became the Nanaimo Fire Department in 1901. All who worked with him praised his ability to sum up a situation and then quickly decide the best course of action. During his years as fire chief he directed firefighters in some of the city's biggest fires.[12] Parkin and two drivers were the first salaried members of the Nanaimo Fire Department.

Parkin was born in Nanaimo on February 4, 1867, to William and Eliza Parkin (née Malpass). Both parents were from England; his mother was a daughter of *Princess Royal* pioneers Lavinia and John Malpass. His father first emigrated to the U.S. before settling in Nanaimo, where he worked as a fireboss in the coal mines until an explosion took his sight only six months after his marriage.[13] The only compensation from the Vancouver Coal Company was a half-ton of coal each month. William had been a prospector in the Cariboo and, after his accident, his Welsh partners in the gold rush gave him a dog that he named Carlo. Unfortunately the dog only understood Welsh but somehow William was able to train him. John was the eldest of 17 children and recalled his home being a happy one:

> We were never allowed out of the house after six p.m. and you can imagine what a bedlam it would be with nine or ten half-grown boys and two girls in the house, with nothing to do. Our mother could do no wrong. She put most of us through school, and I passed for high school, but as there was no such institution here then, I could not go further.[14]

His parents started a grocery store on Commercial Street, next door to the Miner's Hotel. Eliza assumed most of the responsibility, waiting on customers and cooking and mending for the family. Her only help came from a Native woman who came once a week to houseclean. With the help of Carlo the dog, William was able to make deliveries. After leaving school, John worked first in a large grocery store, and later worked as a teamster before joining the fire department. He became fire chief after only three years. John married Rose Ann Hilbert, and they had one daughter, Violet Amelia. The family lived above the fire hall.

Four more fire chiefs served the community: Bramley Benton, 1937–44; James Anthony, 1945–49; Wilfred Wardill, 1950–51; Colin McArthur, 1952–66; and Albert Dunn, 1967–75.[15]

Albert Dunn

Three years after the big fire in 1930 Albert Dunn joined the Nanaimo Fire Department as a volunteer. He became a permanent member in 1939, was promoted to captain in 1950, and became fire chief in 1967, a position he held until retirement in 1975.

Albert was born December 23, 1915, to Charles and Miriam Dunn at the family home on Selby Street during one of the coldest winters in Nanaimo. "It was so bad, in fact, that my father did not get out to register my birth until the following January. For years I thought myself a year younger than I was."[16] The family eventually moved to Milton Street.

His father, Charles, was born in England and was indentured on a farm before he ran away to South Wales and found work in the mines. Charles and Miriam had three children before deciding to come to Nanaimo in 1909. Other family members already worked in the Cumberland coal mines. Of the six children, those born in Wales were Thomas, Charles Jr., and Beatrice; those born in Nanaimo were Albert, Ronald, and Gertrude.

Charles and his three older sons worked in the WFC Reserve Mine developed on the Snuneymuxw No. 2 Reserve in South Nanaimo. The mine operated from 1912 to 1939. Miners' wives worked hard, and Albert's mother was no exception. He remembered her "boiling water on the stove for baths as each miner came home; lunch buckets had to be prepared on a daily basis, and the three smaller children to be fed and sent off to school. I often wondered in later years, when she actually found time to sleep. And she was always singing!"

As a child, Albert fished for cod at the coal wharf and sold his catch to the Chinese laundry, the bunkhouses, or the people in Chinatown:

> Fish sold for between five and fifteen cents and brought in some needed pocket money, or money for the family. Saturday was the great day. Pocket money was 15 cents—10 to go to the Opera House to see the latest film with Tom Mix, Hoot Gibson, or some other popular star, and five to spend at McKenzies for candy. Those were the days when you got six candy suckers for that price, either chocolate or hard ones.

During the Depression, "you never said no" to work. There were seven out of work in the Dunn family. When Albert left school he was determined not to go on relief; therefore he and his school friends began hanging around the fire hall. One day a fire call came in and volunteer firemen had trouble with the equipment. Albert and his friends were able to help them. After the fire was over, he questioned the chief why he and his friends could figure out the equipment while those who were supposed to know how to use it couldn't. "The next thing I knew, he asked me if I wanted to be a volunteer. I said sure." Fire Chief John Parkin told him that he would need a letter from his mother. At that time there were four full-time drivers; most of the firefighters were volunteers.

In the meantime, Albert worked different jobs as a driver, hauler, and tagger of Christmas trees, and for George Pearson in his grocery business. In 1934 he dug out an eight-foot basement in the Bijou Theatre to enable a sound system to be installed. Famous Players took over the Bijou in 1935 and changed the name to the Strand Theatre. Later it became part of G.A. Fletcher Music Co. Ltd.

Albert was on the double-man hose team that sometimes came first in competitions against other fire teams. He fought many other fires in the community but the biggest, the Chinatown fire, was yet to come.

The Trials of Brother XII

Was Brother XII a religious man, or was he a shyster intent on milking his followers of their wealth? So many books have been written and so many stories told about the Aquarian Foundation. It is difficult to separate fact from fiction, but something mysterious did take place in Cedar-by-the-Sea, and on Valdes and De Courcy islands.

This much we know is true—or is it? In 1905, Brother XII, known then as Edward Arthur Wilson, worked as a clerk with the Dominion Express Company office in Victoria. Accounts differ as to his place of birth; one claims that he was born Julian Churton Skottowe in England in 1871. Another that he was born in Wyoming, Ontario, where he ran away from home at age 15 only minutes ahead of an irate father of a pregnant girl. A fellow employee at the Express Company described him as "five foot six in height, slim, sallow and dapper, with a receding chin and large Adam's apple, who often wore a red rosebud in his dark lapel … a smooth talker."[17]

Wilson next appears on the French Riviera in October 1924; he was ill and broke. Later he told the world about this period of suffering, claiming it was here that he had a spiritual awakening, a vision that changed his life. He began using the name Brother XII and identified himself as a Messenger of the Fire, the Whirlwind, and the day of Adjustment.

Sometime in April 1927, Wilson arrived in Nanaimo and found work as a lamp-keeper in WFC No. 1 mine. His job was to make sure all the lamps that went down the mine worked properly and had enough fuel. He lived in a small cabin next to the pithead, which observers noted, "was always stocked with the best of books."[18] Alva Shaw, whose father owned the IXL Stables, said Wilson had worked at the stables "and had made an extraordinary impression upon [her] father and the people of Nanaimo."[19] She claimed he even put on a stage show as a hypnotist in the Orpheum Theatre.

Wilson next boarded with music teacher Peggy Reynolds, where he announced he was starting a new religion. Before long he purchased land in the Cedar-by-the-Sea area, near Boat Harbour south of Nanaimo, with money given to him by wealthy followers. From this home base he began spreading the word about his Aquarian Foundation. In books, pamphlets, and magazines, Wilson persuaded people from all over North America and Europe to endow his foundation with a fortune, which he later converted into gold bars. One book entitled *The Three Truths* later became the foundation's bible. The foundation's monthly magazine was called *The Chalice*.[20] By 1928, approximately 8,000 members were contributing to Brother XII.

Wilson's whole scheme, it seemed, was to instill fear and confusion, so members gladly gave him everything—their money, their property, and anything else of value. Several complained of how he spent foundation money. During an audit, Robert England, secretary of the foundation and former secret service agent, discovered that Wilson had been dipping into foundation money. He charged Wilson with the embezzlement of $13,000 from a donation of $25,000 from wealthy U.S. resident Mrs. Mary Connally. He had used this money to purchase 400 acres of property on Valdes Island for the "Mandieh settlement." Sergeant John Russell of the B.C. Provincial Police arrested Wilson, who subsequently counter-charged England with embezzling $2,800 from the Aquarian Foundation's account. England claimed this money was back wages owed. Wilson refused to withdraw the charges, and the day before the preliminary hearing began, England disappeared, never to be seen again.

Nanaimo was a small town and probably not ready for the international attention that came its way during the next few years. In 1928, downtown was the shopping mall of today. It was a gathering place where people caught up on the latest happenings at home and elsewhere. Families stocked up on weekly groceries at Spencer's Department Store or purchased music for their children at G.A. Fletcher Music Co. Ltd. Miners congregated at Billy Gray's tobacco store to choose from a wide selection of cigarettes, imported tobacco, or pipes. Children loved the Palace of Sweets where they had a choice of their favourite licorice sticks or aniseed balls, while nearby at the Windsor Hotel, patrons quenched their thirst with draught beer and discussed the issues of the day. At the corner of Commercial and Church streets, the impressive columned Canadian Bank of Commerce welcomed businessmen with their take of the day or settled weekly accounts.

Between the years 1927 and 1933 Nanaimo learned the curious details of Wilson and his followers through two trials. In September 1928, Magistrate Charles Herbert Beevor-Potts began hearing the first case in the old city council chambers at the corner of Bastion and Skinner. Lawyer Frank S. Cunliffe represented Brother XII. The lawyer for the prosecution was Thomas Morton, who boldly stated he had no fear of "spirits or ghosts or anything of that kind."[21] Lawyer and former mayor of Nanaimo, Victor B. Harrison, partner in Harrison and McIntyre, one of Nanaimo's leading law firms, and *Province* reporter Bruce McKelvie attended the trial. Harrison attended the proceedings on behalf of the Attorney General R.H. Pooley. Members of the Aquarian Foundation had petitioned the Attorney General to have the foundation dissolved. Pooley waited for the outcome of the trial.

By 10 o'clock, Tuesday, October 30, 1928, the room was jammed with curious spectators seeking a glimpse of the mysterious cult leader. Magistrate Beevor-Potts brought the court to order. Wilson was charged with stealing $13,000 from the Aquarian Foundation. Suddenly Robert England's elderly lawyer, Thomas Morton, collapsed on the bench and others collapsed to the floor. Harrison stated:

> I thought this was a very extraordinary performance; and from out of the audience came Brother XII, [he] strode across the police court floor and held out his hand to shake hands with me and he said, "This is an awful state of affairs. They're trying to prosecute me, but there's nothing in it and you're going to be appointed by the Crown to prosecute this case."[22]

Magistrate Beevor-Potts was so disturbed by the proceedings that in a shaky voice he adjourned the court. There was speculation that Brother XII had hypnotized the people.

McKelvie's report of the hearing was front page in *The Province* the next day, and Nanaimo residents were getting a little antsy at the publicity the case received. Leading the charge was the *Nanaimo Free Press* editor:

> We are indebted to B.C. McKelvie for the assurance that the affair is a local sensation, and this looks like a dirty crack at our rustic emotions. I suggest the scene of court activities be moved to Vancouver, which has had no sensations since good civic government was established there.[23]

Brother XII, fourth from left, was a religious man and a shyster who milked people of their wealth. This photo of him with some of his followers was taken in 1927.

On November 20, 1928, the case came before Chief Justice Aulay M. Morrison. The charges against Wilson and Robert England now included rape, assault, perjury, opium smuggling, and the sexual abuse of a 10-year-old girl. Mary Connally made a surprise appearance in defence of Wilson. She had arrived by train from Reno, Nevada. Crown Counsel Victor Harrison instructed the court that the Attorney General had asked that the charge against Wilson be moved to the next assizes as the principal witness, Robert England, had disappeared. Some believed Brother XII's henchmen had murdered him. The Chief Justice postponed the case until the next morning, but the case would continue with England tried in absentia. The jury returned the verdict no bill (no case). The following day, the jury returned the same verdict in the Wilson case—no bill.

Wilson was a free man and could now concentrate on developing new property on De Courcy Island purchased with Mary Connally's money, with the title placed in the name of Brother XII's secretary-treasurer, Thomas Cranmer Williams.

No story about Brother XII would be complete without mention of his fortification, his navy, and his gold. His vessels were the *Lady Royal* and the *Kleunaten*, and a fast speedboat with a powerful Grey Dart seven-cylinder engine. On De Courcy Island, stone cairns protected guards with guns, who were ready for any assault by government or police. To protect his fortune from the Depression, Brother XII converted money into $20 gold pieces, sealed them in 43 Mason jars, and buried them on the island. Apparently he excavated and buried the jars over and over again to avoid theft.

About this time a red-headed woman named Mabel Skottowe, as strange, bad-tempered, and unscrupulous as Wilson himself, appeared from Florida and became his second-in-command. Wilson legally changed his name to Amiel de Valdes and Mabel changed hers to Zura de Valdes. She was immediately nicknamed Madam Zee. Some described her as a complete sadist. Zee reserved her worst treatment for Mary Connally, who had fallen into disfavour after she lost all her money in the stock-market crash of 1929. Zee and Brother XII made a trip to England; on their return, 12 people, including Mary Connally, were banished from the foundation's headquarters.

This led to another lawsuit in the Supreme Court of British Columbia on April 26, 1933, before Chief Justice Aulay M. Morrison in the Nanaimo courthouse. Connally retained Victor Harrison as her counsel, and Alfred Barley entered a suit against Amiel and Zura de Valdes in an effort to recover some of their money. Once again Nanaimo residents crowded into the courtroom. Mary Connally, or Lady Mary, as she was now respectfully referred to, was considered the key witness to Wilson's fall from grace. Defence lawyer Frank Cunliffe was at a disadvantage, as his clients were not in the courtroom. After a lengthy hearing, the Chief Justice rendered a verdict completely in favour of Harrison's clients. He awarded Mary Connally $26,500 for money she had advanced, $10,000 in damages, and 400 acres on Valdes Island. Barley received $14,232.[24]

In an interview with Nanaimo historian William Barraclough, Victor Harrison explained how he went to De Courcy Island to see Mary Connally after the trial and found her still enamoured of Brother XII.

"Oh my," she said, "it is all terrible. If the Brother would only come back and be his old self again we would all join right in. I would be only too glad to join with him again. Forget all the past."

"Why," asked Harrison, "you've got all these islands back."

"Oh," she said, "that's nothing. I'd give them all back to him. I'd be with him again. If only he'd be his own self again. It's terrible. If he'd only return, I know we'll be all very happy. I certainly would."[25]

Brother XII died in Neuchatel, Switzerland, on November 7, 1934. Mary Connally continued to live on Valdes Island.

Chapter Eight

The Emergence of the CCF

Provincial Politics

Premier John Oliver had been in power since 1918, but by the spring of 1927 his health was failing. Publicly he took a well-earned vacation, but privately he checked in to the Mayo Clinic in Rochester, Minnesota, where he underwent a cancer operation. He returned to Victoria a tired and frail old man, and he told his party to pick a new leader. They refused and instead appointed an interim leader, John Duncan MacLean, a doctor and former school principal. Oliver died on August 17, 1927. His body lay in state in the legislative chamber and was buried in Saanich, north of Victoria.

By all accounts Oliver may not have been a good premier, but he was conscientious, diligent, friendly, and outgoing, and although a little naïve in the beginning, he quickly developed political expertise that astounded some. He summed up his life this way: "My rule of life has been to try and make the best of every condition as I found it at the time. I found out things because I was up against it; adversity was my teacher."[1]

Dr. MacLean called an election for July 18, 1928. His opponent was Dr. Simon Fraser Tolmie, a veterinarian, whose father had worked for the Hudson's Bay Company. Tolmie was a large man weighing almost 300 pounds, and he was a veteran politician, having held a federal seat for the Conservatives since 1921. Tolmie and the Conservatives swept into power taking 35 of the 48 seats.[2]

William Sloan had represented Nanaimo since 1920. After his death in 1928, the riding remained Liberal with voters returning another familiar face, George S. Pearson, the man who had headed up the building committee for the new hospital.[3] His nearest opponent was lawyer Victor Birch Harrison, a Conservative.

This was Pearson's first venture into politics, and he would wait in opposition until the 1933 election when the Liberals were returned. He then followed in William Sloan's footsteps by serving in various Cabinet positions—Labour, Health and Welfare, Mines and Railways and Provincial Secretary. He was MLA until 1952, serving Nanaimo for 24 years.

George S. Pearson was MLA from 1928 to1952, serving Nanaimo for 24 years. He held four different Cabinet posts.

Pearson had left his hometown of Bromley, in Staffordshire, England, in 1889, at 9 years of age. He joined his father, Joseph, who had come to Nanaimo two years earlier with seven other miners. George married Emeline Pearce on March 2, 1904, a union that produced two daughters. In his business life he was owner and manager of Malcolm-Pearson, a retail and wholesale grocery business.

Tolmie's administration dealt with the beginning of the Depression. He established work camps and increased road-building projects. The legislative sessions of 1930, 1931, and 1932 were considered dreary.[4] The high rate of unemployment continued to dominate any hoped-for economic recovery. The 1933 election was a crucial one, for it brought the Co-operative Commonwealth Federation (CCF) into B.C. provincial politics.

The Depression years were particularly difficult in the Prairies. Whole areas of the countryside were affected as soil blew away in the terrible dust storms. Farmers went on relief. Young men, unable to find work, jumped moving freight trains to travel to another location only to find there was no work there either. Out of these disturbing situations a new political party arose.

The CCF was born at a convention in Calgary in 1932. This was a farmer-driven coalition that believed in a mixed economy in which vital industries would be nationalized, and it advocated broad social programs, including health insurance, children's allowances, and workers' compensation. These policies formed the famous Regina Manifesto. Veteran parliamentarian and ordained Methodist minister James Shaver Woodsworth was elected to lead the party.

The CCF grew in popularity in B.C. even though farmers had never really presented a united force. However, unions were quick to get behind it. High unemployment and labour unrest provided fertile ground for the fledgling party. Opposition countered with wild accusations against the socialist ideas being advocated. Newspapers presented anti-CCF commentary about the terrible policies socialists had in mind, such as teaching atheism in the schools and forcing teachers to be socialist.[5]

A look back shows how desperate the financial situation was during the Depression. The Kidd Committee Report of 1932 claimed further taxation was impossible and the only alternative was to reduce expenditures. It recommended reducing the provincial budget from $25 million to $7 million, mostly by getting rid of the civil service, which it described as incompetent. And it recommended that social services be cut back and funding for education restricted to children from age 6 to 13. There was even talk of selling the Pacific Great Eastern Railway, even though it provided the only transportation link for the people in the north of the province, and restricting public works to road building. The Kidd Committee obviously saw that social services were a privilege that could be withdrawn when times got difficult.

The release of the controversial report had ramifications at the next election in 1933, when the contest in B.C. was between the CCF and the Liberals led by Duff Pattullo. The Liberals got 41 percent and 34 seats. Tolmie's Conservatives were just about wiped out.[6] Tolmie resigned and retired to his farm. Although the CCF elected only seven members, it took 31 percent of the popular vote. In Nanaimo, Pearson held the seat for the Liberals, defeating the CCF candidate James Lyle Telford.

Pattullo was sworn into office on November 15, 1933. Pearson was first made Minister of Labour, then later held various other Cabinet portfolios. Another familiar Nanaimo face, Gordon Sloan, son of former MLA William Sloan, became Attorney General.

Gordon McGregor Sloan was born in Nanaimo in 1898. He married Nancy Porter Nicol; they had two children: David Gordon and Flora Betty. Gordon studied law, and he became Attorney General at the age of 35. Four years later he was appointed a justice of the B.C. Court of Appeal, and in October 1944 became Chief Justice of the Court of British Columbia.[7]

Pattullo tried to inject money into a flagging economy by spending on such projects as the Pattullo Bridge and the Alaska Highway. The trouble was that he had no money to spend. Like other B.C. premiers before him, he went to Ottawa pleading the case for the province's financial dilemma. He did succeed in summoning up the old slogan "Better Terms," and he got a subsidy of $750,000 per year until the provincial-federal taxation had been studied.

Pattullo was a third generation Canadian, whose family originated from Fifeshire, Scotland. He earned a reputation for being kind and considerate to friends and enemies alike; however, he could be stubborn, a well-known Scottish trait. History ranks him with Sir Richard McBride, another strong personality from an earlier era. He became increasingly frustrated with the endless struggle to convince Ottawa to take more decisive action in dealing with the effects of the Depression. These tussles undoubtedly contributed to his political overthrow in 1941.[8]

John Hart, an Irishman, was the next premier; he headed a Liberal–Conservative coalition. He took office in a very difficult time, because only a few days before, on December 7, the Japanese had attacked Pearl Harbor and the war in the Pacific had begun. His coalition government continued until the end of the war, since there seemed to be no political will to return to the pattern of straight party government. He resigned in 1947 but remained in the legislature and became Speaker of the House.

Byron Johnson, or Boss Johnson as he was nicknamed, was the next premier and leader of the coalition. His parents were originally from Iceland. He was born in Victoria and named Bjorn at birth, later Bjossi, and from this came the nickname "Boss."

Johnson considered himself a "liberal socialist" and believed in free enterprise.[9] Although criticized by the CCF, he defeated its representatives at their own game by introducing hospital insurance and a medical scheme to be paid for by a new sales tax. The legislation was later modified because the medical profession objected to some aspects of it. The coalition won another term in office in the 1949 election, but Liberals won the majority of the seats. The Conservatives in the coalition were not happy with the situation, and this may have paved the way for the next would-be premier, W.A.C. Bennett.

Federal Politics

Charles H. Dickie, a Conservative, was Nanaimo's man in Ottawa following the election held in 1921. The heated political debate of that election was free trade and a tax on fuel oil. Dickie was 61 and had worked at various jobs—in forestry, mining, and railways. He made some money in the Mount Sicker copper boom and owned a hotel in Duncan. Dickie was born in Beachville, Ontario, in 1859. He came to Victoria in 1885 and married Eliza E. Calvert in 1888. He served three terms as MLA before seeking a federal seat. He was re-elected in 1925, 1926, and 1930 and was defeated in 1935.

In the October 23, 1935, election Nanaimo got firmly behind the CCF by electing James Samuel Taylor. But no sooner had Taylor been elected than he became an Independent, often supporting the Liberals. Taylor was born in Liverpool, England, in 1872 and worked as a printer and publisher. He lost the Nanaimo riding to Liberal Alan Chambers in 1940, who was a merchant in the import-export business. Throughout the war years Chambers continued to represent the riding even though he was in uniform serving overseas. In 1945, George Randolph Pearkes, a Progressive Conservative, was elected and held the riding until 1953 when he was elected in Esquimalt-Saanich.

The next CCF MP from Nanaimo was Colin Cameron, who was elected in 1953. He represented the riding until 1958, then was defeated by Walter Franklyn Matthews, a Progressive Conservative. Cameron was re-elected and served from 1962 to 1968. In 1961, the CCF became the New Democratic Party.

Colin Cameron was a fiery Scot who was considered a figurehead of the radical cause in the province. "The revolutionary nature of the CCF program must be clearly understood," he wrote when he was provincial CCF president. "The first task of a CCF administration will be the swift and ruthless removal of the major sources of wealth production from private hands to those of the community."[10]

Cameron was not someone who adhered to the party line, and much to the dismay of his party he argued openly with the party on foreign and domestic policy. He and Max Saltsman were the economic spokesmen in the NDP caucus. Together they promoted the idea that a Canada Development Corporation should "rationalize" Canadian industry and invest in the industrial heartland. If the Canadian economy was to grow, it must put together firms that were large enough to sell on international markets at competitive prices.

In late July 1968, a month after the federal election, Cameron died suddenly at the age of 71. The Nanaimo NDP riding executive decided immediately that Tommy Douglas should step in, and he agreed. Douglas had just lost in the Burnaby-Coquitlam riding. He moved to Nanaimo and rented an apartment in the Seacrest tower on the waterfront and waited for Prime Minister Pierre Elliott Trudeau to call a by-election.

The Nanaimo Commonwealth Holding Society

The Nanaimo CCF Association needed a home of its own, a place to hold committee and executive meetings, with a large hall for social events. At least that was the dream of the McLellan brothers, Alex and Robert Jr., whose father, Robert, had been a charter member of the Nanaimo Socialist Party and of the Nanaimo CCF. The brothers had been raised in the CCF philosophy and knew the pitfalls. When they tried to rent a room or hall to have a meeting, they were often refused by those not supportive of their ideas.[11]

In 1951 Dave Stupich headed up a building committee and fundraising began. (Stupich ran unsuccessfully for the CCF in the 1949 provincial election.) One of his ideas was to hold bingo games. At this time bingos were illegal but still held despite frequent raids by the RCMP. The Roman Catholic Church and the United Mineworkers of America Union (UMWA) ran two of the largest bingos in town. The latter was held in the UMWA Hall, formerly the St. John Ambulance Hall, on Esplanade. Many union miners were members of the CCF.

In 1951, the association began holding weekly bingo games in a small room in the Harewood Community Hall. These bingos were not well attended and netted only $10 per night. A move into the downtown area was vital if any money was to be made. In 1954 the association decided to buy the miners' hall from Canadian Collieries, renovate it, and take over the union's Saturday-night bingos. The bingos earned up to $100 per night.

The association sold the hall in 1958 and purchased an abandoned funeral parlour at Front and Bastion streets, at the site of the present Coast Bastion Inn. This same year, the Nanaimo Commonwealth Holding Society (NCHS) was incorporated and held legal title to the property. The NCHS also purchased the old Cowie Machine works next door, and later added the rest of the block and the Harewood Community Hall to its real-estate holdings.

By 1974, the NCHS bought more property on Dunsmuir Street and in 1979 began construction on the Commonwealth Centre. This was a co-operative project with the Nanaimo Senior Citizens' Building Society. The project planned to have seniors' housing, stores, offices, and a meeting hall. Plans changed and the building became office and retail space. In 1981, the NCHS had left the old CCF hall on Bastion Street and moved into the new Commonwealth Centre. At this time, the NCHS formed the Bastion Hotel Corporation and planned to build a large new downtown hotel. The project was eventually sold to union and pension fund organizations.

The Commonwealth Centre was lost to the Royal Bank in 1985 due to financial difficulties, although the NCHS retained its lease on the bingo hall and continued to hold four bingos a day, three on Sundays. Funds were given for scholarships and bursaries.

Dave Stupich

Dave Stupich's political career spanned 44 years. He was born in 1921. His father was a coal miner who also owned a small farm. Dave attended South Wellington School and graduated from Ladysmith High School. During the Second World War he joined the Royal Canadian Air Force and spent most of the war years as a pilot instructor. After the war he attended the University of B.C., where he studied agriculture, earning a Bachelor of Science degree. In 1960 he returned to school and completed a course as a chartered accountant.

Stupich first became interested in politics in 1949, urged on by Colin Cameron of the CCF provincial executive. Stupich got the nomination but could not unseat the popular MLA George S. Pearson. Stupich ran again in 1952, but lost this time to Dr. Larry Giovando. This was a minority government, headed by W.A.C. Bennett. Another election in 1953 saw Dr. Giovando squeak in again by only 18 votes. In 1960, Stupich stepped aside to allow Cameron to run, but he lost to former mayor Earle Westwood. Three years later Stupich beat Westwood by 19 votes. In the 1966 election Stupich held on to his seat, running against Frank Ney, for Social Credit. Ney took the seat in 1969.

In 1972 the NDP were elected with Dave Barrett as premier. Stupich was handily elected and served in two Cabinet positions, as Minister of Agriculture and Minister of Finance. During his tenure, he was responsible for creating the Agricultural Land Reserves. He ran unsuccessfully for the provincial leadership of the NDP party in 1984. Stupich went on to represent the riding federally.

The ultimate blemish on such an extraordinary political career was the inappropriate handling of funding for the Nanaimo Commonwealth Holding Society. Stupich pled guilty to fraud and running an illegal lottery involving an estimated $1 million, money that was supposed to have been given to charities. For the 1999 "Bingogate" affair he received a two-year sentence. Stupich died on February 8, 2006, after a lengthy illness.

Chapter Nine

The Depression Years

The Market Crash

The province's economy had been humming along nicely after the recession in the early '20s; then along came Thursday, October 24, 1929. The Wall Street market crash that day is remembered as the beginning of the Great Depression. This was bad news for B.C., which had relied heavily on the U.S. as its major market for coal, forest products, and other goods.

The news was particularly bad for Nanaimo's coal industry, the driving engine of the local economy. When the Depression hit, 2,158 men worked in the mines; when it ended in 1939, only 982 remained.[1] The coal piled up, and when an order did come in, men worked only one or two days a week for $2.25 a day. Jack Ostle remembered how the mine whistle during the Depression signalled if there was work that day:

> We used to have a whistle on the No. 1 mine. Every supper time around 4:00 or 5:00 your dad would say, "Now everybody be quiet and see if there's work tomorrow." If it blew one blast there'd be work, if it blew two you stayed home the next day.[2]

First to be let go were the single men; many of them looked to the city's make-work programs to earn a living. City records tell only half the story—the number employed during the month, or the amount allocated for relief. "Married men with 4 dependents 6 days; married men with 3 dependents 4 days; single men 2 days."[3]

> Those were tough times. The city sometimes gave us some work. The bigger the family the more days you worked. They gave you scrip

> for food instead of pay. But them days you was glad to go and get two or three days' work. And if you spent two bits to go any place you were short on the table.[4]

Between 1930 and 1939, there were 19 small mines opened by private individuals. Some of the mines took the name of their owners: Beban, Biggs, Cowie, Chilton, Fiddick, Westwood, and Renney to name only a few. Another 12 operated between 1940 and 1950, and 10 between 1951 and 1957.[5] These miners worked hard to provide coal for the local market.

Federal, provincial, and municipal governments did devise an Unemployment Relief Scheme. Nanaimo was allocated $76,000, part of which was for labour and materials. The federal government paid 50 percent, or one-half of the total cost; the provincial government paid 25 percent of the actual cost of labour only, and the city paid the balance.

In 1930 the city identified several make-work projects that could be adopted under the guidelines of the Unemployment Relief Act. They included finishing the sewer system of the city, building a subway under the E & N Railway on Comox Road Crossing, repairing South Fork Road, street grading along Albert Street, and constructing the South Fork Dam.[6]

Council was also mindful of the implications for Nanaimo of the use of fuel oil instead of coal. When a newspaper article revealed that the Canadian National Railway Company (CNR) planned to build a new hotel in Vancouver and use fuel oil for heating, council approved a resolution and forwarded it to the CNR. In part it read:

> Whereas it has been recognized by the Provincial and Dominion Governments that the coal industry is in a serious depressed condition brought about principally by the importation of fuel oil and efforts are being exerted to procure a remedy of this condition …
>
> Council deeply deplores the action of the Canadian National Railway Company in deciding to use fuel oil for heating purposes in its new hotel now being erected in the City of Vancouver. More especially in view of the detrimental effect of such action by a Government controlled institution in its influence upon other public and private institutions.[7]

The resolution was probably ignored or filed; council could not stop progress no matter how difficult the situation.

On June 8, 1931, Mayor Hall met with other municipalities on the mainland to discuss unemployment. They met again on June 22 with Senator Gideon Robertson, an aging Minister of Labour, and with B.C. premier Simon Fraser Tolmie. Robertson was on a fact-finding tour of the

West. At this meeting every municipality in the province was represented. Mayor Hall was not the least bit impressed by the Senator, and told his council as much when he reported back to them. "My impression is that Senator Robertson did not fully appreciate the seriousness of the unemployment in the West."[8] Senator Robertson reported back to Prime Minister R.B. Bennett that conditions weren't as bad as he'd feared, despite statistics that showed there were 20,000 jobless men in Vancouver, many of them transients.

Charlotte Whitton was the next federal representative to tour the province to study unemployment relief in the West. She was convinced that "untrained political hacks were costing the government millions through waste and inefficiency."[9] Whitton is best remembered as the formidable mayor of Ottawa. In the '30s she was a director of the Canadian Council on Child Welfare. She reported back to the prime minister that B.C. was in confusion; municipalities were desperate and the province was fertile ground for boondoggle, corruption, and impropriety.

In 1932, the Province took action and set up 27 relief camps to accommodate 18,340 men.[10] The following year the federal government assumed responsibility for the camps, which were usually in remote locations, far away from city centres. These camps became breeding grounds for labour unrest. The men assigned to them felt that they were under military control, as the job of managing the camps fell to the Department of National Defence. In fact, the following year, Prime Minister R.B. Bennett took the vote away from those men housed in the camps. To register to vote, a citizen needed a "domicile," and relief camps were not classed as such.

The newly formed Relief Camp Workers' Union urged the men to go on strike and march on Vancouver. On April 5, 1935, 2,000 men walked away from the camps. Vancouver mayor Gerry McGeer felt this was another communist plot, and when he heard the men were smashing display cases in the Hudson's Bay Company store, he read the riot act. This began the "On-to-Ottawa Trek" that stopped when it reached Regina.

Relief camps were abolished the following year and replaced by a different system. Men who worked in forestry or on the railway were paid $15 a month. The Depression started to lift in 1936—in August, 68,690 people were on relief in B.C., 11,000 fewer than in August of the previous year.[11]

South Fork Dam

It has been said that the best things happen to cities in the worst of times. This was certainly true in Nanaimo during the Great Depression. The city undertook a massive water dam project and built a new assembly dock and a new bridge. At the same time, Newcastle Island became a destination point for day trippers from around the Pacific Northwest.

Construction of the South Fork Dam was a make-work project adopted under the Unemployment Relief Act.

West of Nanaimo and south of the Nanaimo Lakes lies an incredible watershed encompassing 33 square miles. Here two large storage lakes, South Fork and Jump Lake, collect rain and melting snow from the mountains, and through a system of distribution mains, treatment facilities, and pumping stations, water is delivered to the taps in Nanaimo. The South Fork Dam was a Depression-era project that employed hundreds and remains a credit to the city that undertook such a massive project at this difficult time.

When the project started in 1930, Nanaimo had 2,500 service connections and 105 fire hydrants. The water system then served 9,000 people. Water was fed to the 30 miles of cast-iron and wood-stave mains from two storage reservoirs located two miles west of the city. Their combined capacity was 27,000,000 imperial gallons, partly fed by open watercourse and partly by a 12-inch wood-stave pipeline from the intake over 13 miles west, on the South Fork of the Nanaimo River.[12]

During the summer months there was a low flow of water in the Nanaimo River, and with the old pipeline in a decrepit condition, some action was needed to ensure a fresh, adequate, and reliable flow of water to the storage reservoirs. This was something Dr. Drysdale, the Medical Health Officer, had complained about for years.

With assistance from the Unemployment Relief Program, the construction of the South Fork Dam became possible. Before construction began, the city repaired the road to the site, improved several bridges and replaced others, and built a campsite to house 100 men. Construction began on August 1, 1930. The city financed the project with a Waterworks Improvement Loan bylaw, passed in 1930, for $374,000.00.[13]

The chosen site lay in a precipitous canyon 1,000 feet long, 90 feet wide, and 120 feet from top to bottom, situated 600 feet above the old intake structure built in 1910, and 15 miles west of the city.

The city received permission from the Board of Adjustment to operate work crews on 10-hour shifts per day. Larger crews could not be employed, and two shifts were impracticable.[14] Until this time, city engineer A.G. Graham had a temporary appointment from the city, but as he took on more duties as resident engineer for the South Dam project and as building inspector, his appointment was made permanent. The consulting engineer on design and construction was Vancouver engineer H.B. Muckleston.[15] Jamieson Construction Company was contracted to do the work and was required to complete the project by December 17, 1931. When the company defaulted on the completion date, it received an extension to 1932.

When completed the dam could hold about 470 million gallons of water. This was the city's main water reserve until 1975 when Jump Lake Creek was dammed.

Newcastle Island Pleasure Resort

Newcastle Island is a small island of approximately 750 acres located on the north side of Nanaimo's harbour. The island, known for its quarry and its salteries, had always been a playground for residents of the city. The Miners' picnic held every July attracted 1,500 people. Families paid $1 for treats for the children. Families boarded a scow pulled by a tugboat, the *Wee Two*.[16]

At Mrs. Anderson's Reliable Boat House at Wharf and Front streets, you could rent a canoe or rowboat to take you to the island. Canoes rented for 50 cents an hour, rowboats for 25 cents. There were a few permanent residents on the island. On the north end were the Japanese salteries, and on the south end the Cownley family had cleared several acres for farming.

In the '20s, steamship excursions along the coast were very popular. The Canadian Pacific Railway (CPR) felt at a disadvantage because it had no recreational property to attract this clientele. The Union Steamship Company had resorts on Bowen Island, Sechelt, and Selma Park, and the Harbour Navigation Company had a resort at Belcarra Park on Indian Arm. On June 6, 1931, the CPR responded to this growing demand by purchasing Newcastle Island from the Western Fuel Company to develop a "pleasure resort" which would include picnic grounds, a football field, a dance pavilion capable of accommodating several hundred people, and a restaurant.[17] When completed, the resort had a wharf for the coastal steamers to unload their passengers, and a float for the convenience of small boats that ferried passengers to and from Nanaimo. The City of Nanaimo was pleased with the purchase and the proposed development, and advised the CPR "it would co-operate in every way possible ... it [would] be of mutual advantage."[18]

The decision to enter the resort business in the middle of the Depression may have seemed like a strange one, but the CPR had adequate financial backing and enough confidence in the concept to proceed with the venture.

Work began in April preparing the site, and construction of the buildings began in May. Victoria Pile Driving and Construction Company under the direction of Douglas McGary built the pier, the pavilion, and other buildings.[19] Administrator J.M. Cameron supervised the project. Cameron was also the manager of the E & N Railway. Thirty men worked on the initial construction project. Only married men could apply. Wages were 50 cents an hour for an eight-hour shift.

The mayor of Nanaimo, Dr. George Hall, officially opened the resort on June 20, 1931. The inauguration ceremonies began with a luncheon aboard the *Princess Elaine* for officials of the CPR and guests from Vancouver, Victoria, and Nanaimo. Later the group moved to the Newcastle Pavilion, where Mayor Hall declared the Newcastle Island Pleasure Resort open.[20] The mayor said he could think of no better spot on the coast where visitors could enjoy a day's outing or an extended holiday than on Newcastle Island. Representing Nanaimo were the mayor; aldermen Dixon, Drake, Cavalsky, and Inkster; W.W. Mitchell, president of the Board of Trade; and M.C. Ironside, the harbourmaster.

On that day, the *Princess Victoria* brought a large group of day trippers from Vancouver.[21] The CPR's *Charmer* and *Princess Victoria* became floating hotels when they were moored at Newcastle Island. Visitors rented staterooms for $7.50 a week for complete service except food—cooking facilities were provided. This offered an inexpensive option for family holidays. Resort

The CPR's *Charmer* and *Princess Victoria* became floating hotels when they were moored at Newcastle Island.

publicity promoted this alternative: "Meals may be served at the Pavilion Restaurant at moderate rates, or the facilities of the ship's galley are at the disposal of those who wish to prepare their own meals. Provisions may be brought with you or purchased at the Pavilion."[22]

The *Nanaimo Free Press* reported on June 26, 1931:

> The CPR steamers, *Victoria*, *Patricia* and *Joan* arrived in Port this morning with 2,800 excursionists who are spending the day on Newcastle Island, many of their numbers taking advantage of the opportunity to visit old friends in the city. The excursion is the yearly outing of the City of Vancouver's employees and represents all departments in that city's municipal government.

The CPR then had a number of ships serving the Nanaimo–Vancouver ferry route: the *Charmer*, 500 passengers; *Princess Elaine*, 1,200 passengers; *Princess Elizabeth*, 1,100 passengers; *Princess Joan*, 1,100 passengers; and *Princess Victoria*, 1,000 passengers. Most of these ships served Newcastle Island; occasionally the *Princess Patricia* was used as well. The CPR dock at Cameron Island dominated Nanaimo Harbour. From here wharfinger George Brown and his assistant Mr. Archibald arranged excursions. There was a continuous summer ferry service to the island from 1931.

In the summer months, the social life of Nanaimo was greatly improved, particularly on Saturday nights when the Newcastle Pavilion was "the place to be" where you could "dance to the small hours." Many young men owned their own canoes, and one recalled that you had to date a girl who was unafraid of canoes. To claim a picnic table, you had to get there before the ferry from Vancouver arrived.

During the winter months, the Pygmy Pavilion in Nanaimo was the place to be. It first opened on May 22, 1931, just a few weeks before the Newcastle Pavilion. Shelby M. Saunders was reported to have built the dance hall to resemble the famous Grand Palace Ballroom of Coney Island.[23] The hall literally bounced as dancers took to the floor. The Pygmy had a dance floor of 74 by 96 feet, compared to Newcastle's 80 by 40 feet. Saunders promoted the Pygmy as having the only sprung dance floor in western Canada and Vancouver Island's finest bowling—12 lanes of 5 and 10 pins. The Pygmy Pavilion later became the Fiesta Bowling Lanes.

The Newcastle Pavilion was the social centre of the island. Mr. Cook managed the restaurant in very "proper ship-like fashion." Both the linen and the silverware were embossed with the CPR crest, and should the blue-rimmed plates happen to have a crack, they were smashed and thrown away in case someone unconnected with the CPR might retrieve them. The cooks were Chinese from Hong Kong and Canton. Nanaimo high-school

When dancers took to the floor at the Pygmy Pavilion, the hall literally bounced. It was promoted as the only sprung dance floor in western Canada. Shown here is the New Year's Eve dance of 1940.

girls were hired as waitresses to serve the guests on the verandah and in the restaurant. Bill Warwick had a concession to provide boxed lunches, and Lauretta Russell and her sisters, the caretaker's daughters, made about 200 boxed lunches a day. French fries were sold directly from the kitchen to the verandah via a two-way door.

Several picnics could take place simultaneously. Some estimate as many as 12,000 people were accommodated at one time. Every ferry had an upright piano for dancing during the trip. The island resort literally hopped when big bands like Dal Richards came to play at the pavilion. The Nanaimo bands included The Pimlotts and the Stu Storey Band; Vancouver bands included Goodheart and the Vancouver Electric Band. In 1939, when the CPR's Social and Athletic Club visited the island, three different bands were hired: the Bar B. Boys, Marie Abrams Novelty Orchestra, and the West Vancouver Boys' Band.[24]

Everything changed with the outbreak of the Second World War. There was a shortage of ships and gasoline had to be rationed. The resort closed for the remainder of the war, only to open briefly in 1950, but it never again served as a major resort. The city purchased the island from the CPR and turned it over to the Province for a provincial park in 1961. Today the 750-acre provincial marine park remains a popular picnic area for everyone to enjoy.

Nanaimo Yacht Club

On June 19, 1931, the eve of the opening of the Newcastle Island resort, a group of boating enthusiasts met in the Bastion and formed the Nanaimo Yacht Club. The elected officers were Hon. Commodore Charles Ironside, Commodore John (Jack) Charles McGregor, Vice-Commodore Phil Piper, Rear Commodore William Weeks, and Secretary-Treasurer Robert Dunsmore.[25]

There was great enthusiasm over the formation of the club, and everyone hoped it would be strong and healthy. A membership fee was set at $2. The club planned to hold its first regatta on July 1.

This was not the first yacht club—a 1903 charter has been found, and records show Nanaimo had a club as far back as 1897. Members secured a site in 1909, and then built a dock and clubhouse. However, the club as it is known today began in 1931.

Frank Beban—Entrepreneur

Frank Beban is remembered in Nanaimo more for the beautiful house he built on Bowen Road than for the mining, forestry, and horseracing entrepreneur that he was. On February 16, 1934, he announced that he planned to build an export lumber mill on the site of the coal company tie mill, between the old Coal Wharf and the Western Fuel Company No. 1 pithead. The logs for the mill were to come from Galiano and Gabriola islands.[26] The new mill opened on July 27, 1934.

A year later he opened the Beban Mine and started a sawmill at Extension with a daily output of 50,000 board feet. He did this in the midst of the Depression with high unemployment in the city; as well he purchased 173 acres of farmland in Northfield, where he built the family home, known today as Beban House. Frank had just come into a family inheritance of $250,000, which he used to start all these businesses.

Frank was born in Goldsboro, New Zealand, on March 26, 1882, to Stephen and Catherine Beban. At age 24, he travelled to San Francisco, and a year later arrived on Vancouver Island where he found work in Cumberland under contract cutting mine timbers. He settled in Extension, working in James Dunsmuir's mine as mule stable foreman. It was here that he discovered his passion for horses. In 1910 he married 17-year-old Hannah Hodgson, the daughter of John and Mary Hodgson.[27] Like other young couples of the day, they struggled to raise a family. Hannah used flour sacks for her children's diapers. They had four children, Evelyn, Dorothy, Verna, and Jack. The inheritance changed all their lives.

The old farmhouse on the acreage was demolished to make way for Beban House, the lovely rustic half-log house that cost $25,000 to build and remains today a testimony of an earlier time. James Green designed and constructed the house.[28] It had five bedrooms, four fireplaces, three tiled bathrooms, a large living room, a dining room, a panelled den, and enough living area for a growing family. The interior was complete with glass cabinets, ornate chandeliers, inlaid tiles, and coloured bathroom fixtures, reported to be the first on Vancouver Island. A Chinese cook took care of the beautiful flower and vegetable gardens that surrounded the house. There were no maids to do the household chores; Frank's three daughters did these, and it was they who attended when guests came for dinner.

Frank also built a horseracing track and started Emerald Stables with four thoroughbreds he brought over from New Zealand. He purchased a farm off Pleasant Valley Road on Blackjack Lake to use for the mares in foal and for growing hay and feed. It provided accommodation for the Chinese workers employed in the stables and around the farm. According to a family friend, people were welcome on the property, and the barns were always open. Norm Madill remembered going to the stables with his father, Sam, who was a blacksmith, to shoe some of the horses:

> The Beban family had a string of good racehorses and it was a thrill to go there with Dad and see the beautiful stables and racetrack. Mrs. Beban would always bring out tea and cookies to where we were shoeing their horses.[29]

The family owned two horses of exceptional quality: a stallion named Sierra Chief, who won many races, and Big Pine, who stood 17 hands in height. Other horses in the stables were Admit, Compelled, and Sad Henry. The Beban horses were familiar on the horseracing circuit in Vancouver, with the Emerald Stables' green and white racing colours readily recognizable. Frank was known for his generosity, and he treated his employees with dignity and respect. Hannah was a gentle loving woman, who never flaunted her wealth and worked hard even when it wasn't necessary.[30]

The oldest Beban daughter, Evelyn, married Dr. Larry Giovando, one of the city's most respected doctors. They had one son, Larry Jr. The good doctor treated the horses when a veterinarian was needed, as the city had no animal doctor at that time. Evelyn loved to ride and was a frequent visitor to the racetrack. The couple eventually divorced. Dorothy married several times. She died of tuberculosis. Verna married Corporal Joseph Tonelli of Trail. They had one son. She too died of tuberculosis. Jack's marriage to Gertrude Van Houten produced two sons, Frank Beban Jr. and Donald William. Gertrude's family owned a number of drug stores; the Van Houten Block was next to the Bijou Theatre on Commercial Street. The logging and sawmill business was passed down from father to son; Frank Beban Jr. took over when Jack died.

After Frank Sr. died, he left his estate to wife Hannah and son Jack. The daughters received an annuity of $250 a month. Hannah sold the Beban farm in 1956 to the City of Nanaimo for $53,000 and moved to Churchill Street in the Brechin area. The city intended using the property as a replacement for the Central Sports Ground, which it had sold. This became the site of Harbour Park Mall, now Port Place. The farm is now Beban Park and part of the exhibition grounds used for recreation and the Annual Exhibition Fall Fair.

Chapter Ten

Doctors and Their Clinics

The Hall Clinic

There were only seven doctors in Nanaimo when Dr. Larry Giovando began work in the Hall Clinic in 1936, and three were from the same family: Dr. George A.B. Hall, his sons Earle and Alan, and Dr. A.E. Manson. The clinic was at 43 Commercial Street, in the Hall Block. A smaller clinic with only two doctors, Dr. Oswald Grey Ingham and Dr. Carman Browne, was located in the Jenkins Building on Bastion Street. Following the death of Dr. Ingham on October 30, 1935, Dr. Meneely joined this clinic. Dr. W.F. Drysdale, the Medical Health Oofficer, also had a private practice.

Dr. Larry Giovando had been the Granby mine doctor in 1930, taking over from Dr. A.E. Manson who moved into the Hall Clinic. Dr. Giovando attended accidents, made house calls, and delivered babies. After the mine closed, he opened a private practice in Ladysmith, then moved to Cumberland, eventually returning to South Wellington.

Dr. Larry Giovando is seen here with his second wife, Vivian.

The city was small and patients had a close relationship with their doctors. In writing about his early experience in Nanaimo, Dr. Giovando said, "We were taken into their confidence, knew their family problems and were often their financial adviser, psychiatrist, family practitioner, and friend. Older people were reluctant to go into hospital as some still had the idea that hospitals were for the dying. Most babies were delivered at home."[1]

House calls were the norm. Homemaker and nursing care was donated by the family with assistance from the doctor. Babies were either delivered at home or at one of the three maternity homes, such as Mrs. McCree's Nursing Home. The lying-in period was usually 10 days. Doctors kept regular office hours, with one doctor taking calls in rotation, enabling the other to have a day off.

Dr. George A.B. Hall was the city's first resident dentist. After practising for two years, he opened the Crescent Pharmacy. A year later he sold his dental practice to his cousin Dr. W.C. Mason and then completed his medical training, graduating in medicine and surgery.

His first medical practice was in Nelson; he was superintendent of the Kootenay Lake General Hospital for three years. He then moved to Victoria to take the position as Medical Health Officer. After three years of military service in the First World War, he answered an advertisement for a Western Fuel Company physician, and this brought him back to Nanaimo.[2]

The Hall-Giovando Clinic had almost all the Chinatown practice, in part because of the good business relationship the doctors had with Mah Sam, a resident of Chinatown who spoke both Chinese and English. "He translated the fee to the patient, took the money, gave the doctor $2 and kept $1 for himself."[3] The charge for services was $1.75 per month per family, $1 per single person, and $10 per maternity. There were no specialists, and doctors did their own laboratory work.

Dr. Alan Hall and wife, Gertrude, came to Nanaimo in 1929. They lived here for a short time before moving to the U.S. where Alan pursued further studies. They returned in 1933 and joined the Hall Clinic. Gertrude Hall wrote of her impressions of the city in 1929 and 1933:

> I first saw Nanaimo on New Year's morning in 1929. I came from Montreal by train and we were just married. We got on the train and left home, it took four days and five nights. We got to Vancouver on New Year's morning and it was the most dismal sight I ever saw. The streets were littered with all the whoop-de-do of New Year's eve. We got on the boat and I was most impressed with the *Elaine*, it was like a little ocean liner. I couldn't think that that was just a ferry and as we approached Nanaimo, the sun came up and I looked at Mt. Benson and thought what a beautiful place to live.
>
> When we came back here to live [1933] there was a housing shortage and we couldn't find any place to rent and had to live with Alan's parents for a number of months. Finally Mrs. Waygo let us

> have her house at 721 Comox Road, right next to the Benson's nurseries, and the railroad tracks, of course, were just two doors away. I remember the first night I slept there, I thought there was a train coming straight at me because the train blew at the crossing and thundered on and I was left with a palpitating heart. I had never lived in a little wooden house before—it was quite a shock to me.
>
> But the thing that really interested me in driving around town I saw on the street all these small wooden buildings and sheds and I couldn't understand what they were doing there. Alan told me that these were the coal sheds and the coal was delivered to the homes in all these little sheds that stood particularly in the south end of town. I found this very fascinating.[4]

Gertrude Hall was Nanaimo's first female councillor; elected in 1953, she ran for mayor in 1956 and was defeated by Peter Maffeo. She was elected once again in 1966. In 1976 she topped the polls in the Nanaimo Regional District election.[5] On May 25, 1981, Nanaimo awarded her the Freedom of the City.

Ingham and Browne-Meneely Clinics

Dr. Oswald Grey Ingham practised medicine for 38 years. He was born in Fall River, Massachusetts, in 1874 and came to Nanaimo in 1904 to assist Dr. J.H. Hogle for two weeks. At the end of that time Dr. Hogle asked him to stay. Dr. Robert O'Brien also joined Dr. Hogle, in a medical and a dental surgery practice. Ingham later partnered with Dr. Robert O'Brien and with Dr. T.J. McPhee.[6]

Dr. Ingham is remembered for his initiative in being the first doctor to start first-aid and mine rescue classes. He was a lecturer and examiner for 25 years. He was appointed to the Order of St. John and received his insignia and diploma, but he died before receiving his formal investiture.

Ingham was known to be an avid sportsman and was prominent in fraternal and service club work, but most of all the community knew him as a talented musician. For many years he played first violin in the Nanaimo Symphony Orchestra; he later conducted the orchestra. The Gyro Midnight Matinee was one of his many productions, and he also initiated the Nanaimo Male Voice Choir.

Dr. Carman Browne joined Dr. Ingham in his clinic in the Jenkins Building in 1931. Following Dr. Ingham's death, Dr. Meneely joined the clinic, and it became known as the Browne-Meneely Clinic. The clinic was moved to Wallace Street and later renamed the Caledonian Clinic.

Dr. Browne was born in North River, Nova Scotia, in 1906 to Reverend Robert Browne and his wife, Lelia. He graduated from Dalhousie University medical school in 1929, and then moved west to take a position with the Vancouver General Hospital before moving to Nanaimo two years later. Browne is known for his 38 years with the St. John Ambulance Society, which awarded him the Order of St. John of Jerusalem. He was invested as a Service Brother by Governor General Roland Michener in 1967.

Browne liked to sail and was commodore of the Nanaimo Yacht Club; he was also a member of the Nanaimo Pipe Band. His skill as a piper was well known and appreciated, as he often piped in head table guests at social events.[7] He was a member of the Rotary Club for 38 years.

Dr. Seiriol Williams

Dr. Seiriol Williams had a long distinguished medical career. He came from a Welsh mining family. His parents, Llewelyn and Louise, did not want their son to follow his father down the mines. After he quit school in 1920 he worked selling shoes in Watchorn's Store.

Williams left Nanaimo in 1924 to further his education. In Nebraska he finished high school and graduated from college with a scholarship, hoping to become a medical doctor. He was accepted at Harvard University. After graduation, he interned at Montreal General Hospital. He married his Nebraska sweetheart, Wilma Kibben, before accepting an offer to practise in the Hall-Giovando Clinic in Nanaimo.[8]

Dr. Williams worked at the clinic for four years before opening his own practice. The Second World War intervened and he served in the Royal Canadian Army Medical Corp. After the war, he opened a family practice in Vancouver; however, he kept close ties to Nanaimo. In the summertime, the family vacationed at Departure Bay with friends Arthur and Alice Leighton. Forty years passed before Dr. Williams retired and moved back to Nanaimo; his children were now grown and Wilma had died of cancer. He married Ena Smith and moved into the house previously owned by Arthur and Alice Leighton, now deceased.

Fighting New Enemies

Two diseases that gave cause for concern—tuberculosis and poliomyelitis (polio) were the new killers. The year 1947 was particularly bad; 135 cases of polio were registered, just enough to suggest the beginning of an epidemic. No one knew then how polio was transmitted. While the death rate was not high, the disease had devastating side effects on young people. Parents had visions of their children spending the rest of their lives on crutches, in a wheelchair, or in an iron lung machine. This machine helped patients breathe when their own lungs no longer worked.

The Salk vaccine became the most effective way of battling polio. In 1955, Dr. A.J. Nelson of UBC said the vaccine was "one of the greatest scientific advances in medical history."[9] Of 50,000 children vaccinated, not a single one contracted polio.

Tuberculosis was a dreaded bacterial infection that usually attacked the lungs but could also settle in the bones or the brain. Treatment usually meant complete bed rest combined with plenty of fresh air. There were several TB hospitals in the province, the most famous being at Tranquille in Kamloops, known for its dry air. It had been in operation since before the turn of the century. Over the years Tranquille grew into a research and teaching facility with a staff of 450. Later, antibiotics gave a more effective cure, and Tranquille closed in 1958.

During the '30s and '40s, Nanaimo patients were sent to the Tuberculosis Building of Vancouver General Hospital, the St. Joseph's Oriental Tuberculosis Unit, or the Rotary Clinic for Diseases of the Chest Sanatorium, at Tranquille. The annual financial statements for the city reflect the costs incurred by the city on behalf of these patients. The rate ranged from 80 cents to $1.25 per day. There was also a set fee of $5 to cover the cost of an X-ray.[10]

Health Insurance

Following the Spanish influenza epidemic in 1918/19, a provincial Royal Commission recommended a health insurance program for those who earned less than $3,000. Traditionally workers contributed monthly payments towards a fund that paid for a doctor's visit or a hospital stay. In Nanaimo, the coal companies and various lodges administered these funds. No action was taken as a result of the Royal Commission report. Eight years later another commission advocated health insurance, but it was also rejected.

By the '30s, doctors were sympathetic to the idea of health insurance, but when polled they rejected a provincial Health Insurance Act despite a 1937 referendum that favoured the program by about three to two. Premier Pattullo postponed implementation of the act. Three years later B.C. doctors inaugurated a voluntary plan, the Medical Services Association (MSA), with contributions collected by employers. By 1950, about 14 percent of the province's population was enrolled in the MSA.[11]

Premier Byron Johnson introduced the B.C. Hospital Insurance Service in 1948. Then the federal government introduced the Hospital Insurance and Diagnostic Act of 1957, which provided for federal-provincial cost sharing of hospital plans; B.C. joined in 1958. Nationwide medicare came next. With the introduction of medical insurance, doctors had a secure income and patients had protection from disastrous health-care costs.

Chapter Eleven

The Depression Ends

Nanaimo Reviews the Depression Years

In 1937 the provincial government asked each municipality to present a brief showing the effects of reduced government grants and the Province's financial downloading on municipalities. The city's finance and legislative committee, which included aldermen P.R. Inkster, S. Drake, and J.G. Hindmarch, prepared the brief. The trio went back to 1929 to show the city's financial struggle, though the Province had requested only five years.[1]

Their report showed that as the Depression deepened, sources of revenue that might have been expected to continue were cut off, and to add insult to injury, the additional burden of social services, which the provincial government had previously assumed, were piled on the city.

The city also had to grapple with unemployment. The situation became so desperate that Nanaimo was forced to drastically cut down on spending, until only a skeleton of public service remained. Expenditures for unemployment dropped from a high of $68,000 in 1929 to a low of $26,200 in 1933 and to $38,300 in 1936. The city tried to solve the situation by raising taxes. The tax levy was increased from $108,000 in 1931 to $128,000 in 1937.

The report showed clearly how difficult those years were for Nanaimo. The city cut staff salaries by as much as 25 percent, increased water rates by 60 percent, and reduced public services by 44 percent. The city had counted on liquor revenues, but these were clawed back by the Province in 1934. Automobile licences were reduced and the cost of maintaining schools increased. "Figures only show the effect of grant reduction. Public services have been starved in an endeavour to keep the City in a state of financial solvency, of schools which are obsolete and inadequate, and of other conditions which disgrace the City."[2]

Mayor John Barsby and the council of 1933 guided the community through the early years of the Depression. See Appendix V for the individuals' names.

Aldermen Inkster, Drake, and Hindmarch suggested the best solution, and the only satisfactory one, was for the provincial government to assume a greater proportion of services, particularly education and public health. Unemployment relief should continue to be the responsibility of the Dominion government.

Another Bastion Bridge

Towards the end of the '30s, the economic outlook in the province improved. Perhaps it was a frame of mind more than fact, but it was enough to spur the city into undertaking another major project. The South Fork Dam had been a success; now the city planned to rebuild the Bastion Street Bridge. It was another Depression-era project that put hundreds to work.

Dominion Construction Company Ltd. submitted the lowest of 10 bids: $42,076.64, including demolishing the old bridge.[3] The Employment Service of Canada listed the names of the men registered to work on the bridge and indicated whether they were married or single. The list included the number of children each married man had. This determined the number of days of work he would receive: 4 days, 3 days, 2⅛ days, or 1 day. The list of labourers needed on the project was long, and skilled carpenters were brought in from Vancouver to join Nanaimo carpenters T. Nobles, A. Peebles, J. Rowan, and D. Campbell. The bridge was constructed of cement and steel; Arviet Holst was the engineer.[4] On April 27, 1937, Mayor John Barsby declared the new Bastion Street Bridge open. The new structure spanning the ravine opened to traffic on April 30, at 6:30 p.m.[5]

The Coronation Celebrated

Mayor Barsby helped the city celebrate the coronation of their Majesties King George VI and Queen Elizabeth on May 12, 1937. Nanaimo has always had great affection for Great Britain, originating with the city's earliest pioneers who came here to mine coal for the Hudson's Bay Company. It was therefore no surprise to find the community excited about the coronation.

The Nanaimo & District Coronation Celebration Committee, headed by Alderman J.G. Hindmarch, and the Nanaimo Branch of the Royal Canadian Legion planned coronation services in the Capitol Theatre. About 400 people attended and listened to a radio message from King George. G.A. Fletcher Music Co. Ltd. made the radio transmission possible. A special orchestra, conducted by Andrew Dunsmore, provided musical entertainment.

Later 800 people attended the Coronation Ball, and throughout the city, home radio parties were held. Hundreds stayed up all night to listen to the worldwide broadcast. To commemorate the royal occasion, the city planted an oak tree at the northwest corner of the John Shaw High School grounds and gave schoolchildren medallions.

During the broadcast from London, two coronation babies were born at Mrs. McCree's Nursing Home at Albert and Selby streets: a son to Mr. and Mrs. J. Carvin, Victoria Road, and a girl to Mr. and Mrs. Thomas Addison, Prideaux Street.[6]

The Nanaimo School Board sent young student Donald McLellan to the coronation in London, to be part of Canada's student representation. He left on the *Princess Elaine* on April 21. The board held a bon voyage party for him in the gymnasium, hosted by chairman Frederick A. Busby and the staff and students of John Shaw Junior and Senior High Schools. Busby told McLellan, "There is no better way to study the world than by travelling. When you get back, you will realize that Nanaimo is really a worthwhile place in which to live after all."[7]

Within two years, King George VI and Queen Elizabeth paid an official visit to Victoria. Children from central Island schools boarded a Royal Excursion train to see the royal couple in person. On their arrival the children were herded like cattle into Beacon Hill Park, and few saw the royal couple. In an editorial entitled "Draw The Curtains," the *Nanaimo Free Press* reported:

> Complaints regarding treatment of Up-Island children at Beacon Hill Park, Victoria, on the occasion of the royal visit have been made to Victoria City Council and the Victoria Council has replied asking for specific instances. It is too late in the day for this procedure.[8]

The royal visit left a sour note; perhaps the long years of the Depression had taken their toll. However, the visit did give Premier Thomas Dufferin Pattullo the opportunity to express the unswerving loyalty of the province. Many residents were fearful about the future and what was to come in Europe. A certain anxiety had settled over the province. Movie theatres showed newsreels of Hitler reviewing his goose-stepping Nazi troops—everyone knew war was coming and was mentally preparing for the inevitable.

Building the Civic Arena

In 1938 council wrestled with the problem of what to do with a nine-acre derelict waterfront lot covered in rusting machinery parts and old automobiles on Bridge Street between Comox Road and the Millstone. The Bank of Montreal had taken possession of the site from Nanaimo Wood Products in 1935 and now offered it to the city for $6,000. The Nanaimo Lumber Company had previously owned the site and leased the water lot from the Dominion government as a booming ground.[9] Council needed a money bylaw for the purchase of the site and this passed in 1937.[10]

The community was in the midst of a debate on the need for either a civic sport centre, more sports grounds, or an auditorium for art performances. The Franklyn Street Gymnasium built in 1922 by the school board was well used but required enlarging.

The Gyro Club proposed a plan to have an ice arena built on the site and turned into a civic asset. The club envisioned a facility that could be used for skating, curling, lacrosse, or basketball. As an incentive for the city to get involved, the club offered council a $10,000 donation. By February 1938, sports groups had come out publicly in favour of shelving the addition to the gymnasium and building a civic arena instead.

On October 28, 1938, the city put the question of spending $60,000 for such a facility before taxpayers. The plebiscite brought out a record 1,200 of the 1,600 eligible to vote; they voted six to one in favour of spending the money.[11] To the original Gyro Club donation, the city added $21,800 of federal and provincial funds intended for city improvements and unemployment relief. Pete Maffeo, who headed up the Gyro committee, took on the task of selling $60,000 worth of bonds to the community. Other local service clubs such as the Rotary, Kiwanis, and Kinsmen joined the Gyros with contributions.[12]

Perhaps showing faith in their project, Vancouver architects McCarter and Nairne, who designed the building, purchased 500 shares. This was the same company which had designed the Marine Building and the Georgia Medical Building in Vancouver. The construction contract went to Turley Bros., a local contractor that had also built St. Paul's Church. On January 8, 1940, Mayor Victor Harrison turned the first sod.

The civic arena building came with air-heating equipment, a public address system, huge ventilator fans, dressing rooms, and an electric timing clock. An ice hockey team was already waiting in the wings. Don Mills of Seattle, former publicity man for the Seattle Seahawks and owner of the Nanaimo Clippers, had obtained a franchise in the Pacific Coast Hockey League.

On Wednesday, May 15, 1940, the $100,000 Civic Arena at 48 Arena Street opened with great fanfare. The Honorable A. Wells Gray, Minister of Lands, declared the ice arena open.[13] The CBC carried the opening live. According to newspaper reporter Stu Keate, "It was quite a party." He considered the formal grand opening a "spectacular affair," starting with a supper in the Hotel Malaspina and ending with a dance in the new building. A large flag-decked platform was erected at one side of the arena, and 32 loudspeakers kept everyone informed and entertained. George Pimlott's 20-piece orchestra supplied the music, and dignitaries came from all over the Island. Admission to the dance was 50 cents.

Victoria mayor Andrew McGavin and his wife and members of city council also attended. From the sports world, Lynn Patrick, a tall husky forward from the New York Rangers, was also present; he declared it "the finest arena of its size that I have ever seen. I hope it will stimulate the game and we'll see the building packed with fans."[14]

One year later, on a Saturday night, the arena was again packed as Nanaimo Clippers and Fraser Mills opened the coast amateur playoffs. Cars

In 1940 Nanaimo's Civic Arena opened with the traditional grand march and great celebration. The CBC carried the event live.

were lined from the arena to the Hotel Malaspina. Keate described it as being so crowded that one man sitting next to him who wanted to cheer for New Westminster had to go outside, yell, and come back in again.

Keate observed that the combination of an arena, a hustling hockey team, and balanced competition made Nanaimo "hockey mad" and brought about a renaissance of former sporting glories that had made the city famous in soccer and lacrosse. The manager of the arena was Bill Phillips, who also played for the Clippers.

The ice arena could not have come at a better time. Soldiers stationed at Camp Nanaimo had their own hockey team. On a normal night, hockey drew about 800 ardent fans. Within a month attendance figures had doubled. "At this playoff series, for the second week in a row, the 'standing room only' sign was hung out. There were 2,273 paid admissions and probably a few more no one took notice of."[15]

Fans came from all over the island. Their enthusiasm was infectious. Within a year, the Nanaimo Clippers were Pacific Coast and B.C. Champions, winners of the Coy Cup.

In 1940 and 1941, the team manager was still Bill Phillips. He was credited with bringing the team along to become champions. Clipper goalies were Art Davis and Mac Beattie; defencemen were Fergie McPherson, Jim Neilson, Hoppy Hoppus, and Bill Phillips; forwards were Bob Steedman, Red Carr, Herman Wagner, Walt Carry, Geo Gunn,

Within a year of the new arena's opening, the Nanaimo Clippers were Pacific Coast and B.C. champions, winners of the Coy Cup.

Doug Martinson, Jackie Hansen, and Jack McGill. The club physician was Dr. Larry Giovando.

To encourage young people who were not interested in hockey to use the arena, the Nanaimo Rotary Club sponsored the Nanaimo Figure Skating Club. The Rotarians produced the first Ice Carnival in February 1942 with the assistance of the Vancouver Skating Club and the Nanaimo Figure Skating Club. The Ice Carnival became popular and was continued throughout the war, attracting bigger audiences each year. By 1955 the cost of producing the shows, which involved Vancouver professional skaters, became too high. Most of the money raised left the community. Finally faced with an $8,000 production cost with little return, the Rotarians cancelled the Ice Carnival.[16]

The first lacrosse game held in the new arena was between Fletcher's and Spencer's Braves on May 18, 1940. There were nine teams in the Nanaimo Boxla League, four in the senior, three in the junior, and two in the juvenile division. The league executive included president Bob Humphrey, vice-president Vince Crawley, secretary-treasurer Joe Boyce, and executive officers Jimmy Knight and Arthur Jordan.[17]

The senior league playing for the Powers & Doyle Trophy were Spencer's Braves, Fletcher's, Calade, and Orange Crush. The junior league consisted of the Nanaimo Bakery, Howe's Warriors, and Edison Mazdas, while the Hot Points and the Invaders played in the juvenile division.

The Civic Arena is now closing. It served the community well and generated memories of ice hockey, lacrosse, figure skating, curling, and even political meetings. Many will miss the old landmark building.

Nanaimo Curling Club

In 1947 the Nanaimo Curling Club held its first bonspiel in the arena, a 32-rink three men's and one ladies' event. This was followed by other bonspiels in 1948, 1949, and 1950. Regular curling on one sheet of ice started in 1949 during the public skating sessions. This was temporary; but as interest grew, the club recognized the need for its own rink. The club was incorporated as a society on April 19, 1950. President at this time was J.D. Burnyeat. Harry Hutchecroft was secretary, and the treasurer was D.E.S. Smith.[18]

This was not the first time curling had been played in Nanaimo. Records show that in the winter of 1874/75, the newly organized Nanaimo Curling Club played on the swamp just outside the city.[19] The skips for this impromptu match were James Harvey and James Hamilton. The final score was Harvey 37, Hamilton 17. The "roaring game" was a big hit. The *Free Press* reported, "It is certain to be a very successful club. Success to the old Scotch game."

In 1950 the search was on for a site to build a curling rink. The club considered the former drill hall at Camp Nanaimo, as well as building an annex to the Civic Arena and a location at Robins Park. The site finally selected was north of the present rink on Wall Street, opposite Bowen Park. Construction started in 1950 in what is now the parking lot. Hundreds of volunteers contributed their time. By April 1951, hundreds turned out for the opening of the $40,000 rink. Curlers came from Victoria, Port Alberni, Courtenay, and Vancouver and from as far away as Alberta. President Jack Whitham welcomed the guests and made special mention of Art Quinney, a Nanaimo contractor who had voluntarily supervised most of the important construction work.

One columnist paid tribute to the club. "Hats off to Nanaimo," headlined Elmore Philpott's article on February 12, 1952.[20] He wrote that some old-timers who helped with construction had only a vague idea of what curling was all about. "Some thought you had to have skates. But they all got behind the project anyway."

Philpott suggested Victoria take a leaf out of Nanaimo's book. "For was it not Victoria which raised $48,000 for a similar rink, then sent the money back to subscribers because it was not thought to be enough."

There were some fine female curlers in those early years, with perhaps Marg Fuller's Fulsome Foursome heading the list. The Nanaimo Ladies were Western Canadian Champions in 1957 and B.C. Champions in 1961.[21]

The club was running at full capacity, and there was a need for a much larger eight-sheet facility. Fundraising began once again; this time the new rink cost $300,000. The doors to the present Nanaimo Curling Club rink opened in December 1969.

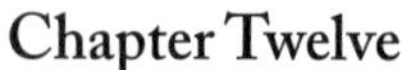

Chapter Twelve

The Harbour, Wharves, and Ferries

The National Assembly Wharf

The coal-mining industry slowly and painfully became a footnote in Nanaimo's history, as the province and the country turned to the more efficient fuel oil. The city, however, did not become a ghost town but underwent a transition to accommodate new economic demands. The Canadian Pacific Steamship Service (CPSS) a division of the CPR, continued to use the docks at Cameron Island, ferrying passengers and freight to and from the mainland. Small boats berthed at the Dominion Government Floats designed as the "Farmers Landing." In 1935, the harbour, one of the city's prize assets, was not being totally utilized and a new direction for the port had to be found. An investigation revealed the need for a lumber loading wharf. From 1920 to 1970, forestry and related industries increasingly dominated the economy of the region. Logging grew due to the demand for lumber exports; this also led to an increase in the number of sawmills in the area.

The building of the wharf during the Depression by the Dominion government was a big factor in rejuvenating Nanaimo's economy. Dredging began in 1935 and construction started the following year. The $73,000 project was financed by a loan under the Municipal Improvements Assistance Act.[1] In March 1937, a 10-year lease was negotiated with Johnston National Storage Company to take over the management of the wharf. This same company managed the Canadian National dock in Vancouver. F.J. Lodge was appointed wharfinger on March 24, 1938.[2] An agreement was also reached to put in a spur line from the main rail line to the assembly wharf. Before long, lumber was being exported from the wharf.

The wharf was a big success. In 1950, city records show 88 deep-sea freighters and 199 American and Canadian tugs cleared the assembly wharf.[3]

Businesses expanded to such an extent that by 1951 the city complained to the federal government about the lack of adequate berthing facilities. Local dealers and shipping agents were forced to load offshore using tenders. This became an added expense for industry, and it put mill owners at a disadvantage with their competitors in Vancouver and Victoria. The city estimated the added costs at approximately $50,000 per year. To make the point for expanded facilities, the city advised that six new mills were under construction and provided pertinent statistics:

> During the year 1949 lumber shipments through this port averaged over 4 million feet per month. Last year the shipments rose to over 6 million feet per month and this year ... the average will exceed 8 million ... the mills have sufficient orders on hand at the present time to keep them operating to capacity for at least 18 months.[4]

Nanaimo MP George R. Pearkes replied to Mayor Earle Westwood, expressing regret that the minister in charge showed little enthusiasm for the project. Pearkes had advised him about the bottleneck in the lumber industry, but he favoured the construction of more loading facilities on the East Coast. "I pointed out that an extension to the assembly wharf at Nanaimo was the most practical solution to the problem."[5]

Five days later, a reply came from Minister of Fisheries R.W. Mayhew stating that in the past week he had received requests from Crofton, Chemainus, and Ladysmith for an assembly wharf. The Nanaimo request was being investigated.[6]

The letters continued back and forth between Nanaimo and Ottawa. There seemed to be some hope when a letter from Pearkes advised in February that a cost of $470,000 had been attached to the request. He suggested, however, that the present facilities were not being used to their full extent and asked for further clarification.

> Apparently there is an agreement with the Longshoremen's Union that if a second shift is employed, that second shift must receive overtime pay, a condition which the shipping companies are not prepared to meet. The Dept. argues that if the present loading facilities are not used for eight hours each day, it is unreasonable to ask for public funds to provide extra facilities when the present ones lie idle for 16 hours each day.[7]

The agreement between the International Longshoremen's Union and the Shipping Federation was the same one applied to all wharves and docks in the province, except Victoria, which was on similar terms with the

American Federation of Labour. There had been no difficulty in obtaining sufficient longshoremen and stevedores to work. The city advised that it was not discriminating against labour.[8] Finally the good news came June 18, 1951, and Pearkes praised the city:

> I am certainly elated to hear that the Honorable Mr. Fournier is recommending the construction of an additional berth at the Assembly Wharf … the biggest hurdle has now been overcome. Most of the credit for it will belong to you, as it will be mainly by your assistance and advice that it is brought about.[9]

The assembly wharf was expanded just in time to take on the added shipments from Harmac, the new pulp mill being built south of Nanaimo.

While the assembly wharf was an improvement to shipping, there was still a need for a place where fishermen could tie up to purchase supplies. The argument was made in 1942 that float accommodation might encourage some of the bigger fishing companies on the mainland to moor their boats. The city "was sadly in need of some industry" because there were very few coal miners employed now.[10]

The most obvious location for improved docking facilities was the old Hirst wharf that dated from 1874, at the time of the city's incorporation, when pioneer merchant John Hirst purchased the wharf from the Vancouver Coal Company. The wharf and the tract of land on which the Hirst warehouse was built were located at the end of Bastion and Wharf streets and were of strategic importance to the city. After Hirst's death, the Hirst Estate Land Company Ltd. was formed and the wharf was rented out to James Renney, then later to J. Kneen.[11] Records show the wharf had been rented continuously for over 60 years. However, the city limits did not extend into the harbour until 1936 when an extension bylaw was approved.

Federal authorities advised the city in 1942 that efforts were being made to purchase the old wharf and asked if the city had any objection to a deed being given for the land. The city objected because of the two city streets.

In 1943, the city clerk, Harold Hackwood, wrote to MP R.W. Mayhew advising that the public landing facilities in Nanaimo Harbour were "altogether inadequate," and that farmers and fishermen were severely handicapped because the congestion was so bad. "Only extreme necessity forces them to dock here."[12]

The Hirst Estate Land Company threatened to take the matter to court to establish its rights, but remained hopeful of avoiding litigation. City council concluded it had no objection to the lease being granted regarding the water lot provided that nothing obstructed any of the city streets.[13] When the Hirst property was put up for sale, the city expressed interest.

The city leased the water lot from the Department of Public Works Canada and the old Hirst warehouse became the home of the Nanaimo Harbour Commission. In 1947 Commercial Inlet was deepened to 10 feet and a new set of floats was constructed for the fishing fleet.

Until 1960, the Department of Transport in Ottawa managed the harbour. Ben Abrams collected harbour dues from his office at Bastion and Front streets. There was a movement to establish a Nanaimo Harbour Commission led by Nanaimo Chamber of Commerce president Don Cunliffe, who lobbied Ottawa to have the commission formed. The commission became a reality in 1960 when the first three commissioners, former mayor George Muir, Max Blunt, and John Thompson, were appointed. Blunt owned a car dealership and Thompson was in the lumber business. Their first office was shared with Captain Bill Higg's towing company. Then in 1968, the commission purchased and renovated the old Hirst building, formerly used by Stannard Flour & Feed Store. This remains the home of the Port Authority today.

CPR's New Ferry Terminal

The face of the harbour changed once again when the CPR built a new two-berth terminal for its ferries. The transportation terminal cost $1.7 million and could handle road, rail, and water traffic. It was judged the most modern travel terminal on the coast and proved its worth in 1949 by daily handling 11,200 passengers and 400 cars, as well as the Vancouver Island Coach Lines traffic.[14]

The shipping berths were 380 feet long and had two elevators, one for passengers, the other for freight. The passenger service terminal, a two-storey concrete building, had a waiting room for 3,000 people, a restaurant, restrooms, and offices for rail, steamship, and bus lines. The coach line garage had space for 30 buses.

The CPR dock at Cameron Island dominated Nanaimo Harbour.

The CPR Ferry Terminal officially opened May 18, 1949. The city praised the CPR "for endeavouring to meet and assist in the remarkable growth and prosperity of the B.C. Coast."[15]

The CPR purchased two new ferries, the *Princess Marguerite* and *Princess Patricia*. During the winter the *Marguerite* ran daytime service between Victoria and Vancouver and also made a Vancouver to Nanaimo trip in the evening, returning the next morning. Either the *Princess Joan* or *Princess Elizabeth* made a daytime return trip from Victoria and Seattle. Later the *Princess Elaine* filled in on the winter service.[16]

The *Princess Marguerite*, the first of the new steamers, was launched in May 26, 1948. The *Princess Patricia* was launched October 10, 1948. The Clyde shipyards in Glasgow, Scotland, built both vessels. Maritime historian Robert D. Turner wrote, "They were coastal liners, not ferries, and the distinction was clear in every line and curve of their design."[17] The new steamers were popular, but there was not enough traffic to warrant using them all year round.

Another vessel, the *Princess of Nanaimo*, was added to the fleet in 1951; she was also built in Scotland and was impressive, modern, well built, but almost obsolete by the time she came into service. She could carry only 140 cars and was still designed for side loading and unloading.

A big blow to the CPR passenger service was the arrival in 1953 of the Black Ball Line, a Canadian subsidiary of Washington's Puget Sound Navigation Company that began a fast, no-frills ferry service designed for quick loading and unloading. The service was punctual and frequent between Departure Bay and Horseshoe Bay in West Vancouver.

Nanaimo Towing Company Limited

Nanaimo Harbour was the home port of the Nanaimo Towing Company Limited, which began with two small gasoline tugs and had by the mid-'40s grown to include 12 tugs of various sizes, 41 employees, and an annual payroll of $100,000.[18]

Following service in the First World War, Captain William (Bill) York Higgs worked for a few years with the Canadian Pacific coastal service, then later had a stint in the sawmill industry. He soon discovered that his love was with the sea, not in manufacturing lumber. In 1926 he established the Gulf Islands Transportation Co. Ltd. Two years later, he inaugurated the Shoal Harbor Marine Service, at Sidney, north of Victoria, and in July 1931, with his brother Captain Thomas L. Higgs, began the Gabriola Island Ferry Company with the *Atrevida*, which could carry passengers and cars. The ferry service was inaugurated on August 15, 1931.[19]

In 1936 Higgs changed the name of his company to Nanaimo Towing Company Limited while continuing to add subsidiary companies: the

North American Towing and Salvage Company Limited, for marine salvage; the Nanaimo Piledriving & Dredging Co. Ltd.; the Ladysmith Booming Grounds; and the Sechelt-Jervis Towing Company. The headquarters for the Nanaimo Towing Company was at Bastion and Front streets in Nanaimo.

There were few places on the coast that the Higgs operation did not touch. Eighty percent of his business was in log towing, and 95 percent of that trade was in the area bounded on the west by Seymour Narrows and on the east by the U.S. boundary, including the mainland inlets, Vancouver, the Fraser River, and the Gulf Islands. Higgs knew the Gulf Islands "like a housewife knows her kitchen," and he looked upon Nanaimo as one of the future busy ports of British Columbia.[20]

The assistant manager of the company was Captain J.H. Marshall, a former marine superintendent of the War Assets Corporation of B.C., an ex-naval lieutenant commander with considerable deep-sea experience. His dispatcher was Captain M.A. Corfield, who joined the company in 1929 and was a well-known figure in the marine and sawmill industries, and among loggers along the B.C. coast. The marine salvage superintendent was his brother Captain Thomas L. Higgs.

As well as creating one of the largest towing and salvaging operations on the coast, Captain Bill Higgs was particularly interested in safety at sea. He designed radio distress frequency buoys and survival vehicles. Transport Canada approved his special float-free radio buoy in 1973 for use on seagoing tugs. Higgs also designed a rapid embarkation lifeboat. In 1984, at a ceremony in New York, he received the Halert C. Shepheard Award for achievement in merchant marine safety. He was also honoured with a fellowship from the Nautical Institute of London, England, and he received special recognition in Germany from the Nautical Association of Seamen. He was an honorary life member in the Canadian Merchant Service Guild.

Captain Bill Higgs moved to Gibsons on the Sunshine Coast. He was president and managing director of Intercontinental Marine Ltd. of Gibsons and a member of the master mariners of Canada. He died in 1989.

The Gabriola Ferries

The Gabriola Island ferry *Atrevida* did yeoman service, carrying passengers, cars, and freight. The 70-foot-long ferry could transport about seven cars each trip. Initially she docked at Degnen Bay, on the east side of the island, but this was quickly changed to Descanso Bay, on the west side, to shorten the run to the CPR docks in Nanaimo. The ferry's name was fitting, for she was named after the famous Spanish corvette *Atrevida*, one of two vessels on the Malaspina expedition to the Pacific that anchored near Gabriola Island.[21]

The islanders appreciated the ferry, for farmers could now take their produce to market in Nanaimo and residents could drive to any part of Vancouver Island. The Sylva Bay Resort, and the Laws, Milwards, and Taylor Bay resorts also benefited from the new link.[22]

When Nanaimo incorporated in 1874, Gabriola Island had only 19 settlers; in 1931 there were approximately 200. Three schools served the population at the south end, the central island, and the north end. There were also two churches, one a United Church and the other Roman Catholic. The Nanaimo Board of Trade and other organizations were credited with lobbying to improve the transportation link between the island and Nanaimo.

After the *Atrevida*'s engine failed on January 15, 1955, the ferry was sold to Captain Bert Davis, of the Davis Shipping Co., Nanaimo, which had operated the service since 1947. The next ferry to service the island was the *Eena.* She was 20 feet longer than the *Atrevida* and could carry between 10 and 12 cars.

The *Eena* was built in 1919 at Yarrows Shipyard in Victoria for the provincial government. For many years she worked on the Fraser River until the George Massey Tunnel (a.k.a. Deas Island Tunnel) opened, and at the Agassiz-Rosedale and the Albion–Fort Langley crossings; then she was retired to New Westminster. She became the Gabriola ferry in 1955.

Parker Williams joined the three-man crew of the *Eena* in March 1957 as the engineer. During the winter, the ferry made four return trips a day, with an extra late-night trip on Friday; an extra sailing was added during the summer. Parker recalled that trips in fog were always difficult; there was no radio or radar, only a magnetic compass and a wind-up alarm. The ferry used the CPR dock at Cameron Island. Returning to Gabriola Island, she headed to Gallows Point foghorn on Protection Island, which was operated by a lighthouse keeper. After that it was full speed ahead for about 13 minutes until a whistle echo was picked up from the bluffs on the island. "This would get us close enough to pick up the shoreline and follow it into Descanso Bay." Other vessels using the waterways whistled their presence during foggy conditions. It was just as difficult finding the CPR dock on the return trip, as it had no navigational aids.

Vehicles boarded through the side of the ship. Drivers had to make a sharp 90-degree turn to get into the fore and aft lanes. Local residents were very proficient at this manoeuvre, but strangers found it a little intimidating. This also limited the size of trucks that could be carried. When a new dock was constructed in 1957 it was possible to end load, at least on the Gabriola side. A new dock was built on the Nanaimo side in 1960. It was still a difficult operation, as all the ramps were raised and lowered manually.

In February 1962, the provincial government purchased the *Eena.* The sailing was then under the administration of the Department of Highways.

Several years passed before the Nanaimo–Gabriola run became an integral part of B.C. Ferries Corporation.

The *Eena* was replaced by the *Garibaldi II*, which was renamed *Westwood*, in honour of Earle C. Westwood, the MLA and former Nanaimo mayor. This popular ferry lasted eight years. The guest list at the ferry's inauguration ceremony included many well-known politicians such as Earle Westwood, the Honorable Phil Gaglardi, MLA David Stupich, and Nanaimo mayor Pete Maffeo. However, the honour of christening the vessel went to Gabriola Island resident 77-year-old Mrs. Norman Poyner, who first arrived on the island by canoe. Darryl Bate, president of the Ratepayers Association, and Rev. Chris Jack were also present.[23]

Since then other vessels have served the run: the *Kulleet*, the *Klatawa*, the *Kahloke*, the *Quinitsa*, and the *Quinsam*.

Chapter Thirteen

The Second World War: Defending Freedom

Twenty-five years after the First World War plunged the world into a conflict that cost millions of lives, Europe was once again an armed camp. Within weeks, Germany's Adolf Hitler plunged Europe into another war. The Pope pleaded for peace. Great Britain mobilized her fleet. Schoolchildren were evacuated from London, and French children were whisked out of Paris, while Europeans waited for the inevitable.

After a German force swept across the Polish border on September 3, 1939, Great Britain and France declared war on Germany. The first British attack was on September 4, when the British air force bombed a German fleet in the North Sea. The German domination continued throughout Austria and Czechoslovakia. Canada was slow to react; most politicians were still at their cottages enjoying the last remnants of summer. Parliament did not meet until September 7 and it was not until September 10 that the declaration of war was approved and $100,000 allotted towards war expenses.

Air Commodore Raymond Collishaw

Only months before, as war with Germany became imminent, the Royal Air Force (RAF) in Egypt was strengthened. On April 18, 1939, Nanaimo's First World War hero Raymond Collishaw, aged 45, credited with bringing down 60 enemy planes, was appointed Air Officer commanding a new group in the Middle East, the Egypt Group, with headquarters in Cairo. This group became known as the Desert Air Force.[1] For his work in Egypt, he was made a Companion of the Order of the Bath.

Collishaw's next appointment was in March 1942 to Fighter Command in Scotland, with headquarters in Inverness. He was now air vice-marshal

Raymond Collishaw, Nanaimo's First World War hero, is shown here with his family. From left to right are his daughter Felicity, his mother, Raymond, wife Juaneita (née Trapp), and daughter Mary in May 1945.

and was responsible for the air defence of Scotland and of the Fleet at Scapa Flow. He remained there until the summer of 1943, when, after nearly 27 years' service with the Royal Naval Air Service (RNAS) and the RAF, he retired and returned to Vancouver to join his wife, Juaneita, and two daughters, Felicity and Mary.

Returning to civilian life was a difficult transition; he commented, "I had been constantly in uniform of one sort or another since 1908, and a straight diet of civilian dress was at first strange."[2] He considered his command in North Africa his best effort.

His father, John Edward Collishaw, had an interest in mining and had conducted many prospecting ventures. He died in the Australian gold fields in 1923. Like his father, Raymond turned his abilities to placer mining and set up an operation in the Barkerville area but was forced to close because of the low price for gold. Over the years he was associated with a number of mining operations in the Interior; outstanding among them was Craigmont Mines Ltd., for which he served as president for five years. A previous illness that affected his eyesight ended his mining career. The man who had remarkable eyesight as a young man and who could see distant objects that friends could see only with binoculars, was now almost blind.

Collishaw was inducted into Canada's Aviation Hall of Fame in 1973. He died in 1975 in Lions Gate Hospital, North Vancouver, at age 82.[3] The Raymond Collishaw Terminal at Nanaimo Airport was named in his honour.

Building an Airport

In 1938 Mayor Victor Harrison wrote to Captain Entwistle of the Air Ministry in London, England, promoting Nanaimo as a possible air base. Entwistle had visited Vancouver, but the mayor had missed meeting with him in person. However, Harrison found the subject had already been brought to the Air Ministry's attention. He was prepared to follow up with blueprints and other relevant data and wrote a glowing report about Nanaimo's attributes. He advised that Nanaimo was on the U.S.–Alaska route for air traffic and was 36 miles by water from Vancouver.

> There is a steam boat service twice daily in winter and four times daily in summer to the latter city. We are on the all red route. The All Red Cable to Australia passes through the city and under the Bastion Street Bridge. This harbour has been recommended very strongly in the past as a most suitable place for the landing of air and seaplanes, mainly due to the absence of fog. The city recently acquired some waterfront property which could be made a most suitable place for water landings. An additional three thousand acres at the head of this harbour (the Nanaimo River Flats) could be acquired from the respective governments, which would afford suitable location and ample space for present and future development.[4]

The waterfront property Mayor Harrison referred to was the nine-acre lot on which the civic arena was eventually built. The mayor put Nanaimo on the Air Ministry's agenda, but it was a couple of years into the Second World War before the Dominion government decided to build more airports for defence purposes on the west coast. There were several RCAF "aerodromes" built on Vancouver Island. They included Cassidy, Tofino, and Comox.

On September 20, 1943, the Crown purchased land from Thomas William Cassidy for $20,000. More land was expropriated from Nora Kathleen Anglin for $13,000.[5] The Tofino airport had already been completed when Gordon Gibson's logging crew was asked to clear land at Cassidy, south of Nanaimo. No tenders were called for on the project. When asked about the financial arrangements, Gibson was told, "Just start and send the bills to us. Get the kind of men you need, regardless of the wages … the project must be completed as quickly as possible."[6]

Manpower was the biggest problem at the time. Most young men had already signed up for military service; however, Gibson had unlimited funds. The men were seconded from nearby logging camps. He first approached Jimmy Sheasgreen, manager of the Comox Logging Company, with a list of requirements—100 men, 10 donkeys, and 10 Caterpillars. Gibson said,

"Jimmy saw the sense of the offer, for we could have wrecked his logging camp by stealing away all his men, so he co-operated by sending his good men and equipment."

A gravel road was put through the middle of the site. Every 600 feet a spur road went 600 feet in either direction, thus dividing the entire site into 600-foot squares. Within each square all the saleable timber was retrieved and poor timber and stumps burned in a giant bonfire. Before long, an official from the B.C. Forestry Department ordered the crew to stop burning the huge piles. They told him where to go in no uncertain terms and advised they were working in the interest of national security. The Comox Logging Company and other small contractors built the airport for less than the approved cost and twice as quickly. Gordon Gibson and his crew moved on to build another airport at Port Hardy.

Before long RCAF aircraft were landing and taking off from the Cassidy airstrip.

Pacific Command: Threats from Japan

The greatest threat to B.C. did not come from Germany but from the Pacific Ocean. Japan entered the conflict by bombing Pearl Harbor, Hawaii, on December 7, 1941. War was immediately declared, and four days later the United States also declared war against Italy and Germany. This was now a world conflict.

Alarm was felt across B.C. because of the large number of Japanese living here. Various organizations, service clubs, trade unions, and municipal and provincial governments pressured the federal government to provide some military protection for the west coast. When the Japanese forces invaded the Aleutian Islands in June 1942, the fear only grew. The War Committee in Ottawa authorized the formation of an 8th Division.

Major General George R. Pearkes was brought back from Europe in September 1942 to take charge of the Pacific Command, which by the spring of 1943 included 35,000 officers and men.[7] It also included the reserves of 15,000 officers and men of the Pacific Coast Militia Rangers, an organization of rangers, miners, loggers, and others who were scattered around the province. These volunteers served without pay, provided local defence, gathered intelligence, and, if the need arose, were able to assist in a major attack.

Major General Pearkes was born February 26, 1888, in Hertfordshire, England, and moved to Canada in 1906 to attend an agricultural school at Red Deer, Alberta. At 25, he joined the Royal North-West Mounted Police and served in the Yukon before enlisting in the First World War. He was awarded the Victoria Cross. Between wars he was deputy commandant at the Royal Military College, Kingston, and Director of Military Training in Ottawa. In 1925, he married Blytha Copeman; they had two children, Priscilla and John.

Pearkes was promoted to colonel in 1934, and brigadier in 1938. From 1939 until 1942, he served overseas training the 2nd Brigade and later the 1st Division troops; then he was recalled to Canada.

Camp Nanaimo

Mayor Victor Harrison's earlier request for an army camp to be located in Nanaimo was finally realized on May 29, 1940, when Prime Minister Mackenzie King announced that a training centre for the fighting forces would be located here.[8]

City Council decided it should be named "Camp Ralston" after the Minister of National Defence, the Honorable J.L. Ralston. A quick reply came from the department stating, "The Minister would prefer it if some other name than his own be used."[9] It was named Camp Nanaimo. The camp came under the Pacific Command of Major General Pearkes.

The establishment of Camp Nanaimo, which became known for its small arms and infantry weapons training, brought hundreds of young servicemen here. The impact on the city was enormous. The military camp was located at Wakesiah Avenue and 5th Street, on the old Western Fuel Company's farm now owned by Canadian Collieries Co. The camp extended from Jingle Pot Road to Nanaimo Lakes Road.

Over the course of the conflict, a total of 36 regiments of approximately 10,500 troops completed their training at Camp Nanaimo. The regular force units of the 13th Infantry Brigade, including the Canadian Scottish Regiment's 196th Battery of the 66th Light Anti-Aircraft Regiment and the Duke of Connaught's Own Rifles, trained here. The camp was also used as a combined operations base for the training of army and naval groups, but this section closed in 1943 when it was centralized in Comox.

The first regiment of 1,000 officers and men to arrive was the 1st Battalion of the Duke of Connaught's Own Rifles on October 1, 1940. They were part of the 3rd Division formerly stationed at New Westminster and North Vancouver now under the command of Lieutenant Colonel Carmichael. The troops arrived on the *Princess Joan*, bringing with them several truckloads of baggage and a refrigeration system. It took almost four hours to unload the *Joan*. Hundreds of residents gathered at the dock to welcome the troops.[10]

An advance party, which had made the camp ready for the soldiers, met the regiment at the dock. "How's the camp?" called the men. "Swell, if a bit up and down," was the reply.[11] The soldiers may have been surprised to learn they would be living in tents for the next while. Camp Nanaimo, or Tent City, as the soldiers dubbed it, was not the best place to be on a cold

Camp Nanaimo, or Tent City, as the soldiers dubbed it, became known for its small arms and infantry weapons training.

wet winter day on the west coast. Floorboards were installed under the tents until new buildings could be completed.

The platoons formed at the wharf and then were marched in threes to Camp Nanaimo, led by their bugle band. This scene was repeated many times during the war. The following week, an equal number of men from the South Alberta Regiment arrived from Dundern Camp.

Soon construction began on more permanent accommodations, including canteens, messes, living quarters, training buildings, and a hospital. The camp military hospital may have been better equipped than the city hospital. There were 225 beds, four X-ray machines, an examination laboratory, inspection rooms, canteen, quartermaster stores, and quarters for a staff of 90. The hospital was equipped with a physiotherapy department and was steam heated throughout.[12]

Edith Pinkett worked at the Salvation Army Red Shield Centre on Wallace Street when the first soldiers arrived at Camp Nanaimo. "After marching from the wharf to the camp in the pouring rain, they discovered to their dismay that there were not enough huts ready. Hastily pitched leaky tents did not prove an adequate alternative."[13] She recalled their soggy clothes hanging all over as they temporarily retreated to the Red Shield Centre, which could sleep up to 100 people. Soldiers visited there on their days off or met there with girlfriends or wives. The centre served meals and had a library with writing paper available. In July 1943, an annex opened beside the Salvation Army Citadel on Nicol Street; it took the overflow from Wallace Street. Here another 75 men could sleep.

Connie Filmer kept a scrapbook of the camp activities during the war years. Her collection, now in the Nanaimo Archives, shows there was a social aspect to the young servicemen being stationed in the city. Miss Filmer received many invitations to dances held in the Officers' Mess on New Year's Eve and Remembrance Day, and invitations to dances held around town.

The dances held in the Pygmy Pavilion were well attended by camp soldiers. Young women who could dance were in high demand for the well-chaperoned events, and there were never enough of them. Many young Nanaimo women learned to dance with men in army boots. Stu Storrie's house band played every Saturday night from 1943 to 1951. No liquor was allowed. Al Campbell played in the band and later recalled the dance hall days:

> You couldn't bring liquor into a dance hall and the Pygmy didn't sell it. People would keep a bottle stashed in their cars and go out and have a swig. Even some of the band members kept liquor behind the musical stands we had. We used to play from 8 p.m. to 2 a.m. every Saturday night. It was a long night. Then the province brought in the Lord's Day Act and they wouldn't allow entertainment past midnight.[14]

Stu Storrie's house band played at the Pygmy Pavilion every Saturday night from 1943 to 1951. No liquor was allowed. Standing at the sides are announcer Gordon Theedom (left) and bassist Stu Storrie (right). In the back row, left to right, are Chuck Hewitt, Spud Murphy, and Al Campbell. In the front row, left to right, are Cyril Kilner, Don Sutherland, Jack Sneeden, Jack Norrish, and Ted Bramley. Pianist Johnny Nielson is in back.

Another article in the Filmer collection notes that Nanaimo had "the nicest girls, [and] the best beer in all Canada," according to the soldiers of the South Alberta Regiment.[15] After the regiment had put in seven months' training, the soldiers were transferred to Vancouver. Spectators cheered the kilted band as they paraded through downtown Vancouver streets in full battle dress.

The military staff also liked the camp. When Lieutenant J.W. Worthington of the Duke of Connaught's Own Rifles, Vancouver regiment, was guest at a Nanaimo Junior Chamber of Commerce luncheon, he congratulated the city "for the excellent camp site at the Wakesiah Farm." He added, "The battalion had no idea it was coming to so pleasant a camp when it left New Westminster."[16]

Civil Defence

As Pearkes took over Pacific Command, Nanaimo went on wartime alert. Blackout restrictions were imposed and driving was restricted to emergencies only. A Civil Defence Organization was formed under First World War veteran Pete Maffeo. This group took control of fire halls, trucks, and equipment and divided the region into 12 districts from Cedar to Wellington North.

Maffeo was the right man to rally the community in the war effort. He was a born in Nanaimo in 1897, was orphaned at an early age, and was raised by his aunt and uncle, Mr. and Mrs. J. Fontana. At age 10 he began working in the mines. After his war service he purchased the Davenport Ice and Ice Cream plant. On December 15, 1923, he married Vera Akenhead. They had one child, Joyce.[17]

Maffeo began the home defence by establishing first-aid posts throughout the district under the chairmanship of Charles Wharton, St. John Ambulance Association. Two hundred people formed the main casualty response service. In addition, Wharton and his captains trained 1,015 people for new first-aid certificates and re-examined 678 others. The Nanaimo team was regarded among the best in the province.

Schoolchildren also trained in civil defence. The district found homes in town for all out-of-town students. Parents consented to have their children remain at their new homes until the all-clear sounded. This was done to avoid parents rushing into town looking for their children.[18]

The students of Wellington School were trained for a disappearing act should an enemy approach the school ground, either by land or air. When the principal, Arthur Peake, called ARP (Air-Raid Precautions), the students ran from their seats, gathered under squad leaders who accounted for each of them, then vanished into the nearby forest. Anyone passing through the area would never see them, but the principal knew where to reach any one of them.

When the all-clear signal was given, the students emerged from every nook and hollow in the ground. Even the previously empty brush contained 70 students. The students cut trails and always hid in the same spots, where they camouflaged themselves perfectly.[19]

Air-raid sirens were established on the Nanaimo Free Press Building, South Ward School, Brechin School, Harewood School, and on the roof of Jameson's Bakery in Wellington.

Maffeo's civil defence team also had the use of Tommy Naylor's homing pigeons to carry messages to and from any district. This service was the only one of its kind known in civil defence.[20]

The carrier pigeons were put to good use on May 26, 1944, when a RCAF crew of five crashed on 4,600-foot-high Mount Whymper, about 20 miles southwest of Nanaimo. Maffeo was in charge of the rescue party that included game wardens Frank Greenfield and Jim Dewar and RCMP officer Bert Lannock. They flew over the area in a Canso floatplane before finding clothing hanging in the trees near the top of the mountain. The plane had been fully loaded with bombs and had exploded on impact. Pieces of the plane and men were scattered over a half-mile radius.[21] A ground crew of six men was dispatched from Jump Lake on May 29, along with four of Naylor's pigeons. It took until June 3 to reach the site. The birds carried the information back to Nanaimo.

A major ARP exercise was carried out along the east coast of Vancouver Island in May 1942. The area extended from Oyster River to Duncan and included the operations of six unit areas. The exercise revealed only a few villages without an organization. Neighbouring communities would take these into their fold. There were 2,500 men and women in the exercise that included wardens, first-aid ambulances, public utilities, and Canadian Red Cross disaster committees.[22]

While the residents of the city were used to the militia marching through town, the city wanted to be reimbursed for the damage done to local streets by tractors while the camp was being built. The city accepted $700 as full settlement.[23]

Nanaimo was bulging at the seams. The city instituted rent control because of the conditions created by the military camp presence.[24] Wives of soldiers came to the city to be near their loved ones.

After St. George's School closed, Shelby Saunders, who built the Pygmy Pavilion, purchased the building. During the war he converted the old doctor's house into suites for soldiers' wives and "camp followers." Children were amused to see Mrs. Saunders collecting the rent accompanied by her servant, an African-American woman wearing a big white apron and a bandana.[25] After the war, the house was converted into apartments.

Housing was in such short supply that the city complained to federal authorities that several families shared the same house, thus lowering living standards and family life.[26]

In 1942 the city was ordered by the Minister of Pensions and National Health to chlorinate its water supply as a war measure act.[27] The Chase River watershed had been subject to pollution for some time, and the city had gone to great expense to lay a large supply main from the South Fork Dam. In 1943 Shanahan's Limited supplied the chlorinating equipment at a cost of $6,982.[28]

Even the local post office felt the strain from increased business. There were complaints about service but most people tolerated the inconvenience; however, as soon as the war ended, the city began lobbying the Dominion government for a new post office.[29]

In 1942 Nanaimo Hospital added a new wing with 86 beds and accommodation for 15 nurses on the top floor of the original south wing. The nurses' quarters were soon converted into 15 single-patient rooms. A new boiler house and laundry were built in 1947/48. The Nurses' Home continued to function as before, but the building had seen its best years and was closed in 1961.[30]

War Affects Everyone

Everyone felt the effects of war. Ottawa curtailed the number of telephones being installed in private homes because of the shortage of copper and other metals. Nanaimo launched a "vigorous protest against the shipment of copper and other war materials to Japan."[31] This resulted from a press report stating that the entire production of Copper Mountain, south of Nanaimo, was to be shipped to Japan.

Gasoline and sugar were rationed from 1942. The amount of sugar allowed was a half pound per person per week. In August 1943, when meat was added to the ration list, housewives found meat-extending recipes and restaurants introduced "meatless Tuesday." Wage and price controls were mandated between 1939 and 1944, and income taxes increased more than 10 times as Canada ran up a $15 billion bill for the war. Women were lucky to get a pair of nylon stockings, and liquor was hard to come by. Canadian factories employed over 1.1 million people in the war industry.

Barbara Samarin (née Lawson) attended North Ward School during the war years. These were her recollections of that time:

> I remember the gas mask drills and never really learning how to put one on properly, which of course worried me half to death. We bought war savings stamps at 25 cents each and pasted them in booklets, we collected scrap newspaper and empty toothpaste

> tubes, we lived on rationed food, we did without candy and gum, but in spite of it all we survived.[32]

The National Selective Service (NSS) registered women from coast to coast to maintain the wartime workforce. Women entered the job market in large numbers and moved from poorly paid positions to those with higher wages. This was probably the first time the government had intervened in the labour supply since the First World War.[33] Some men regarded the women as intruders in a male-dominated workplace, but as the war progressed and more and more men enlisted, women became vital in factories across the province.

Without government support, the B.C. Women's Service Corps made their own military-style blue uniform and trained themselves in practical skills likely to be needed in the war. Women in other provinces formed similar groups. After some lobbying, some by Joan Kennedy of Victoria, the Dominion government co-ordinated these groups into a national army unit. On August 13, 1941, the Honorable John Ralston signed an order-in-council authorizing the formation of the Canadian Women's Army Corps.[34]

Nanaimo urged all enemy aliens to register. Before long applications for naturalization were heard in court. In June 1940 government notices stated "All Italians naturalized after September 1, 1929, are required to register with RCMP authorities. All Italians in the above category are required to turn in their firearms to the same authorities."[35] The Italians swore allegiance to Canada.

The Nanaimo Branch of the Canadian Red Cross collected items to send overseas. During the month of June 1944, the branch collected 4,983 items and donations. These included 126 wool comforters, 4,712 surgical items, 99 pieces of civilian clothing, and 36 knitted items. The Women's Auxiliary donated five items and 543 hospital supplies. The press release from the branch asked for help:

> British civilians are once again suffering because of the robot bombings. There are quantities of children's clothing ready to be made up at the workrooms. Grey flannel pants for little boys, and blue shirtwaist frocks for little girls.[36]

Music and movies gave everyone a respite from the grim war news. This was the era of swing. Glen Miller's big band was the most popular dance band in the world during the war. His music was played in every venue from dance hall to military camp and came to symbolize a time and place. Miller went missing in December 1944 on a flight from England to France during a trip to entertain the troops.

Miller never played Nanaimo, but the "Trumpet King of Swing" did. On July 20, 1944, Louis Armstrong and his orchestra and singers gave a concert in the Pygmy Pavilion to an estimated crowd of 1,000. Armstrong, accompanied by 18 musicians, won the hearts of local dancers.

At Nanaimo's Capitol Theatre, Mickey Rooney and Elizabeth Taylor starred in *National Velvet*. *Casablanca,* starring Humphrey Bogart and Ingrid Bergman, was released just prior to Pearl Harbor but remained a hit throughout the war years.

Nanaimo Builds Minesweepers

In 1941 Mayor Harrison lobbied to have wartime wooden-ship-building contracts come this way. The Newcastle Shipbuilding Co. Ltd., located adjacent to the Civic Arena, took up the challenge. Frank Hanna was president of the company, Elmer Bradshaw was secretary, Jack Gilmour was superintendent, and Henry Ericksen was foreman.[37] In 1942 when they started building the wooden ships, Gilmour and Eriksen were the only two trained shipbuilders. Over the course of the project, they trained and hired 100 men from Ladysmith and Nanaimo.[38] The company built a total of three minesweepers and six air-force auxiliary vessels.

The first ship to be launched was the HMCS *St. Joseph*, a 105-foot minesweeper. They handed the ship over to the navy on Victoria Day, May 24, 1944, as "the white ensign [was] unfurled at the masthead to the shrill whistle of the bosun's pipe."[39] Lieutenant Alec B. Plummer, Royal Canadian Naval Volunteer Reserve (RCNVR), took command of the new ship, which had been named for the town of St. Joseph de Grantham, Quebec.

The *St. Joseph* was the first major vessel built here since September 1882, when the barque *Nanaimo* was launched at almost the same spot. Building wooden ships depended on a reliable lumber supply, and that Vancouver Island had in abundance. The stem, keelshoe, and guards of the *St. Joseph* were made of Australian gumwood; the deck hatches and doors were of Burmese teakwood, and the remainder of the ship used 350,000 feet of Douglas-fir that was processed in the nearby sawmills.

Another minesweeper launched was the HMCS *Coquitlam*. Mayor Harrison and his council joined Coquitlam's mayor and council, and several naval officers for this ceremony.

Two months later, on July 21, another ship was handed over, this time to the air force. This was the seventh ship to be launched in Nanaimo and the eighth neared completion. The ship was a 114-foot Royal Canadian Air Force supply vessel. These vessels were sturdy and reliable craft and very much appreciated by the men who served on them. Mrs. F.V. Heakes, the wife of Air Vice Marshal F.V. Heakes of the Western Air Command, christened her the *Hesquiat*. As the ship took her initial plunge into the water of Newcastle Channel, whistles and sirens of boats in the harbour mingled with the cheers of a crowd that had gathered on Front and Comox street heights to witness

In January 1942 the crew of the corvette HMCS *Nanaimo* was sent out in the howling Atlantic to save sailors adrift in an open boat who had abandoned their sinking ship. The *Nanaimo* crew was given a slim chance of finding them, but they rescued all 10 men just as darkness fell.

the launch. The shipyard workers assembled around the vessel as Mrs. Heakes gave her the traditional champagne blessing.

Elmer Bradshaw introduced the guests and emphasized how important these small vessels were on the east and west coasts to the men who flew. Other shipyards in the province built corvettes for the Royal Navy. Canada built more than a hundred of them and sent them into the Atlantic to seek out U-boats and provide an armed guard for ships carrying essential equipment for the war in Europe. The city was advised that one of them would be named HMCS *Nanaimo*. The Minister of National Defence for Naval Services noted:

> The idea of having ships adopted by the city or town has been found to be very advantageous in keeping up the morale of ships' crews, as well as giving the citizens of the community an opportunity to give expression to help in the winning of the war.[40]

A young sailor aboard the HMCS *Nanaimo*, A.V. Hodding, wrote to his mother, Mrs. A.M. Hodding, in Duncan about the heroic action of the ship's crew in January 1942. She in turn informed Mayor Victor Harrison of the bravery of the city's namesake ship. The ship had been sent out in a howling gale in the Atlantic to save sailors adrift in an open boat after abandoning their sinking ship. The *Nanaimo* crew was given a slim chance of finding them, but they rescued all 10 men just as darkness fell. Mrs. Hodding asked:

> If any kind person in Nanaimo has a warm pullover, or part-worn overcoat to give away, some poor sailor would be very grateful for it. We owe so much to the Merchant Navy and so few people ever give it a thought. My son tells me that the Red Cross supplies corvettes with warm clothing for merchant seamen, only with no overcoats, and all clothing is only on loan. On reaching port such things have to be handed back. The men are given money with which to buy new clothes, but it does not go very far, and the cold on the Atlantic in winter is terrible.[41]

The corvettes played a major role in the war, but according to those who sailed on them, they were hell to live in as they raced through the mountainous grey seas of the Atlantic.

Just as the wooden ships were being launched, a young Nanaimo man received the Distinguished Service Medal in recognition of "bravery in saving the lives of shipmates." King George VI gave stoker Thomas H. Forrester, RCNVR, the award. Forrester had seen action in every allied invasion of Europe, North Africa, and France. He was the son of Mrs. Jeanie Forrester, of 4th Avenue, and was one of 11 children.[42] Two other brothers also served in the Royal Canadian Navy.

In 1942, Forrester, 19, had just started work at the Nanaimo Airport when he received his draft papers to join the army. With two other brothers in the navy, he didn't want to join the army, so he enlisted in the navy. He trained in Detroit before being sent overseas to serve with the British landing craft infantry.

Forrester's war was spent in the Mediterranean, transporting troops between Europe and North Africa. Bombing was a common occurrence, so the crew paid little attention to it until the night of January 22, 1944, when the bombs hit the ship. Asleep in the top bunk, Forrester was blown out of bed. The ship rolled, trapping some men beneath.

The first casualties were men who had been dangling their legs over the side of the boat—they lost their legs. Forrester devised tourniquets to stop them bleeding to death. Then he heard someone tapping below the overturned vessel. He and other rescuers cut a hole in the ship and hauled the sailor out. Forrester saved the lives of five men. He received not only the Distinguished Service Medal, but also the African Star, the Italian Star, and the French and German Stars.[43]

Chapter Fourteen

Peace with a Price

Attack on Alaska

Th United States and Canada worked hand in hand to protect the west coast. In October 1942, the 1,576-mile Alaska Highway neared completion under the direction of the U.S. Army Engineers at a cost of $138 million, and joint Canadian and U.S. forces completed a road up the Skeena Valley. Prince Rupert doubled in population when the U.S. military forces used the port as a base.

Major General Pearkes visited Camp Nanaimo on July 5, 1943, accompanied by Lieutenant General John L. DeWitt, to observe training. DeWitt was the commanding general of the U.S. Fourth Army and Western Defense Command at San Francisco. He commanded the troops both to the north and south of Pearkes's Pacific Command. DeWitt was extremely pleased with the soldiers training at Camp Nanaimo.

Japanese forces, which now occupied Attu and Kiska in the Aleutian Islands, were seen as a threat to the west coast. Pearkes was informed in April 1943 that he had permission to attack Attu, and possibly Kiska later on. He informed Camp Nanaimo that those units at the camp must be moved out to make way for the 13th Brigade to start training for Operation "Greenlight."

Before dawn on July 12, 1943, truck convoys roared through Nanaimo, while the 13th Brigade marched to the wharves where U.S. ships waited to embark them. Pearkes was there with his senior staff officers to wish them good luck. The *Nanaimo Free Press* reported:

> It was an historic day for Nanaimo … the departure of a military expedition for a destination then undisclosed. And the Canadian force in this case, under the command of Brig. Harry Foster was to become part of an amphibious armada bound for the misty isles

> of the Aleutian Chain that stretches like a necklace almost to the shore of the Japanese owned Kuriles.[1]

Now 5,300 Canadian forces joined 30,000 Americans to take Kiska. The island was heavily bombed; then the troops stormed ashore only to find there was no one there. The Japanese had left two weeks earlier.

The only Japanese attack on the west coast of Canada came on June 20, 1942, at Estevan Point, when a Japanese submarine surfaced opposite the lighthouse. The enemy vessel was sighted two miles offshore. It began shelling the lighthouse at approximately 9:40 p.m. and continued for 40 minutes. None of the shells hit their target; most exploded on the beach, and the lighthouse suffered no damage. The attack was enough to alert the Home Guard and the Airplane Detection Corps in Victoria. The next morning local people scoured the beach looking for souvenirs, while planes searched the ocean for the submarine. A few months later, when a Japanese submarine was sunk off the New Zealand coast, the first thing the crew said when rescued was that it was they who had shelled the Canadian lighthouse.

The Japanese tried another type of bombing—balloons designed to explode on impact. The theory was that the balloons would land in forests and start fires. The prevailing winds were strong enough to carry the balloons across the ocean in a few days. Hundreds of balloons were set adrift towards the continent but, fortunately for Islanders, the timing was a bit off—from November to March, B.C. forests are cold, damp, and highly unlikely to ignite.

Nanaimo military authorities came into possession of one such balloon. The potential fire starter had dropped months before in an inaccessible area. Someone found it and reported its presence to authorities. It was found to be a complete stratosphere-borne experimental balloon. Bomb disposal officers extracted the explosive and combustible contents, rendering it harmless. Another one was found near Yellow Point. This balloon eventually went on display in a department store window in Toronto.[2]

Japanese Interned

Feelings about the Japanese had simmered in B.C. since the turn of the century, so when the war in the Pacific erupted, there was a growing unease at their presence. The Japanese who had settled in Nanaimo had worked hard, raised their families, and established roots in the community. With their birth country at war it was inevitable that action would be taken, but how swiftly it happened took many by surprise.

> It was a shock beyond words. From Port Alice south to Victoria, the unexpected stunned the nikkei community. That night, tomato growers on Mayne Island, shopkeepers in Duncan, mill workers

> in Port Alberni and a community leader in Chemainus—eleven men, all Japanese nationals—were arrested and interned but never charged. Within 24 hours, language schools were shut, Japanese-owned logging assets seized and nikkei workers at Victoria's Empress Hotel fired without notice.[3]

The day after Pearl Harbor, newspapers reported that all fishing vessels owned and operated by Canadian citizens of Japanese origin must report to naval authorities for a "routine check and examination."

On December 17, 1941, all Japanese older than 16, male and female, residing between Qualicum and Ladysmith, were required to immediately register at the Provincial Police office in Nanaimo. The order also applied to all male Germans and Italians between the ages of 18 and 45 who were not naturalized. This order was province-wide. The only exceptions were native-born descendants or residents who were naturalized before September 1, 1922.

On January 3, 1942, Vancouver City Council proposed that the entire Japanese population of the province, estimated at 24,000, be removed to communal work camps east of the Rockies.

On January 13, 1942, Prime Minister Mackenzie King announced that enemy aliens of whatever racial origin, except those holding police permits to remain, were to be removed from the defence areas of B.C. All Japanese fishing operations on the Pacific coast were prohibited, and the fleet of 1,100 vessels immobilized pending negotiations for their transfer to Canadian operators. For the duration of the war, the Royal Canadian Mounted Police controlled the sale of gasoline and explosives to Japanese people. They were also forbidden to possess or use short-wave radio receiving sets, radio transmitters, and cameras.[4]

Fisheries Minister Michaud ordered that people of Japanese origin were prohibited from fishing in Canadian waters, serving on Canadian fishing boats, or buying fishing licences, "for reasons of national defence and security." The Japanese fleet was valued at between $2 million and $3 million; some 980 boats were impounded in New Westminster. All Japanese-owned fishing boats were placed under detention, and plans were underway to turn a large number of them over to White crews for the next fishing season.

A dusk-to-dawn curfew was imposed, and cameras, radios, firearms, and motor vehicles were confiscated. Police could search without warrant any place occupied by a Japanese person. A ban was imposed on liquor and beer; all mail was censored and long-distance telephone calls prohibited. All people of Japanese origin had to carry a registration card, and any movement within the province required a police permit.

Newspapers reported that resources such as mines and timber owned by alien Japanese were subject to seizure by federal authorities. Prior to this, the B.C. government had refused to sell Crown timber to Japanese, although there was no legal basis for doing so.

Finally the inevitable came: exile for everyone of Japanese descent. On January 16, an order-in-council authorized the Minister of National Defence to evacuate all Japanese nationals.[5] The British Columbia Security Commission carried out the evacuation. John Shirras, Nanaimo's former chief of police, now deputy inspector of the B.C. Police and a member of the Securities Commission, attended an executive meeting of the Union of B.C. Municipalities on March 12, 1942, to discuss the Japanese situation. The group passed a resolution that each province should take a percentage of the people within their boundaries for the duration of the war.[6]

The exodus began in mid-March, starting with the men. By the end of April 1942, all 3,400 had been removed from Vancouver Island. Every Japanese family dutifully packed up the belongings that would be left in the care of the Custodian of Enemy Property. Their homes were boarded up and contents sealed. Then they made their tearful farewells to neighbours, school friends, and others before boarding the steamer that would take them to the mainland.

On April 21, 1942, 470 Japanese boarded the *Princess Adelaide* at Chemainus. Included were those from Chemainus and those bused up from the Cowichan Valley. Special trains brought Japanese people from Tofino, Ucluelet, Clayoquot, and Port Alberni to Nanaimo, where they were shipped to the mainland. Their first stop was Hastings Park, in Vancouver, where men and women were separated. One wife sent a note to her husband in the men's dormitory:

> It is bedlam here. Tired children crying, the noise of people taking in this huge building with no walls to cut the sound; The terrible odour of animals mixed with disinfectant desperately trying to make it smell better. I can hardly breathe.[7]

Some spent months in Hastings Park before being moved to New Denver and Greenwood in the Kootenays, or to farms in Alberta and Manitoba, and elsewhere in Canada. Across Canada an estimated 20,881 Japanese were forcibly removed from their homes and communities. Nothing would ever be the same for those Japanese families that had lost everything. There was reluctance by some in fishing and forestry to allow them to return, because it was feared they would again dominate those industries. As for the politicians who were pleased at the Japanese redistribution across Canada, their mood soon changed when claims were made for confiscated property.

Peace Celebrated

Peace was declared on Monday, May 7, 1945, and part of the world breathed a lot easier. The German forces in Italy surrendered on April 29. Hitler shot himself in Berlin the following day, and the Red Army took over Berlin two days later. The main German forces in the west surrendered to Field Marshall Montgomery on May 4. Young men and women who had fought to preserve peace would be coming home. But some would not. The Second World War added 60 new names to Nanaimo's cenotaph.

Most residents of Nanaimo had just sat down to breakfast when at 7:10 a.m. three sets of ARP sirens alerted the community that the war in Europe was finally over. Mayor George Muir immediately declared a civic holiday. In the evening all churches held services of thanks. War veterans gathered at the cenotaph for a short service and then marched to St. Andrew's United Church to participate in the service with Mayor Muir and his council.

The morning shifts at the coal mines were already below ground when the sirens sounded, so they continued working, but the miners were allowed to quit early to join in the community celebrations. Newcastle Shipyards declared a two-day holiday; all retail outlets closed for the day. The *Free Press* recorded that wonderful morning:

> It was a sunshine-swimming morning with all hearts gladdened, folks of Nanaimo seemed to hustle through with the housework and daily chores and get out into the brightened atmosphere of the streets. Adults and young folk thronged the sidewalks, while Dad, Mom and the kids, in numbers rolled through the main streets in the family automobile, horns honking and cheery cries of congratulation sounding. The Silver Cornet Band, in full uniform and glittering instruments, boomed its way in a victory parade up and down Commercial Street, while sidewalk crowds beamed happily as the musicians passed.[8]

The editorial on VE Day spoke for everyone:

> We rejoice for the many Nanaimo homes wherein today's news means so much joy because of the loved ones who will be released from bondage, and for the still stalwart ones who will return unharmed. But in our joy we must not forget those homes wherein there will be vacant chairs and heart-spots which are still aching and sore because there can be no return of the ones held so dear.

A monster Citizens' Church Parade was held at the Civic Arena the following Sunday. Camp Nanaimo soldiers and cadets from both sea and air joined veteran organizations, the Silver Cornet Band, the Salvation Army Band, and a massed choir made up of all community church choirs in a Sunday of thanksgiving.

While the celebrations continued, Peter Bell urged the community to contribute just another $63,950 to reach the $1-million mark of the Nanaimo Unit Eighth Victory Loan drive. As the local organizer, he said he was confident that before the end of the week that goal would be reached. B.C. Telephone Company sponsored a large advertisement in the *Free Press*; it was a sketch of Sir Winston Churchill smoking his trademark cigar, with the words, "Remember, the war is not over yet. We still have to finish the job. Buy Victory Bonds now."

The Victory Loan headquarters invited the public to visit Cassidy Airport on Friday afternoon when the famous overseas Mosquito Bomber "F," for "Freddie," would be on display. The aircraft had made more than 200 operational flights over Europe. The public was warned, "Do not be alarmed by the sound of the engines ... The Mosquitos are notoriously noisy planes, but very effective. Authorities have strictly instructed pilots there is to be no stunting."[9] This referred to an incident in Toronto where a warplane had alarmed residents by circling skyscrapers in the downtown business district.

For those living on the west coast, VJ Day was as important. They celebrated victory over Japan on August 15. Japan surrendered after the U.S. atomic bombs destroyed the Japanese cities of Hiroshima and Nagasaki.

Air-raid sirens broke the news and the silence. Mill whistles, the horns of ships in the harbour, and the sirens of police cars joined them. Those with automobiles cruised through town with their horns blaring, and young and old cheered the end of the war.

Nanaimo's downtown thronged with people celebrating. Three big dances attracted a record number of people "who sought terpsichore and light fantastic as the means of self-expression."[10] The Kinsmen held the biggest dance at the Newcastle Island Pavilion. The Pygmy Pavilion brought in a band from Victoria. There was an almost spontaneous street dance conceived by George Pimlott, Nick Wright, and a group of residents who just wanted to dance in the open air. Bastion Street, between Commercial and Front streets, was blocked off and a loudspeaker set up—dancing continued from nine o'clock to midnight. The celebrations brought out the usual "rock-hurlers." They broke two windows of the liquor store on Church Street and stole liquor.

Reverend J. Wright conducted a more solemn service of remembrance at the cenotaph, attended by the military, Canadian Legion, cadets, Women's Auxiliary, and veterans of the First World War.

The Spencer's advertisement in the *Free Press* proclaimed "Peace Around the World":

> Today the peoples of fifty-one nations rejoice in the surrender of the last of the Berlin-Rome-Tokyo war-mongers who ganged up to put the world under the blood-and-torture tyranny of totalitarian oppression. Today for the first time in all but six years, the guns are silent and this bomb-battered world breathes again in Peace ... let us be truly thankful in our longed-for job.[11]

Children were the future, and they were not forgotten. On September 12, the Gyro Club held a Victory Day celebration just for them; this was the first Kiddies Picnic in four years. Approximately 2,000 children of all ages whooped it up in one giant picnic held in the Gyro playground on Haliburton Street. They consumed 80 gallons of ice cream, 2,500 hot dogs, and 100 gallons of Orange Crush. Some of the children showed up at the picnic wearing gas masks, souvenirs of the war given to them by ARP Warden Pete Maffeo. The Silver Cornet Band topped off the day with a community concert at Dallas Square.[12]

Adults may also remember this as the day they bade farewell to the Protection Island mine. For years the 85-foot pithead had stood as a reminder of the glory days of coal mining in Nanaimo. The structure had also guided mariners into port for more than half a century.

The Celebration Committee received permission from Canadian Collieries to set fire to the pithead. The structure had been a danger to anyone

The Nanaimo Concert Band, once known as the Silver Cornet Band, continues to entertain at community events as it has done since 1872.

tempted to climb it. The old timbers were full of dry rot and soaked in oil and coal dust. When the fire was lit, the pithead literally exploded. The two men chosen to set it ablaze were almost trapped in the high framework. The fire could be seen for miles. In just over an hour the old pithead toppled. Unfortunately, once lit, the fire was harder to put out, as the coal ignited underneath and burned for several weeks afterwards.

Chapter Fifteen

The Postwar Period

After the Fighting

The province emerged from the war in a better financial position than it had been in going into the conflict. In many ways the war erased the tough years of the Depression and heralded a new era of prosperity as men moved to the province to work in shipbuilding, airplane construction, and a host of other industries essential for the war effort.

The military army camps and airfields brought thousands to Vancouver Island, and every city and town experienced a housing shortage. The shortage did not diminish after the war, for there was an urgent need to accommodate returning veterans. For families with enough wartime savings for a down payment, the National Housing Act guaranteed low-cost mortgages. Unemployment Insurance, which took effect in 1941, helped make the transition from war production to peacetime jobs virtually painless.

Young men who had so gallantly gone to war, many away from home for the first time, found comfort in the companionship of war-weary young women. They met in dance halls and pubs in Britain. Some married, and after the war 44,886 of those "war brides" came to Canada to join their husbands' families. The Canadian Wives Bureau arranged their passage, delivered them to their ships, and distributed information. Red Cross volunteers tended to their needs in the hostels where they stayed awaiting departure.

After the war brides arrived in Halifax, the Canadian Red Cross escorted them across the country, and people turned out to welcome them. It was a difficult transition for those who had lived in cities and now found themselves in rural communities or on farms. Compounding the difficulties of their new lives, the housing shortage kept many living with their husbands' families for some time. Most adapted and grew to love their new country.

After the war, the War Assets Corporation sold the buildings of Camp Nanaimo to the city and other groups such as the Canadian Legion, the Nanaimo Golf Club, Canadian Vocational Training, and the Navy League. A large number of the buildings were taken over by the Central Mortgage & Housing Corporation, which turned them over to Housing Enterprises Ltd.[1] All the buildings were put to good use. The Canadian Legion used a number of the huts for emergency shelter for veterans and their families. Some were even used to accommodate delegates to the International Woodworkers of America convention held in June 1946. The school board also purchased land that would become the site of Nanaimo District Secondary School.

The old military hospital became a Department of Indian Affairs TB (tuberculosis) hospital, known locally as the Nanaimo Indian Hospital, which served Native people from all over the Island. The 200-bed hospital was almost always at capacity. The patients were of all ages from babies to elders. During their stay, which in some cases lasted 18 months, patients occupied their time doing crafts such as leatherwork, weaving, or basketry. The hospital also trained women for home nursing careers.[2] Nanaimo Indian Hospital was the first Indian hospital to become accredited in B.C.

Those who worked there describe it as friendly. "Patients and staff established a warmth of feeling and close personal relationship that was unique," Miss E. Robb, the housekeeper, recalled. "Our patients were not people of a different colour or race to us. They were individuals. We grew very fond of them."[3]

The hospital employed 100 people, and like the military hospital, it came well equipped with its own operating room, X-ray department, laboratory, and laundry. Hospital doctors were Dr. Campbell and Dr. Gamble. The patients were very ill; the hospital had three or four deaths a month. Many of the patients did not speak English. One Native woman had never lived in any other building than a tent.

The standard of care was mainly custodial. Patients had poor reactions to the first trials of the new TB drugs. Hallucinations were common—some thought they could fly and went out the window. Other patients were so old that the drugs did nothing for them.[4]

The hospital operated for 20 years and literally never closed its doors. When it came time to lock up permanently, it was found the door had no lock and had never had one. When the hospital closed, most of the staff found other jobs in other hospitals. Some went to the DVA hospital in Victoria. What emerged in its place was a new health and welfare program with trained workers who visited Native communities to help improve housing, family life, sanitation, employment, and whatever else was necessary. These public health nurses, technicians, and advisors, many who were themselves Native, were trained in the field.

Nanaimo's Man in Ottawa

Major General George Pearkes retired from the military three months before the war in Europe ended. He left military service under a cloud, after a disagreement over the government's conscription policy. Mackenzie King thought that voluntary enlistment was the best policy, but by 1944 the military was convinced that voluntary recruitment had failed to produce the required reinforcements and wanted conscription.[5] Only the year before Pearkes had been made a Companion of the Order of the Bath, a citation for "outstanding service, devotion to duty."[6] After he demanded that he be relieved of his command, he got his wish on February 5, 1945. The War Committee decided in its wisdom, or lack of it, that he should be retired, as there was "no suitable employment" for him in the Canadian Army at his present rank.

The military's loss was Nanaimo's gain. At that time, the large Nanaimo riding included Saanich, rural Esquimalt, the Gulf Islands, Duncan, and Ladysmith. Liberal MP Lieutenant Colonel Alan Chambers then represented the riding and was still serving overseas. The Conservatives wanted Pearkes to seek the nomination of their party. Frank Cunliffe, a Nanaimo lawyer and former Conservative candidate, made it clear he did not want to run again.

At the first nomination meeting held April 14 in the Knights of Pythias hall in Duncan, Pearkes was unanimously voted the Conservative candidate. It had been 10 years since the Conservatives had been in power in Ottawa, and 5 years since the last election. Another was expected soon.

Frank Cunliffe and Dr. Stanley Morrison opened an office in Nanaimo, and got supporters organized. Pearkes had the name recognition factor in his favour; there was no need to make him known in the area. Frank Davie, the former president of the Nanaimo Progressive Conservative Association, knew the riding well, so when the federal election was called for June 11, 1945, Davie arranged for Pearkes to speak at coffee parties, teas, and various other community events.

The all-candidates meeting hosted by the Nanaimo local of the United Mine Workers of America was one of the largest during the campaign. When a crowd estimated to be 700 showed up, the meeting quickly outgrew the UMW hall and the debate had to be moved to the Civic Arena. For three hours the candidates argued their positions on various issues. The Liberal incumbent, Alan Chambers, campaigned in uniform and praised the people's war and Prime Minister Mackenzie King's leadership. Pearkes had little praise for the Liberal war policies. The CCF candidate, Dr. J.M. Thomas, a principal of Mount View High School in Saanich, suggested that Canada was living under an economic fascist society and would continue to do so if either the Liberals or Conservatives were elected.

Pearkes was a popular candidate; veterans liked him and his Victoria Cross gained him a few votes. On election day, when the final results came in, his nearest competitor was the CCF candidate. Mackenzie King's Liberal government remained in power.

Pearkes worked hard as Nanaimo's MP in the postwar years to help veterans, and kept close contact with the Canadian Legion. As a member of the Parliamentary Committee on Veterans' Affairs, he had a strong voice on the Veterans Land Act, the War Service Grants Act, and the Pensions and Veterans Rehabilitation Act. In his estimation this was the most important committee on which he served. Fishing and forestry also received his attention, and he championed the cause of Native people. One speech he gave in the House in June 1948 drew attention to the situation on the Nanaimo Reserve No. 1.

> I wish to express my regret that such a meagre amount is being provided for the improvement of Indian reserves ... I object to only $500,000 being spent for the maintenance of the reserves and provision of houses for our Indians. Right in the heart of Nanaimo is Nanaimo Reserve No. 1. I went there last Fall at the invitation of the chaplain of the reserve. I drove up to the boundary line and was told that I would have to leave my car. I stepped off a paved road onto a dirt track full of potholes. I left houses where there were electric lights, sewers and water and I went in among hovels where there were no lights, no water, no sewer. This is right in the heart of Nanaimo.
>
> I pleaded with the Department to do something to improve the roads and they generously granted $100, making it $300 instead of $200 for maintenance of roads. This enabled the Indians to bring in a few cartloads of cinders to put in the worst mudholes. This is all I have been able to get from the Department and it is not good enough.
>
> Another matter I brought to the attention of the Department was the fact that the children on Nanaimo Reserve No. 2, some eight miles away, had not been able to obtain any education for the last five or six years simply and solely because the Department will not bring the few Indian children on that reserve into the school at Nanaimo.[7]

At the 1948 Conservative leadership convention, Pearkes nominated John Diefenbaker, a man he knew and respected and believed would make a good leader. Pearkes was handily re-elected in 1949, 1953, and 1957. When Diefenbaker became prime minister on June 21, 1957, Pearkes was appointed his Minister of Defence.

In the autumn of 1959, a federal-provincial conference on civil defence was held in Ottawa. Fear of an atomic bomb convinced many to build bomb shelters. Pearkes stated that there would be no hope for citizens in an area hit directly by the blast of a nuclear bomb, but he said those beyond the immediate area could be saved, especially if they were shielded from radiation. There was not enough money for the government to build shelters to protect everyone, and Pearkes's "do-it-yourself basement shelters," or "every-man-for-himself" approach, did not sit well with the public. The following year, Diefenbaker published a pamphlet, "Booklet for Survival," on building fallout shelters. Most Canadian dismissed the idea.

Nanaimo got the biggest shelter of all in 1963. Authorities were careful to clarify a popular myth; it was not a "bomb-shelter" but a "fallout shelter." Today it is easy to scoff at the paranoia that lurked everywhere during the Cold War era. The "Diefenbunker" as it was nicknamed, was built on the grounds of Camp Nanaimo to house government and civil defence authorities in the event of a nuclear strike on B.C. It could withstand a near hit by a nuclear warhead and remain in operation while fatal levels of fallout and radiation contaminated the area surrounding it.[8]

The shelter was operated by Emergency Preparedness Canada, with room for 321 very important persons, federal and provincial politicians, military and civil authorities, a health centre, and broadcast and communications services. The kitchen was stocked with enough food to feed 300 people for a two-week stretch. The food was rotated on a regular basis. The intent was to provide continuity of government if all hell broke loose.[9]

During Pearkes's years in parliament, he was involved in many highly charged debates and decisions on the Cold War era, including Bomarc, NATO, NORAD, and the Arrow. The cancellation of the Arrow project in February 1959 was the beginning of the end, both for Diefenbaker and for Pearkes. The Avro Arrow was a magnificent airplane, but it was more expensive and problem-plagued than Diefenbaker's government on the verge of a recession could afford. Pearkes never doubted his decision to scrap the project. However, the storm of protest from across the country would not go away, and Deifenbaker's and Pearkes' actions became a political embarrassment. Pearkes decided he would not run again; he did not want a senate seat, nor did he wish to stay in parliament as an ordinary member. A happy solution to the situation came from B.C. when he was appointed Lieutenant-Governor on October 11, 1960.

Pearkes, with Blytha by his side, carried out his duties as B.C.'s Lieutenant-Governor with grace and dignity. He retired on July 1, 1968, at 80 years of age.

Shake, Rattle, and Roll

Sunday, June 23, 1946, was a morning few would forget. At 10:15 a.m. an earthquake with the magnitude of 7.3 on the Richter scale rocked Vancouver

Island; its epicentre was on land but close to the shoreline of the Strait of Georgia.[10] It was one of the few documented B.C. earthquakes to generate a tsunami. This tsunami produced waves of about eight feet near Texada Island. This resulted in a large submarine slide and the loss of a lighthouse on Comox Spit. One man drowned at Deep Bay when the tsunami swamped his small boat. There was extensive property damage throughout the mid-Island region. The earthquake was felt on the Lower Mainland, and as far south as Portland, Oregon, north to Ocean Falls, and east to Kelowna. The heaviest damage resulted in Courtenay, the Albernis, and Kildonan, where showering bricks and shattered glass fell onto the streets.

Near Campbell River, a hillside moved 35 feet closer to the water. In the Courtenay–Comox and Campbell River area, about 75 percent of chimneys collapsed. At Kildonan a pier and a cold storage plant were wrecked. A man who had been working on the ice crusher fell 15 feet and injured his shoulder. In Alberni, one in three chimneys toppled, and the Motion Block was hit hard. Nanaimo escaped relatively unscathed.

The earthquake took everyone in Nanaimo by surprise. Fortunately it happened on a Sunday when most people were at home, and there were no public gatherings or events that might have resulted in panic. Meteorologists noted it was fortunate the earthquake was of the "rolling or undulating" type and not the usual "hard shock" type, or there might have been more casualties.[11]

Throughout the 600-mile circle affected by the tremors, the damage to property was light. Brick and plaster walls cracked in several of Nanaimo's oldest buildings. Telephone lines jammed as people rushed to check on friends and neighbours. Merchants on Commercial Street surveyed the damage to their displays.

The quake also generated amazing stories. Constable G. Weeks of Rosehill Street was up on the roof of his two-storey home extinguishing a chimney fire with a garden hose. Despite being shaken up he remained on the job, and reported he saw a wall at the side of the house bulge with the shaking. A woman crossing the Bastion Street Bridge went down on her knees, unable to keep her balance at the height of the quake. In another part of town, a man jumped out of bed thinking his wife was shaking him to get up for breakfast. He yelled at her because it was Sunday morning, and he wanted to sleep in. He soon realized she was not in the room and got up in a hurry. Another resident had a grandfather clock that had been silent for many months. After the tremor subsided, the family heard the familiar steady "tick-tock." They found the big pendulum swinging to its usual beat.

Details of the death of Daniel Fidler emerged soon after. He was a Vancouver fisherman, one of the crew of the fish boat *Scapa Flow*. The crew, which included Daniel's nephew Robert Annal was fishing near Deep Cove when they decided to load rock and boulder ballast. They ran the nose of the boat onto the outer end of a 300-foot sand spit, anchored her, and then boarded an 8-foot dinghy. They were in the dinghy when the water surface became rippled as the disturbance went on below and the sand spit began to sink. The dinghy was capsized by a wave high enough to engulf the wheelhouse of the fish boat, which swung around under the impact. Annal managed to reach the larger boat, but Fidler swam around in circles dazed, then disappeared beneath the water.

The only physical injury in Nanaimo was to Mrs. Austin Wright of Machleary Street, who suffered a severe bump on the head. She fainted and fell from the top of a flight of steps when the quake hit.

Vancouver Islanders had been awakened from their complacency regarding earthquakes. This time casualties and property damage were light. However, authorities have forewarned Islanders to prepare for the catastrophic "big one."

Paul Robeson Visits Nanaimo

Paul Robeson, one of America's most influential performers and political figures, appeared in Nanaimo on February 13, 1947, along with pianist William Schatzkamn and tenor Lawrence Brown.

The Upper Vancouver Island Concert Association sponsored his visit. Two buses full of music lovers came from Port Alberni to attend the concert in the Army Drill Hall. President of the Concert Association, Dr. R.E. Foerster, introduced the artist.

Robeson, from Princetown, New Jersey, spoke Russian, Spanish, and Chinese; he was a commanding figure at 6 foot 6 and 275 pounds. He had one of the best baritone voices of his day and was an equally impressive actor. He was the first African-American to attend Rutgers University, where he earned a Master of Arts degree in 1932, and Columbia Law School, in 1939; Hamilton College awarded him an Honorary Degree of Doctor of Human Letters.[12]

Robeson was an advocate of socialism and went to Spain during the civil war there. Because of his open admiration for the Soviet Union, he became ostracized in his own country during the Cold War and the period of the McCarthy hearings.

Obtaining a passport to travel was a big achievement for the singer. He had been denied the document because of his communist sympathy. Robeson's program had an international flavour, but the most crowd-pleasing numbers were the songs he made popular in his appearance in the movie *Showboat*. His rendition of "Ol' Man River" was a request number, and it brought loud applause. He sang several folk songs such as "Weepin' Mary" and "Swing Low Sweet Chariot." The crowd was so appreciative he gave them encore after encore, and then ended his program with a portion from Shakespeare's *Othello*.[13]

Pete Maffeo hosted Robeson and his troupe and members of the Concert Association to an Italian spaghetti dinner in his own home.

CHUB Radio Goes on the Air

On May 17, 1947, George Randall of the Hotel Malaspina sent an application to the Controller of Radio, via MP George Pearkes, to have broadcasting facilities located in Nanaimo.[14] On May 24, 1949, CHUB 1570, Nanaimo's second attempt at a radio station, officially opened in the Hotel Malaspina. Crowds jammed the hotel to witness the launch by B.C. Premier Byron I. Johnson.

The station, owned by Standard Broadcasting Company Limited, was a dream come true for many Nanaimo businessmen. The station went on the air with a staff of 16 announcers, writers, and technicians filling the airwaves from Cowichan to Campbell River. The 250-watt transmitter was located on Jingle Pot Road; the studios were housed in the Hotel Malaspina.

This was a busy day for Premier Johnson, who that day had already opened the CPR terminal and watched the Empire Day parade. He paid tribute to George Randall, chairman of the board, and Donald Cromie, of the *Vancouver Sun*, which had financial interests in the station, as well as the engineering and technical staff of the new radio station. Other tributes came from MLA George S. Pearson, MP Major General George Pearkes, and Mary Sutherland of Parksville, who was a member of the CBC Board of Governors and a newspaperwoman formerly with the *Regina Leader Post*. She and her business partner, Eileen Allwood, owned the Island Hall Resort in Parksville.[15] CPR vice-president George Baillie, Mayor George Muir, and *Vancouver Sun* assistant publisher John Lecky were also present.

The staff of the first station were Joan Orr, manager; Dorothy Plant, programming and promotions; Bill Dobson, news; Glen Kristjan, program director; Gordon Theedom, announce staff; Joy Andrews, secretary and scripts; and Edgar Weber, studio engineer.

In 1951 the station boosted its power to 1,000 watts. Larry Thomas joined the staff at this time, along with interim manager Mary Sutherland, until the new brother-and-sister management team Chuck Rudd and Sheila Hassel from the *Vancouver Sun* arrived. Rudd came with the experience of four years in the Canadian Forces Radio Services. He had broadcast to the troops from London, England, and Hilversum, Holland. After the war he managed the radio station CJAV in Port Alberni, then came to take over management of CHUB.[16]

Under Rudd and Hassel's management the station developed new programs such as *Treasure Chest* and *Around the World*. *Treasure Chest* was a money give-away program that lasted four years. *Around the World* offered an expense-free prize trip to Honolulu every two months. Rudd also composed and donated the song "March of Dimes." The B.C. Association of Broadcasters distributed the song to all stations in the province for their fall March of Dimes campaign.

By 1958 the station was heard all over Vancouver Island and the mainland, thanks to another boost in power in 1958 to 10,000 watts. The transmitter was moved to a site in Cedar. Mayor Pete Maffeo inaugurated the new signal linking satellite studios in Duncan and Courtenay. The CHUBMOBILE and the fleet of CHUB cars were familiar sights around Nanaimo and on the Island Highway.

Over the years, CHUB fostered many talents and personalities. Larry Thomas started as an evening disc jockey, then moved to morning man, then to news and sports director. Nanaimo audiences knew him as the voice of the intercity lacrosse and Nanaimo Clippers games. Lyall Feltham was the open line host for many years as well as sales representative. Pat O'Neill was news director. Bill Dobson left Nanaimo to become the CBC provincial news editor; Reid McLeod went to Los Angeles.

George Lawlor joined CHUB Radio as manager in July 1966.

In the '60s, the Rudd-Hassel team retired, leaving the door open for new talent like the trio of Bob Giles, Jack Kyle, and Joe Lawlor, who kept listeners informed on traffic conditions. Joe's brother George joined the station as manager in July 1966. Ted Kelly joined as program director and later Merv Pickford as engineer.

On April 15, 1968, CHUB built a new home at 22 Esplanade, where it continued broadcasting for many years. In 1994 the AM stations CHUB, CKEG, and CHPQ in Parksville merged into a new FM station, CKWV 102.3, The Wave.

Petroglyph Park

In August 1948 a rocky area two miles south of Nanaimo which was known for its Native carvings of fish, birds, and animals became the newest provincial park.

Canadian Collieries Ltd. general manager H.R. Plommer handed over the deed to the 3.84 acres of land in perpetuity to the provincial government. Nanaimo MLA and Provincial Secretary George Pearson accepted the gift on behalf of the Province. This allocation of land did not come without controversy. Edison White, chief of the Snuneymuxw, expressed his displeasure that the petroglyphs were passed into the hands of the White man. He said the carvings constituted hundreds of years of Snuneymuxw tradition, a visible history of the creation of their race.

> These are drawings giving truth to the fact that we Indians believe man was originally created here (as Christianity claims that original man was created elsewhere). The man who made this work on the rocks was one of the originals who saw the miracle of creation. As the forms of life of those days emerged from the waters, they came in forms and shapes we do not know today. Then came the Great Creator of the Universe to see his handiwork. He found that the "guardian" had upon the face of the rocks created images which invested himself with several powers of physical strength and skills which alone belonged to the Creator. In his displeasure the Creator said "Because of your insulting attitude I will cause you to disappear, and also will disappear your water."[17]

Chief White explained that the circular excavation in the stone on top of the petroglyph area was the rim of the well "which the Great God caused to dry up, as he tapped the Indian upon a shoulder and caused him to entirely disappear." He said his grandparents told him that "local Indians, until a few decades ago, made annual pilgrimages to the spot for prayers."

Historian Bruce McKelvie, who was present at the ceremony and who had worked to have the park preserved, presented a different opinion on the origin of the carvings. He said, "The prehistoric art was the handiwork of a vanished race of sun worshippers that occupied this area from 10,000 to 15,000 years ago." In Victoria, other well-known authorities on Native folklore, A. Newcombe and Mrs. W.C. Cryer, discounted McKelvie's theory.

The provincial government was happy to dedicate another park for the public to enjoy, and Canadian Collieries felt it had made a contribution to the preservation of a historic site. All expressed hope that safeguards would be taken to stop vandalism in the park.

Plommer's final comments mentioned the coal-mining industry in the area. "After all," he said, "coal is older than the petroglyphs."

> These petroglyphs bring home to us the passage of time, and the ever-changing times. It will be reminiscent to some of the alleged passing of the coal mining on Vancouver Island. But I would like to say that, although the mining activities may change from place to place, and perhaps some of the coal deposits be left unspoiled for the next or later generations, there are still thousands and thousands

> of acres of coal bearing lands on Vancouver Island which have never even been prospected. In my opinion there is no person now living who will see the end of coal mining on this island.[18]

Following the opening, the Province installed interpretive signs, added picnic benches, and created natural trails through the forest to the carvings. The park is a popular spot for visitors and those interested in studying the ancient stone carvings.

Nanaimo Airport

The Nanaimo military airstrip at Cassidy continued to function after the war, and in 1946, Harry McCracken, Jack Beban, the son of Frank Beban, and Bus Mathews, who later became Nanaimo's Member of Parliament, formed a small flying club. Nanaimo City Council supported the initiative, and the Nanaimo Board of Trade said it was "decidedly a good move" to establish the Nanaimo and District Flying Club.[19] The club operated from a small building in the infield near the Island Highway. It had two Tigermoth planes; the first item of business was to secure airplanes for training purposes. The group held discussions with Nanaimo and Ladysmith and hoped that with municipal collaboration the Cassidy Airport would be available for training and commercial airplane use.

The early airlines and the pilots who flew them are legendary on the west coast, for without today's technology they managed to deliver a much-needed service to outlying communities. The first scheduled passenger airline at Nanaimo Airport was Canadian Pacific Airlines in 1947. This company later enlarged by absorbing Canadian Airways Ltd. and the Ginger Coote Airlines. It operated out of Nanaimo Airport for only six months.

Next came Queen Charlotte Airlines, which ran from 1949 to 1955 using rebuilt wartime water and bush aircraft. Before long this small airline handled 85 percent of the passenger traffic to the west coast with aircraft that were seldom more than 40 percent full.[20] The flight to Vancouver in 1953 on a DC 3 cost $3.45, and during the month of June every woman passenger got a corsage.[21]

In September 1950, the airline applied to federal authorities to have the lighting improved at the airport. The city urged consideration of the application in a letter to Major General George Pearkes, with a copy to the District Supervisor of Airways.[22] It was the following spring before Pearkes replied that in the opinion of the Air Services of the Department of Transport "lighting alone would be inadequate and it would be necessary to provide full equipment for night flying if any value was to be obtained in the further development of Cassidy airport." Pearkes doubted Treasury Board would provide the funds.[23]

A string of electric bulbs had been strung on a line along the runway for emergency night landing. Eventually Sam Madill and Ken Griffith privately bought 20 flare pots for use in emergency landings.

It is doubtful that extra lighting at Nanaimo Airport would have helped the troubled Queen Charlotte Airline plane that crashed on October 17, 1951, onto a cliff on Mount Benson, immediately behind the sub-station of the B.C. Power Commission on Jingle Pot Road. It was one of the worst airplane crashes in the history of the province. The seaplane, a twin-engined Canso, was en route from Kemano, B.C., to Vancouver with 20 passengers and a crew of three. The crash caused such an explosion and flash of flames that some Nanaimo residents saw it. All aboard perished.[24] The cliff was several hundred feet high, and after the crash the plane fell about 50 feet onto a ledge about 100 feet wide. A wristwatch on one of the victims gave the precise time of the tragedy. It had stopped at one minute to seven.[25]

The next day there was speculation the plane had either developed engine trouble as it neared Vancouver or had just lost its way. The plane was first spotted at 6:55 p.m. circling the Jingle Pot Road substation. Keith Price, the night operator there, said it circled twice over the station; the second time it just missed the high-tension wires. Then it gained altitude, rose about 50 feet, then zoomed toward the jagged mountain. Within seconds a sheet of flame followed the roar of an explosion.

Eighty rescue workers spent the next morning recovering bodies. Corporal Vickers of the RCMP directed operations. School board employees, members of the Dominion-Provincial Youth Training School, and members of the Civil Defence committee helped him. Dr. Jack Tully was in charge of the recovery. Queen Charlotte Airline employees removed portions of the wreckage looking for clues to the cause of the crash. Game Warden Frank Greenfield blazed a trail from the crash scene. It took three hours to bring the bodies from the mountain; the terrain was treacherous and several cliffs had to be negotiated. Salvation Army personnel supplied sandwiches and doughnuts for the rescue workers.

One of the casualties was Eric Mellanson of Vancouver, the chief project engineer for Kitimat Construction, builders of the Kitimat townsite for Alcan. Most of the victims were from the Vancouver area; one was from Victoria. Gordon Graham had been on his way to visit his six-week-old daughter, whom he had never seen. His visit was meant to be a surprise; he had not told his family he was coming.

Queen Charlotte Airlines Ltd. was eventually sold in 1955 to Pacific Western Airlines.[26] Cassidair, a forerunner of Pacific Coastal Airlines, used the airport for two years from 1959. Air West ran intermittently for five years from 1966 and again in 1976.[27]

In 1953, the Aeradio Office, or Flight Service Station, was constructed with Bob Gibson the officer-in-charge. Each radio station had an operator and a radio range operator. Stations were constructed within a 100-mile distance of each other; radar technology was still very limited.[28]

The Nanaimo Airport was a child of the Second World War, owned by the federal government and operated by the City of Nanaimo under a lease agreement with Transport Canada after 1952. The city never received any operating funds from Transport Canada. All improvements were funded through airport revenue. Today the airport is owned and operated by the Nanaimo Airport Commission.

Chapter Sixteen

A Growing Forest Industry

The New Economy

Vancouver Island is blessed with an abundance of forests—rich old-growth forests that were a boon to companies seeking to exploit and export the wealth. The growth in the forest industry caused concern about whether it was sustainable. In May 1940, Vancouver Island was the principal log-producing region in the province, with over 1,800 logging operations active during the previous year. The total scale of the industry for the province was at an all-time record of over 3 million board feet.[1] There were now approximately 40,000 men working in the forest industry in British Columbia. In 1948 there were at least 15 logging companies with offices in Nanaimo.

Chief Justice Gordon Sloan began a one-man inquiry in 1945, the Royal Commission on Forest Resources. His report resulted in the establishment of Tree Farm Licences (TFLs) and the revision of the Forest Act of 1947. TFLs required an operator leasing Crown land to replant, guard against fire, and restrict the harvest to a sustained yield capacity. After cutting, the company paid a fixed price for the Crown timber (stumpage) that was set by a formula annually. This provided for long-term planning in the forest industry.

Forestry giant Harvey Reginald MacMillan had timber holdings valued at $11 million; he owned sawmills, plywood plants, and logging operations. Others saw a future in the forest industry and began creating their own wealth. John Coburn sold his New Ladysmith Lumber Company to Texan Shelby Saunders, who endeared himself to the community by building the Pygmy Pavilion dance hall. Saunders changed the name of the company to the Nanaimo Lumber Company.

Saunders was a decorated veteran of the First World War, having fought in France and later in Russia with the U.S. Army. He came to Nanaimo in the '20s with his wife, Mary. He was active in the community with the Chamber of Commerce, Navy League, Nanaimo Yacht Club, and Royal Canadian Legion No. 10. He was also a member of the Ashlar Lodge and the Nanaimo Shrine Club.[2]

Strait's Lumber Company at Red Gap (Nanoose) still exported lumber around the world. A fire in 1940 caused considerable damage to the sawmill, but it was able to continue operating. Declining markets due to the war with Japan caused the mill to close permanently. In the spring of 1942, the old buildings that once housed the Japanese, Chinese, and East Indian labourers were torched, as they were considered a fire hazard. The workers remaining at the mill had moved to more suitable housing.

Frank Beban, who had operated a small sawmill at Extension in the early '30s, expanded by building a new sawmill, Frank Beban Lumber Company, on Nanaimo waterfront in 1934 using logs from Gabriola and Galiano islands. The Beban Logging Co. Ltd. office was on Commercial Street.

After Frank died, son Jack took over the family business and expanded logging operations. Jack used his own plane to transport loggers up the coast. He parked his plane at Nanaimo Airport.

Thompson Lumber Co. Ltd. began as Inkster & Thompson Lumber Co. Ltd. with partners John Thompson Sr. and Peter Inkster. Both men had worked for the New Ladysmith Lumber Company owned by John Coburn. Inkster had been the manager at Boulder Creek mill near Nanaimo Lakes, and Thompson Sr. managed the sash and door department of that company. Thompson had previous experience as a mill owner in Sheffield, England.

Thompson became the sole owner when Inkster withdrew from the partnership to open his own operation in Courtenay. Then John Thompson Sr. brought his two sons, John and Noel, into the company. Thompson Lumber Co Ltd. manufactured all types of building supplies from its plant on Prideaux Street.

More logging companies had opened offices by 1958. They included the Cedar Logging Company, Grandview Logging, and Malpass R. Logging. There were also companies selling lumber and supplies, such as Stewart & Hudson, Dietrich-Collins Logging Supply, and Kneen's Building Ltd.

Comox Logging Company Moves South

The Comox Logging and Railway Company logged in the Courtenay–Comox area and shipped its logs to Canadian Western Lumber Company at Fraser Mills on the mainland. A windstorm in December 1934 that devastated Island forests brought the logging company south to Ladysmith and Nanaimo. The storm toppled giant trees and snapped others off at the trunk; everything that was not secure the wind picked up and hurled through the air. In Chemainus, the wind tossed lumber around like straws, or threw it like javelins; roads were choked with debris. Lands previously owned by John D. Rockefeller were put up for sale because the fallen timber had to be quickly harvested or it would rot. Comox Logging purchased these holdings in 1936, and the staff moved to Ladysmith. The company bought the Abbotsford Hotel for use as a bunkhouse and office; it had a dining room that could accommodate 100 men. A new office opened in 1947.

The storm put Ladysmith on the map as the largest truck-logging outfit on the coast. "There were windfalls as far as the eye could see—miles of them. It needed a tremendous amount of knowledge and experience to cut logs among all those huge roots and criss-crossed fallen trees."[3]

In 1942, logging operations were expanded into the Nanaimo Lakes area and the logs were hauled out by rail. The company purchased the first 9 miles of rail from the harbour to the Nanaimo River trestle from Canadian Collieries, then added another 14 miles of new grade along the north side to Nanaimo Lakes. At the peak of production the railway equipment consisted of seven locomotives, 80 logging and tank cars, and several speeders.[4] Comox Logging cut only the very best old-growth timber; everything else was left behind—stumps, snags, branches, and timber with imperfections.[5]

In 1958 Comox Logging Company and Canadian Western Lumber Company Limited merged with Crown Zellerbach Corporation, a U.S. integrated lumber and pulp operation.

Mayo Lumber Company

Mayo Singh built his own forest empire beginning at Paldi and Cowichan Lake, near Duncan. The small community of Paldi was named after the Sikh community in India's northern Punjab State. More than 5,000 Sikhs emigrated to B.C. between 1904 and 1908. Word spread that there was work in the woods in B.C., news brought to the state by Punjabi soldiers of the Hong Kong regiment who travelled through Canada during Queen Victoria's Diamond Jubilee in 1897. Singh arrived in 1908; he first farmed and logged at Rosedale, B.C. before coming to Vancouver Island in 1916.[6]

Singh was also a partner in Kapoor Lumber Co. on Sooke Lake, and he built a new mill at McKay Lake, near Cassidy, south of Nanaimo. Frank Rowbottom managed the logging operations at McKay Lake where loggers travelled daily from Nanaimo.

In 1958 the company purchased land in Nanaimo and began construction on one of the first fully integrated medium-sized forest product companies on the coast. The operation, on 11 acres of waterfront south of the Snuneymuxw Reserve, had a sawmill with debarking and chipping facilities, a particle board plant, dry kilns, plus a large store on Nicol Street South with display facilities for building and industrial supplies. Before long the company's trademark "Diamond M" was recognized for its quality.

After Mayo Singh's death in 1955, his children carried on the business; son Kajindi became president and daughter Jagindar Kaur Mayo became secretary. Jagindar's husband, Karnail Singh Saroya, managed the lumber and building wholesale firm in Duncan.

S. Madill Limited

From a simple beginning as a blacksmith, Sam Madill started one of the largest companies serving the forest industry on Vancouver Island. His sons Norman and Charles (Chuck) joined him in the business as it evolved. Norman became president and general manager; Chuck did sales and design work and managed the shop. Today the name Madill is recognized around the world for its logging equipment.

Sam was born in Manitoba. After apprenticing as a blacksmith, machinist, and wheelwright, he came to Nanaimo in 1911 and began working in the Wilkinson's blacksmith shop shoeing horses. A few years later he opened his own shop on Ravine Street, adjacent to Akenhead's livery stables. Ravine Street is now known as Terminal Avenue. As the use of horses disappeared, the business evolved into a welding and general machine shop. Most of the work came from the logging industry, so the shop began specializing in logging equipment.[7]

Norman joined the business in 1936 and Chuck in 1946. A year later the family bought the Newcastle Shipyards building next to the Civic Arena and remodelled it as a heavy-duty machine shop. While Sam continued to work hammering out logging hooks, tongs, and other equipment, workers at the other end of the plant constructed hundreds of steel boom boats designed by Norman Madill. The little dozer boats could turn on a dime; they did the work of boom men with pike poles, and were powered by Chrysler gas engines.[8]

After the Second World War the company built bunks, bulkheads, draw bars, and water tanks for logging trucks, and they designed and manufactured one of the first steel-heel booms for loading logs with a power shovel. The Madills also pioneered the manufacture of portable spar trees in Canada. While they did not invent the portable spar, they did adapt it for use on trucks. The portable spars and hydraulic yarders were shipped to all parts of B.C., Alaska, and New Zealand.

A fire wiped out the machine shop and most of the waterfront manufacturing plant in 1960; it was then that the Madills took a bold step and purchased the five acres of land north of Nanaimo at the corner of the Island Highway and Bowen Road. They built a huge concrete building to house the main factory, then built an addition to bring the total floor space to more than 40,000 square feet. Other buildings housed the warehouse and wire rope division of the company. The new shop was better equipped to manufacture the famous portable Madill spar trees, mobile spars, and yarders.

After Sam's death, the brothers took over the company and continued their father's commitment to serving customers.

Harmac

While dining at home over caribou steaks with company officials in 1947, Harvey Reginald MacMillan decided a waste wood pulp mill would be built near Nanaimo and named Harmac, in his honour.[9] He decided to build in Nanaimo because of a ready water supply, a good harbour, accessibility to transportation, and the opportunity for workers to build new homes. When the official announcement was made on January 29, 1948, everyone must have cheered from Lantzville to Ladysmith, because it meant hundreds of jobs, and it used waste wood.

Most of the pulp mills built during the 1940s and 1950s were tied to a large allocation of Crown timber; however, 50 percent of Harmac's waste wood came from chips shipped in barges from his four sawmills and two plywood mills. The remainder came from the company's six logging camps harvesting small low-grade logs that were more suitable for pulp than lumber.

Construction began in August 1948. Alex Menzies, who later was the shipping foreman, joined the construction crew that summer. The site was cleared and underlying rock blasted out to form a natural foundation for the mill. He and Bill Shaw, later a pipe fitter, carved the road from the main gate up and around the arboretum. Consulting engineer H.A. Simons designed the mill, and J.S. Bates supervised the utilization of waste wood; he was the former head of the Forest Products Laboratories of Canada. The major contractor was B.C. Bridge and Dredging Company, which also built the steel tanks, digesters, and other units.

In June 1950, the $19 million MacMillan Export Company Harmac pulp mill opened with great pomp and ceremony before 400 guests that included Premier Byron Johnson and two of his cabinet ministers. Mayor Earle Westwood represented Nanaimo.[10] The mill employed 200 workers on three shifts, seven days a week, producing 250 tons a day of unbleached kraft pulp for corrugated boxes, bags, and brown wrapping paper, mostly for the U.S. market. Most of the crew had pulp-mill experience so the mill started without a hitch and produced its first bale of unbleached pulp on June 10, 1950. The initial product went to Chile, Columbia, and Cuba.

The pay was a $1 an hour, plus a Christmas bonus of 5 percent of gross earnings in the first year of operation. The second year, the company paid a $50 bonus to all married men and $25 for single men. By the third year, it was a turkey for everyone—a gift the company became known for.

Joe Annau began working at the mill on June 24, 1950, on the No. 1 machine. "When the coal mines closed in Nanaimo, the miners were quite happy to work at the mill," he recalled the day he met H.R. MacMillan.

"No one was allowed near the machine wearing a hard hat because of the danger of the hard hat falling off onto the machine. When this man appeared wearing one, I ordered him to take it off. I didn't realize until later that this had been H.R. MacMillan."[11]

No sooner had Harmac opened than Nanaimo residents rose up in indignation and howls of outrage at the smell. MacMillan told a luncheon meeting of 200 of the city's leading citizens that the company would do what it could to alleviate the stench. Then he painted a rosy picture of the city's economic possibilities, which included an implied threat to take future investments to a more appreciative community. When he finished, his listeners leaped to their feet in thunderous applause.[12] At least that was how the press reported it.

The smell may have been the smell of money to some, but others were concerned about clean air. One man wrote a letter to the editor using the nom-de-plume Airwick; he was not enamoured by MacMillan's speech. He said the crowd had applauded because MacMillan had finished speaking, not because everyone endorsed his speech.

> Can you imagine an officer of any corporation having done an injustice, coming here and adopting the attitude he did, and ending his talk "Shall we pull it down or double it." If it was pulled down we would still be able to live just as the Indians did before we came here and after all there are other big corporations looking for locations that operate businesses that do not smell."[13]

Joe Annau thinks the smell was worse in those days. "I remember one worker retired and as a parting gift was presented with a photograph of Harmac from mill manager. As he received the gift, the manager pointed out to him, 'See that smoke coming out of the chimney—if you work here longer, you won't see it.' Well, the smoke is still coming out of the chimney and it still smells."[14]

The *Harmac News* of December 1951 reported that three large expansion programs were underway, which when complete would provide another 500 jobs. The biggest project was a $20 million extension to the pulp mill. The company built a deep-sea wharf, added another three silos to bring the total to 10, and installed eight more digesters to supplement the four already operating. The warehouse also doubled in capacity. The total cost of the plant after the expansion was completed in 1953 was approximately $40 million. The now bleached sulphate pulp was used to produce tissue and towelling and writing papers. High-grade Bible paper was also one of the many final products.

Attempts to start up the mill's No. 2 line in 1953 did not go well. George Syrotuck was fired along with the rest of the machine crew while trying to start it. The colourful mill superintendent Einar Walloe fired everyone in desperation after months of doing battle with the machine. Reason won out and Einar stopped the crew at the gate and sent a cab into Nanaimo for meals; then they sat down and ate quietly in the technical building. Einar then politely asked the crew if they would try the machine again. More failure! The crew was again sent home and urged to try again the next morning. Eventually they succeeded. The mill's tonnage doubled and Einar gave out cigars.[15]

The site of the giant mill was a wooded shoreline with a gently shelving beach. Within four years, tons of rock had been blasted out and used in a pier 380 feet long and 60 feet wide. Harmac spent more than $1 million on a dam and tunnel to bring water from 15 miles away and installed a network of wells and collecting pipes near the mill. Tremendous quantities of water were used; each ton of pulp required approximately 225 tons of fresh water in the manufacturing process.[16] The mill required 67 million U.S. gallons of water daily; this was supplied from a reservoir on the Nanaimo River at Fourth Lake and from wells along the Nanaimo River.

The complex known as "The Wells" included two pump houses, an office building, monitoring and control equipment, and five wells. Mill water attendant Roy Stupich and his assistant Joe Annau manned it. When they needed relief help, Joe Manzini joined the crew. Their territory included the dam and reservoir. The reservoir was over two miles long, and according to Annau, it was "a good fishing spot, with plenty of pan-sized rainbow, cutthroat and Kokanee."[17]

There were 56 men in the original start-up crew; 9 were still there in 1985. The following were mill managers: C. Crispin, 1948–1951; L.G. Harris, 1951–1960; E. Walloe, 1960–1964; J.S. Rogers, 1965; A.M. Van Allen, 1966; D.H.R. Blake, 1966–1970; G.F. Woram, 1970–1975; R.B. Findlay, 1975–1980; G.I. Bender, 1981–1986; G.A. Edgson, 1987; R.D. Tuckey, 1987–1989; and R.A. Killin, 1989–1996. Doug Eamer is the present manager.[18]

H.R. MacMillan Export Company merged with Bloedel, Stewart & Welch on October 1, 1951, to form MacMillan & Bloedel Ltd. The merger made the company one of the largest firms in the world engaged in both the production and sale of lumber. The amalgamation with the Powell River Company in 1963 made the newly formed MacMillan, Bloedel and Powell River Company one of North America's largest producers of newsprint. The name Powell River was removed from the corporate title at the annual general meeting of 1966, and the company became MacMillan Bloedel Ltd. (MB). By 1962 the company had 13,000 employees.

In March 1963, adjacent to Harmac, Hooker Chemical began construction of a plant to produce the bleaching agent for the pulp mill.

The sprawling, giant Harmac mill, shown here in 1963, provided hundreds of jobs as the mining industry declined. Its economic impact was felt throughout the region.

During construction it employed 250 workers. After completion, the plant provided work for 22 unionized employees, all members of the Pulp and Paper Workers Union, Local 8.

In 1970, Harmac employed over 1,000 workers. Everyone felt the impact of the plant and the forest-related industries. Wood had replaced coal as the economic driving force in Nanaimo.

There is a footnote to the history of Harmac. Periodically sea monsters have been reported along the coast. Victoria is known to have had a sighting, and there have been others around Vancouver Island. Just as Harmac began operations there was a rare sighting in Northumberland Channel.

In February 1951, Rolly Tait and two other workers said they saw what they thought was Cadborosaurus, or Caddy, emerge from the depths of Northumberland Channel. They said it had a head like a horse. The *Nanaimo Daily Free Press* quoted the men's description: "The body emerged from the water in a rolling manner. It was about 20 feet long and the colour of a pig. But Caddy slipped away within seconds."[19]

Bob Swanson's Whistle Farm

Bob Swanson barely needed an introduction in B.C., for he had always been associated with engines and whistles, and his skill was known across the country. He was born in Reading, England, on October 26, 1905, and lived for a period of time in South Africa before coming to B.C. His family settled in Wellington, where he became fascinated by a train that ran on a narrow gauge track near his home. He took his first train ride at age three. At 12, he helped his father build chimneys in Nanaimo and clean and repair boilers at the Jingle Pot mine. His father had a contract with Strait's Lumber Company at Nanoose Bay to do brickwork and boilers, so Swanson grew up loving trains and steam engines.

His first job was firing up a steam donkey at East Wellington; then he repaired engines and soon earned enough credentials to get his fourth-class steam papers. But it was the steam whistle that held his interest and became a life-long passion. At the Boulder Creek mill near Nanaimo Lake, he worked for Pete Inkster, who needed a whistle for his mill and asked him to build one. He was hooked! The whistle he built was so strong that anyone within five miles could hear it as the sound echoed from one mountain to another. Someone mistook it for a fire alarm; Jack Miller, an owner, arrived with 40 Chinese workers with axes, shovels, and buckets of water.[20] Swanson stayed with Nanaimo Lumber Company when it took over the No. 3 mill at Boulder Creek.

By 1936 Swanson had his first-class steam engineer certificate; by this time he was working as chief engineer for the Port Mellon pulp mill on Howe Sound. From there he came back to the island to be chief engineer at Chemainus. Here he designed and built a huge mill whistle, the biggest whistle in Canada, weighing more than a ton. On May 10, 1940, he opened up the whistle for the first time, toning it down to allow people to get used to the sound, then opening it up just a bit more every day. The whistle is now on display in the Chemainus museum.

During the war, Bob Filberg, manager of Sitka Spruce Logging, drafted Bob Swanson to repair steam engines on the Queen Charlotte Islands. His salary in 1943 was $750 a month, plus board and travel expenses; he repaired five locomotives, 43 boats, and 38 steam donkeys.[21] Spruce logging had high priority, as the wood was perfect for building the light wooden frames of Mosquito bombers. Hundreds worked in the Queen Charlotte Islands logging the Sitka spruce.

As the E & N Railway began using diesel locomotives, the steam whistle was silenced. The new diesel horn was not too popular with the public, for it sounded a bit like a sick moose. When a logging truck driver was injured in a railway crossing accident after mistaking the train horn for just another logging truck, Swanson was challenged to find an alternative that sounded like a steam whistle. He did just that and patented the first five-chime horn and launched his whistle company that became known as Airchime, which is still going strong today in Aldergrove, B.C.[22]

When he first started designing whistles, orders came in from England, and he needed a place to test them. The idea of a whistle farm took root among the mountains to the west of Nanaimo, near Second Lake. Swanson built living quarters where his family could come and stay, and it was a place for him to entertain visitors from around the world who came calling for him design a whistle or two.

After the war, he worked in various positions, usually associated with trains and whistles. In retirement, he helped the Forestry Museum at Duncan restore old logging donkeys and locomotives, and in Port Alberni he helped the Industrial Heritage Society restore the old Two Spot locomotive. He is also known as the designer of the Gastown Steam Clock. Swanson was an engineer and a poet. He left not only a legacy of whistles around the world but also poems about logging and life in the woods. He sold thousands of copies of his *Rhymes of a Western Logger*. He died October 4, 1994.

Chapter Seventeen

Mayors and Aldermen, 1920–1967

Changing Boundaries

Nanaimo's boundaries had changed considerably since incorporation in 1874. As the city grew, its boundaries expanded to include the Fairview District west of Pine Street in 1927, the remainder of the area known as the South End in 1946, and Brechin and Acacia districts in 1952; this latter inclusion almost doubled the area of the city. Beach Acre Park was added in 1960. At this time the Brechin/Departure Bay/Island Highway intersection came under the control of the Provincial Department of Highways.[1] In 1975, expansions included the Improvement Districts of Harewood, Chase River, East Wellington, Northfield, Departure Bay, and Protection Island. Each of these areas had a fire department. After amalgamation they became part of the Nanaimo Fire Department.

By 2005 the City of Nanaimo covered 34 square miles (88 square kilometres) within the Regional District of Nanaimo (RDN). The district stretches from just south of the Nanaimo airport in Cedar, to Deep Bay in the north, to Mount Arrowsmith on the west, and to Gabriola Island off the east coast; it is one of the fastest-growing regions in the province.

Regional districts were created throughout the province to ensure that all residents had access to commonly needed services, regardless of where they lived. The RDN was established in 1967; Nanaimo has five representatives; Parksville and Qualicum Beach have one each, as do each of the eight electoral areas that make up the rural portions.

As the city expanded, its population also increased. In the three decades between 1921 and 1951, the population increased only by 892. Then it jumped to 14,135 in 1961 possibly due to the increased workforce at Harmac and forest-related industries. Ten years later, the population was 34,029. There was another increase in 1981 to 47,069.[2] B.C. Statistics has projected the 2006 city population to be approximately 78,874.

Seven mayors served the city from 1920 to 1967. They were mayors Busby, Hall, Barsby, Harrison, Muir, Westwood, and Maffeo.

Frederick A. Busby served as mayor from 1920 to 1924 and from 1927 to 1929. He retired, or was ordered to retire because of ill health, in 1926 as manager of Pat Burns & Company. This did not stop him filling the mayor's chair for another two years. At age 57, when the market crashed in 1929, he had already given much to the community as alderman, mayor, and school board member, and he served on the committee that built the new hospital. His successor as mayor for the next two years was Dr. George A.B. Hall.

Dr. Hall's term as mayor was brief, only two years from 1930 to 1931. He was more recognized for his medical practice and the establishment of the Hall Clinic. However, he was mayor during two difficult years at the beginning of the Great Depression. In 1931 he met with federal ministers and other mayors to discuss unemployment in the west. Perhaps one of the more pleasant tasks during his term in office was to officially open the Newcastle Island Resort in 1931.

John (Jack) Barsby, a plasterer by trade, followed Dr. Hall as mayor. He served as alderman from 1920 to 1931, then as mayor until 1937. He led the City of Nanaimo through some of the most difficult years since its incorporation. Barsby was born in Derbyshire, England, in 1883, one in a family of 13 children. At age 24, he moved to Canada and worked for a short time in the coal mines of Nova Scotia, then moved to Fernie, B.C., before finally settling in Nanaimo and establishing a plastering business. He was a member of Haliburton United Church and served as Sunday school superintendent; as well he sang in the church choir. He and wife Martha Ann had five children: three sons and two daughters—Ernest, Jack, Edward (Ted), and twins Phyllis and Iris.[3]

During the early history of the Upper Island Music Festival, Barsby served as president and continued to support Andrew Dunsmore in his work with the festival. He at one time sang in its competitions and was often a prizewinner. In later years when the festival hit a low point, Barsby helped revive it.

Barsby was an all-round good citizen of Nanaimo. His list of accomplishments is long, especially in relationship to education; he served first as school trustee then at various times as chairman of the board. Each election he was returned to office. His interest in education extended provincially through the B.C. School Trustees Association where he was first elected vice-president in 1941 then president in 1942, eventually being honoured with a life membership in that association when he retired in 1950. John Barsby Junior High School, which opened in 1956, was named in his honour.

The Nanaimo Rotary Club welcomed him to its group in 1938, and he served as president in 1947/48. (Barsby's son Ted was Rotary Club president in 1971/72.) He was also chairman of the Greater Nanaimo Water and Sewer Board from its inception in 1953.

In Barsby's spare time, if he had any, he played sports, and won a gold medal for trap shooting and another in football. He enjoyed the outdoors and was an active member of the Nanaimo Fish and Game Club. For all these accomplishments, the City of Nanaimo honoured him with the Freedom of the City award.

Mayor Victor B. Harrison took over from Barsby in 1938 and carried the city through the Second World War years. Harrison had already served as mayor between 1925 and 1926, and also as police commissioner. He whetted his appetite for politics by running unsuccessfully for the provincial Conservative Party in 1920.

In 1923 when he was a candidate for alderman in the North Ward, he offered his thoughts on municipal government in his election campaign. Harrison said he wanted a businesslike approach to civic affairs and an efficient system of maintaining the roads. He also questioned which government should maintain the trunk roads passing through the city, and he wanted a better water works system.[4] Roads and water were always points of aggravation with Nanaimo taxpayers. He was elected. Harrison again held the position of mayor from 1938 to 1944, and is credited with lobbying the federal government to have a military airstrip located near Nanaimo and to have the wooden minesweepers built here.

Harrison was born in Nanaimo in 1884. He was one of four sons of Judge Eli and Eunice Harrison, the first County Court judge appointed on Vancouver Island. All four boys entered the legal profession. Victor was called to the bar in 1908 and began his career in the law firm of Drake, Jackson, and Helmcken in Ladysmith. He served as stipendiary magistrate from 1909 to 1912, then moved to Nanaimo and became a partner in the law firm of Harrison and McIntyre.

The young lawyer became a household name in Nanaimo during the trials of Brother XII when Harrison acted on behalf of Mary Connally, a wealthy U.S. resident who had loaned money to the Aquarian Foundation. He also represented Nanaimo residents seeking legal title to their property under the Vancouver Island Settlers' Rights Act.

From 1945 to 1956 two men took turns serving as Nanaimo's mayor: George Muir and Earle C. Westwood. Muir followed Victor B. Harrison in 1945 and served until 1950 when Westwood became mayor. He gave three years to the position before Muir was again returned to office to serve until 1955. Westwood again became mayor for one year before resigning to seek the provincial seat for the Socreds in 1956.

George Muir, Scottish by birth, was a veteran of the First World War. In his business life, he was an agent for the Metropolitan Life Insurance Company. He had served 13 years as alderman (1933–1945) before becoming mayor. He also was a member of the School District 68 board of trustees and was a member of the B.C. Municipalities executive for four years. He enjoyed boating and took part in the International Cruiser race. In 1949, he was a member of the crew of the famous *Eileen* that won the Capital to Capital race from Olympia, Washington, to Juneau, Alaska, the only Canadian ship in the race.

Earle C. Westwood's family dates back to 1860 in Nanaimo when his great-grandparents arrived in Victoria on the steamship *Pacific*. His father was Joseph Arthur Henry Westwood, son of William Joseph Westwood, who left England in 1849 for St. Louis, Missouri, then followed the gold rush to California in 1853. In 1864, he opened up a blacksmith shop in Nanaimo and acquired a 2,000-acre farm. Westwood Lake is named for the family.[5]

Earle was born in Nanaimo in 1909. His marriage to Dorothy Planta produced two children, Brenton Earle and Susan Mary. He operated Westwood Funeral Home, and his spare time was devoted to civic affairs and education. He was also active in the Rotary Club, Nanaimo Yacht Club, Chamber of Commerce, Pioneers' Association, Native Sons, Post No. 3 Doric Lodge, Loyal Order of the Moose, and Canadian Red Cross. Following his political career as MLA, he was appointed Agent General for B.C. at British Columbia House in London, England.

On November 3, 1958, Westwood and mayors Barsby, Harrison, and Muir were honoured with the Freedom of the City award.

Throughout this period in the history of Nanaimo, from 1920 to 1967, Peter Maffeo's service to the community stands out. His friends called him Pete. He operated the Davenport Ice and Ice Cream plant on the property where he was born on Machleary Street. With his wife, Vera, by his side, he turned his free hours into community service. The citizens of Nanaimo recognized they had a good and dedicated representative when they elected him mayor in 1957, then again and again until 1966, even though he came to the job without council experience.

After completing his war service with the Sixth Field Canadian Engineers, during which time he was athletic instructor, he carried on with athletics in Nanaimo. He joined the Gyro Club in 1922 and helped in the campaign to build the Franklyn Street Gymnasium and establish the Gyro playgrounds. He also was a member of the Masonic Lodge No. 18 and the Native Sons Post No. 3.

Maffeo was one of 26 directors and businessmen who built the Hotel Malaspina, and in 1938 he headed up the Gyro Committee to sell bonds to help build the Civic Arena. He was called on again during the Second

World War to take charge of the Civil Defence organization, and for his efforts he received the Order of the British Empire from His Majesty King George VI. Maffeo also campaigned vigorously for War Saving Certificates, Canadian Red Cross drives, and Red Shield drives, and he fully supported the community Empire Days celebration.

Racism and prejudice were two words not in the vocabulary of Pete Maffeo. When the Harlem Globetrotters basketball team first arrived in Nanaimo in a battered old Model A Ford and were refused accommodation at the Hotel Malaspina because of their colour, Pete Maffeo stepped forward and offered accommodation and a spaghetti dinner. Three decades later the team honoured him with a silver award.[6] He similarly welcomed Paul Robeson to Nanaimo, topping off his visit with a spaghetti dinner.

These were only a few of his activities before he became mayor. Afterwards, from 1957 to 1966, his name appears time and time again as he fulfilled his civic duties. When interviewed by William Barraclough in November 29, 1963, Maffeo talked about some of the interesting people he had met and said how proud he was of the guest book at city hall.

His highlights included the visit of Princess Elizabeth and Prince Philip in 1951 and the opening of the new city hall. Others were the visit in 1955

Nanaimo's city council is shown here in 1958, B.C.'s centennial year. Back row, L-R: Aldermen Eddie Blackburn, John Cook, Haig Burns, Bill McGregor. Front row, L-R: Phil Piper, Mayor Pete Maffeo, George Bryce.

when Princess Mary signed the city guest book, and in 1958 when Princess Margaret visited the city during the B.C. Centennial celebrations and cut the largest cake in the world with a sword. He also met the Lord Mayor of London, Sir Denys Colquhoun Flowerdew Lowson, on September 2. The following year, Elizabeth, now Queen, and Prince Philip made a return visit to the city.[7]

The end of Maffeo's public life came suddenly and shocked those who had worked with him over the years in various community projects. A fall during a curling game at Courtenay, on March 27, 1966, caused severe head injuries. A year later on December 7, 1967, at a dinner in the Tally-Ho Hotel, 185 citizens paid a special tribute to him for his outstanding public service to Nanaimo over the years. On January 8, 1968, Maffeo was named a Freeman of the City. He died on June 7, 1968, at age 72 years.

Aldermen are the unsung heroes of city affairs. They take positions on committees, often thankless jobs, but important nevertheless to the workings of the city. Few are called on to cut ribbons or open city facilities, or have their name attached to a community event. Most Nanaimo mayors served terms as aldermen, the exception being Pete Maffeo, who went directly into the mayor's chair.

Edward George Cavalsky served 17 terms as alderman, being first elected to the South Ward in 1908. His last term was from 1930 to 1935. His is the longest service of any alderman. Born in Denmark, he came to Nanaimo in 1880, and for a time worked for Canadian Pacific Navigation Company before he and wife Laura turned their energies to operating a grocery store. Later in life he operated his own insurance and accounting business. As alderman he headed the finance committee and earned a reputation for being frugal with the city books.

John Kerr served as alderman from 1932 to 1946. He was a carpenter by trade and operated the Nanaimo Cabinet Shop. Joseph Dixon, a miner working for Canadian Collieries, gave nine years as alderman: 1926 and 1929 to 1936. John G. Parker served nine years, from 1959 to 1967. Parker was instrumental in the formation of a society responsible for building the Nanaimo District Museum as a centennial project.

George Addison served from 1941 to 1953 as alderman, and as school trustee from 1936 to 1953. In private life he was a plumbing and heating contractor and a charter member of the Nanaimo Kiwanis Club. He and wife Jane came from Scotland. They had three children. George was also a member of the Grand Lodge AF and AM of Scotland (Freemasons) and was on the board of St. Andrew's United Church. He represented the City of Nanaimo at the coronation of Queen Elizabeth in London, England, 1953.[8]

George Bryce was alderman from 1953 to 1964. He was born in Bathgate, Scotland, and came to Canada in 1927. He worked in Granby,

Northfield, and No. 10 South Wellington mines, and was secretary-treasurer of the United Mine Workers of America, Nanaimo Local 7355. Later he held the same position with the Nanaimo Local of the Beverage Dispensers and Culinary Workers' Union. He married Mildred Knowles in 1935. The couple had three children, Georgina Beryl and twins James Robert and Arthur George. Bryce served on the board of the Vancouver Island Health Unit and was instrumental in bringing the Victorian Order of Nurses to Nanaimo.[9]

William Charles McGregor was alderman from 1954 to 1963, and also served on the Parks and Recreation Commission for 14 years. He was born in 1911 to Jack and Catherine McGregor, and was the grandson of the pioneer mining family of John and Mary McGregor, one of the first mining families in Nanaimo. He married Angelina Clovis and they had one son, Malcolm. In his younger days McGregor was an avid soccer player. He was a member of the Doric Lodge and a member of the Nanaimo Downtown Development Committee.[10] He was chairman of the Parks and Recreation Commission when Bowen Park was officially opened in 1967.

Samuel Drake, a grocer by trade, served as alderman from 1930 to 1940. He was born in December 1895 to Rhoda Malpass and Samuel Drake Sr. His mother was the daughter of *Princess Royal* pioneers John and Lavinia Malpass.[11] Samuel and wife Ethel had two children, Thelma and Dorothy.

Chapter Eighteen

The Fabulous Fifties

In B.C. the 1950s were an amazing time of growth and prosperity. The Depression and war years were left behind, and a new feeling of optimism emerged. Nothing seemed impossible! Those veterans who had entered university after the war ended were now graduating with degrees and starting families. The biggest house-buying spree was on, and no one was content with the small postwar cottages that were built to supply an immediate housing crisis. Now husbands and wives dreamed of split-levels, and all wanted brand new cars. The trend was towards lower, bigger cars with lots of chrome. Studebakers were popular.

Ormond Plumbing and Heating and Hardware, at 60 Bastion Street, with a staff of 30 employees, could supply electric stoves, refrigerators, freezers, sawdust burners, or air conditioners. The Ormonds also did sheet metal work and roofing, and installed hot water heating. The business was so successful the family opened branches in Port Alberni and Duncan.[1]

Nanaimo families tuned into CHUB radio broadcasting from the Hotel Malaspina. The age of television broke into the entertainment scene in the early '50s. Rabbit ears and TV antennas were all that was required to get "good" reception. *Spies and Buys* magazine advertised in 1951: "Sparton gives you the best television reception. If Jack Holman feels your neighbourhood will give good TV reception, he'll install a Sparton Television Set in your home for Six Days' Free Trial. If you don't like it, he will take it out, no questions asked. What have you got to lose? Garden Supplies, Fitzwilliam Street."

Parents worried about their teenagers who were "going steady." Women's skirts were long, their hair was short, and hats and gloves were in vogue. Women wore hats to church, weddings, and social gatherings. Jean Burns' Ladies' Wear on Commercial Street was "the" place for ladies to shop. Her Nanaimo store was so successful that she opened others in Courtenay, Port

Commercial Street in downtown Nanaimo was a bustling place in the mid-'50s.

Alberni, and Victoria. What began as a dressmaking business evolved into one of the largest ladies' wear stores on the Island.

People still went to the movies, and in Nanaimo they had a choice of the Capitol Theatre on Bastion Street or two drive-in theatres. If you wanted to watch under the stars there was the Starlite Drive-in at Departure Bay and the Cassidy Drive-in, south of the city. The Starlite offered the feature movie plus a cartoon and special shorts, and there was a talent show every Thursday at 9:00 p.m. On July 22, 1951, Yvonne De Carlo and Peter Ustinov starred in *Hotel Sahara,* and on July 26, Errol Flynn and Olivia de Havilland starred in *Captain Blood.*[2]

The big bands were still swinging, and the most exciting sound was that of Stan Kenton. By the mid-'50s, rock and roll almost put an end to swing. Elvis Presley gyrated his way into millions of homes on the *Ed Sullivan Show.* Presley's rendition of "Hound Dog" and "Love Me Tender" catapulted him to fame. Johnny Ray sobbed "Cry," and young people danced cheek-to-cheek. Local musician Ed Gibney, who taught youngsters how to play brass instruments from his studio in G.A. Fletcher Music Co. Ltd., formed the Vancouver Island Junior Band with young people aged 8 to 16 from Nanaimo, Ladysmith, and the Albernis. The band played at May 24 celebrations in Nanaimo, July 1 at Ladysmith, and Labour Day in Port Alberni.

The Silver Cornet Band, renamed the Nanaimo Concert Band, continued to entertain as it had done since 1872. There were few events in the history of Nanaimo that did not benefit from the music played by these talented musicians.

The Starlite Drive-in offered cartoons and shorts before the feature movie. It was located at the end of Long Lake, near the junction of Departure Bay Road and Norwell Drive.

A Premier with a Vision

Few political figures have dominated provincial politics like William Andrew Cecil Bennett, fondly known as "Wacky Bennett." His term as premier from 1952 to 1972 brought profound change in the province, with new roads, railways, dams, power stations, two universities—Simon Fraser University and the University of Victoria—and the British Columbia Ferry Corporation. Somehow along the way he founded a provincial bank and turned the country's largest private power company, B.C. Electric, into a publicly owned crown corporation: B.C. Hydro and Power Authority. He had a vision for the province of opening up its interior and providing roads for the movement of goods and services. Still today, the mention of his name in provincial politics brings a smile or recollection of the boom times during his tenure.[3]

W.A.C. Bennett was born in Hastings, New Brunswick, on September 6, 1900. As a young man he moved to Edmonton, where he began his working career in a hardware store, Marshall Wells Ltd. In 1927 he married May Richards and became a partner in a hardware store in Westlock, Alberta. After selling this in 1930 he settled in Kelowna, B.C. and again purchased a hardware store. Community service was important to him, and soon he was associated with the Kelowna Board of Trade and other organizations.

Bennett's first venture into politics was in 1941 when he was elected as the Conservative member for South Okanagan, becoming a backbencher in the minority Coalition–Liberal government of Premier John Hart. Bennett was re-elected in 1945. Three years later he resigned his seat to run for the federal Conservatives, but lost. In 1949 he returned to provincial politics and was re-elected in South Okanagan as a Conservative in the coalition government of Premier Byron Johnson. In 1951, Bennett resigned from the Conservative Party to sit as an Independent. In December of that year he joined the Social Credit League (Socreds), a movement which at that time did not like to be called a party.

Premier Johnson called an election for June 12, 1952. Former Nanaimo MLA George S. Pearson (Liberal) did not run in this election. He had given 24 years of service to the city as its provincial member, and for this the city honoured him with the Freedom of the City award. Dr. Larry Giovando (Conservative) became Nanaimo's newest representative.

If the Conservative Party needed a recognized name in the 1952 election, it had that in Dr. Giovando. Everyone in town knew the doctor, either through his medical practice, his club work, or his interest in sports, or from his real-estate holdings in Qualicum, Ladysmith, Port Alberni, and Nanaimo. His nearest political contender was David Daniel Stupich (CCF).

This was an odd election, for in the final days of the Coalition government, an amendment was made to the Elections Act in preparation for the 1952 election. The Liberals and Conservatives knew their coalition was in trouble, and sensed the CCF might win a minority, perhaps even a majority. To forestall this, they designed the preferential ballot. Voters were asked to rank the candidates in their ridings. If your first choice finished last, he was eliminated and the vote went to your second choice. The procedure was repeated until there was a clear victor. No candidate could win with a minority of votes under this scheme.

On June 12, 1952, B.C. voters tackled the preferential ballot system. It was several weeks before the vote was finally calculated. The CCF got 34.3 percent of the votes and 18 seats; the Socreds had 30.2 percent and 19 seats; the Liberals 6; Conservatives 4; and Labour 1.[4] Premier Johnson lost his seat and retired from public life. On July 15, the 19 Socreds chose Bennett as their new leader. On August 1 he was sworn in as the province's 24th premier.

Bennett knew he would have difficulty keeping power with only one seat more than the CCF had. Within a year everyone was back on the campaign trail trying to attract new voters. The election of 1953 was a close one in Nanaimo; Stupich (CCF) took 4,358 votes and Giovando (Conservative) took 4,376. Another man waiting in the wings ran in this election; he had been mayor of Nanaimo since 1950; Earle Cathers Westwood (SC) took 2,626. Giovando held the seat until the 1956 election when he declined to run; then Westwood gained the seat for the Socreds.[5] Westwood was appointed to cabinet as Minister of Trade and Industry,[6] and in 1958, he became Minister of Recreation and Conservation.[7]

Premier Bennett became well known for his personal style, which combined the skill of a veteran salesman with that of a master politician. For the next two decades he took the province on a roller-coaster ride, opening up the Interior to new investment. Tommy Douglas, the New Democrat Party leader, described Bennett as "the only man I ever knew who could get money from the rich and votes from the poor with the promise to protect them from each other."[8]

A New City Hall

On February 17, 1951, Lieutenant-Governor Clarence Wallace officially opened Nanaimo's new city hall on Wallace Street. The first council meeting was held in the new council chambers two days later on Monday, February 19, 1951. The building was described as a "gem on a hillside," a "thing of beauty inside and out."[9] It was built by contractor Doug Robinson and designed by architect Thomas B. McArravy.

The new city hall commanded a sweeping view of Nanaimo Harbour, Protection Island, Gabriola Island, and the mountains of the Lower Mainland. The two-storey concrete building, faced with Haddington Island stone, was constructed and furnished at a cost of $200,000. The main entrance was on Wallace Street, but there was also access from Dunsmuir Street. Placed above the entry was the year of opening, 1951, and the city's new coat of arms in heavy bronze.

Shortages of materials delayed the completion of the building. By August 1950 all work came to a standstill while the contractor waited for the steel-framed windows being imported from England.

Mayor Westwood spoke at the official opening, saying how proud his council was of "this beautiful building, the finest city hall for a city of its size in all B.C. and some say Canada." He drew attention to the city's new coat of arms symbolic of the early history of Nanaimo, depicting the early Hudson's Bay Company fort, the discovery of coal, and the landing of the first coal miners. Below the arms was the motto, "Faith and Labour." The coat of arms, designed by city engineer, Arthur Leynard, was officially registered by the College of Arms in England on September 28, 1951.

The principal colour of the arms of Nanaimo is red, taken from the red cross on a silver field on the arms of the Hudson's Bay Company. The first quarter of the shield is a barque commemorating the arrival of the early settlers from Great Britain. On the fourth quarter is a pattern of "black diamonds" representing Nanaimo's coal-mining industry, and the second and third quarters indicate the unfulfilled future.[10]

Past mayors were not forgotten; they were listed on a bronze plaque. The work of former Mayor George Muir was acknowledged, for during his term in office, both as alderman and mayor, he worked diligently in planning and laying the groundwork for the new city hall. The opening was an impressive ceremony. The Lieutenant-Governor inspected the Guard of Honour. The Nanaimo Concert Band played "God Save the King."

The old city hall that had served the community well since 1864 was demolished in February 1951. No one was sad to see it go; its long life began as the Nanaimo Literary Institute Hall. It had long since passed serving the city as viable council chambers.

The city got a chance to show off its new city hall to a series of important visitors from Great Britain that year. First to visit was the Lord Mayor of London, Sir Denys Colquhoun Flowerdew Lowson, on September 2. On this occasion he was given the Freedom of the City award. Next to visit were Princess Elizabeth and Prince Philip, the Duke of Edinburgh, on October 26.

The royal couple made a trans-Canada train journey, stopping at towns and villages along the way. The city was well prepared for the royal visit. A red carpet had been purchased for the occasion. Streets were cleaned, street banners installed, and retail stores decorated.

Mayor Westwood had the honour of welcoming the royal couple to Nanaimo City Hall. Here they were introduced to the mayors and their wives from Port Alberni, Courtenay, Duncan, Ladysmith, and the Reeve of North Cowichan. Even the weather co-operated; it was a glorious sunny day with citizens from all over the island lining the streets to welcome them. The royal procession then made its way to the Civic Arena where 4,500 children patiently waited to sing the royal anthem, "O Canada," and "The Maple Leaf Forever." "The ovation given the visitors was tremendous."[11]

Mayor Westwood then welcomed them to the arena. He remembered the Princess's ailing father, King George, and paid tribute to "the noble characteristics" that had marked their public and private lives.

> The health of your gracious father, His Majesty King George, has been one of deep concern to us and it is our fervent hope and prayer that he may again be blessed with good health and that he will long be spared to continue his noble reign.[12]

In his speech, the mayor explained how Nanaimo celebrated the birthday of Princess Elizabeth's great-great-grandmother, Queen Victoria, each year on May 24, and how each year a May Queen was crowned. He said that the children of Nanaimo and district "had saved pennies, nickels and dimes for weeks, to buy a present for Bonnie Prince Charles and Wee Princess Anne." He then asked May Queen Penny Pederson to present a gift from "our children to your children with all their love." The gift was two sterling silver mugs engraved with an inscription and the city coat of arms.

The first council meeting was held in the new council chambers on February 19, 1951.

Twenty minutes later the royal party left for the CPR wharf to board the HMCS *Crusader*. This was a short whirlwind visit to Nanaimo, but one that christened Nanaimo's new city hall and gave children something to remember. Within a few months, Princess Elizabeth became Queen, following the death of King George.

New Federal Building

As the new city hall opened in 1951, another building of importance was being planned. Since the Second World War, the city recognized the urgent need for more space in the Dominion Post Office building. The desperate situation was tolerated during the war, but afterwards, letters flew back and forth to Ottawa pressing the need for a new federal building. Some money was allocated to improve the crowded working conditions, but it did not solve the problem.

While plans for the new post office proceeded, there was one old-timer who thought the old post office building should be saved. He was W.A. Owen, who had been city engineer in 1914. In a letter to the editor on June 6, 1953, he made the case for preservation:

> Is there no last minute persuasion that can be directed to avert the destruction of this splendid building which was erected in 1884,

> and represents a type of masonry construction which together with the Provincial Court House are built with Newcastle Island Quarry stone? It is a typical Victoria example of that period of solid masonry in building construction, which has now disappeared entirely, and to tear it down is a sacrilege. The Anglican Church, the war memorial, the Pioneers Memorial, the Post Office and the Bastion ... create this harmonious setting. The Post Office building has been very intimately tied to Nanaimo's history for 65 years. It is a landmark that can never be replaced.[13]

The old post office with its familiar clock tower and "Big Frank" chimes had served the city well. Owen's plea may have registered with some, but nothing could stand in the way of progress, and the new Federal Building went ahead. A two-year lease on the Pygmy Pavilion was signed with the owner, Shelby Saunders. The 8,400 square feet of dance floor provided plenty of space for temporary headquarters for the post office. Partitions divided the area and a long counter was installed along with offices for the postal staff. A new stairway led directly to the office floor.

On Monday, August 31,1953, staff began moving out of the old post office on Front Street into the newly renovated Pygmy Pavilion. The lobby and wicket of the old post office had officially closed two days earlier. In preparation for the demolition, the clock and the machinery in the tower were acquired by former alderman Phil J. Piper and presented to the city. The old building was demolished in 1954.

The new $850,000 Federal Building was constructed adjacent to the Hotel Malaspina. On February 28, 1956, the *Daily Free Press* headlines read, "Nanaimo Is Proud of Its Federal Building—New Million-Dollar Edifice Now Complete." The contractor was E.H. Shockley & Son Ltd., of Vancouver. "The building of limestone and granite is one of the handsomest in the city and a splendid addition to the commercial heart of the city," reported the *Free Press*.

The elderly postmaster, Ernest Banks Booth, did not live to see the new building; he died two months before it opened. Booth had worked in the post office since 1910 when Adam H. Horne was postmaster. Horne held that position from 1890 to 1928; Walter Thompson succeeded him from 1928 to 1938; then Booth took over. Those postmasters who followed Booth were James Dean, W.F. Mulligan, W.H. Hewlett, M. Gordi, L. John, and D.H. Anderson.[14]

The past decade had been a difficult one for Booth for he had to cope with the influx of 10,000 soldiers to Camp Nanaimo, plus thousands more in other parts of Vancouver Island whose mail passed through the Nanaimo office. This more than doubled the volume of business.

The new building accommodated a number of federal offices, including the postmaster James Dean and postal officer M. Gordi, plus 15 postal clerks and 11 letter carriers. James Fox headed the Unemployment Insurance Commission office with a staff of 19. Customs collector was Leigh White with a staff of 6. H.E. Palmer, the Fisheries supervisor, had a staff of 7, and Immigration inspector was Desmond Craddock.

The old clock Big Frank was turned over to St. Peter's Roman Catholic Church holding committee. In 1960, the four-faced clock found a new home in the bell tower of the new St. Peter's.

Had it been saved, the old Dominion Post Office building sitting across from the old courthouse would have been a wonderful representation of the heritage buildings of downtown Nanaimo.

While the city was a virtual construction zone in the early 1950s, a new bridge spanning the Millstone River was erected, connecting Nanaimo to Newcastle Townsite. This improved the movement of goods and services as the city expanded its boundaries; it also improved connections with the new Black Ball Line ferries operating out of Departure Bay.

On August 11, 1954, the Honorable Phil A. Gaglardi, Minister of Public Works, officially opened the $250,000 George S. Pearson Bridge, named for the former MLA. Mayor George Muir introduced the flamboyant energetic member of the Social Credit Party. Where there was a road or bridge to be opened, Gaglardi was there. His frequent use of government airplanes and his many speeding tickets earned him the "Flyin' Phil" nickname. He certainly added colour to any ceremony. Also present at the opening were aldermen William C. McGregor, Elsie "Happy" Hall, George Bryce, Robert E. Fawdry, Haig Burns, and MLA Dr. Larry Giovando.

The Black Ball Line Ferries

In June 1953 the Canadian Pacific Steamship Service (CPSS) ferry fleet received some stiff competition when the Black Ball Line inaugurated a ferry service between Departure Bay and Horseshoe Bay. For a few years the Black Ball Line had provided transportation for cars and passengers travelling between Victoria and Seattle with the luxury liner *Chinook* (meaning "warm wind").

The Black Ball Line, established by Captain Alexander Peabody, had a history dating back to February 16, 1816, when it began a cargo and passenger sailing ship service travelling between New York and Liverpool, England. The company house flag, a black ball on a crimson field, was chosen because this was also the U.S. Navy "Meatball" insignia, an emblem of efficiency.[15]

The new ferries could not go into downtown Vancouver or Nanaimo because the CPR owned and controlled the land. The Black Ball Line had no alternative but to use its own terminal at Horseshoe Bay in West

Vancouver, then used for the service to Gibsons. This was expanded and a new terminal was built at Departure Bay. Colonel George Paulin, president of Black Ball Lines, quoted the passenger rates at $2 one way and passenger cars $5. Trailers were assessed according to length. Commercial and other vehicles were charged a basic rate of eight cents per 100 pounds for vehicle load. There were special discounts to operators of commercial vehicles using the service frequently.[16]

The first Black Ball ferry on the Departure Bay–Horseshoe Bay route was the *Kahloke* (meaning "white swan"). The ferry made five round trips daily, with special buses transporting foot passengers between the Vancouver bus terminal at Cambie and Dunsmuir and the Horseshoe Bay terminal. The connecting bus service was available to all passengers on the run in either direction at no additional charge. The *Kahloke* carried 500 passengers and 100 vehicles, and for the first time "house trailers" were accommodated.

Two years later the *Chinook* joined her sister ship on the Nanaimo–Horseshoe Bay service, bringing the schedule to 10 round trips daily with a ferry leaving every two hours, on the hour, from 6:00 a.m. to midnight. The *Chinook* also carried 100 vehicles and 500 passengers. Another Black Ball ship, the *Bainbridge*, served Horseshoe Bay and Gibson's Landing, while the *Quillayute* was on the Earl's Cove–Saltery Bay (Powell River) route.

John Dunham managed the Vancouver Island branch. He was a welcome addition to Nanaimo community affairs, serving as director of the Nanaimo Chamber of Commerce and the Rotary Club. He was also chairman of the Association of Chambers of Commerce for Vancouver Island. Dunham lived at 45 Cavan Street with his wife and two children.[17]

The Black Ball Line set new standards for ferry travel; it was so punctual that Departure Bay residents could set their clocks by it; the food service was good and prices competitive and the personnel were well trained and courteous.[18]

For a few years all went well for the Black Ball ferries. Then in May 1958 the CPSS employees, members of the Seaman's International Union, walked off the job and four days later the Black Ball staff, members of the Canadian Merchant Service Guild, and the National Association of Marine Engineers gave strike notice. Both companies were dealing with three unions. Most of the union contracts expired toward the end of 1957, and by mid-1958, problems at the negotiating tables brought things to a standstill.[19] Premier W.A.C. Bennett could not take action in the CPSS dispute because it fell under federal labour laws. However, he could do something about the Black Ball dispute; he invoked the Civil Defence Act ensuring the Departure Bay–Horseshoe Bay route came under provincial control. Defying a court injunction and the Civil Defence Act, the Black Ball workers still went on strike, effectively isolating Vancouver Island.

When it became clear that the problems were not going to be resolved, Premier Bennett decided to take control of the situation by getting into the ferry business. In 1958, Bennett announced the province would start its own ferry system, ensuring a ferry connection between the Island and the mainland. Provincial highways minister Phil Gaglardi was put in charge. Bennett said, "The government of B.C. is determined that in the future, ferry connections between Vancouver Island and the mainland shall not be subject either to the whim of union policy nor to the indifference of federal agencies."[20]

The B.C. Ferry Corporation was created. Its first two vessels were the MV *Sidney* and the MV *Tsawwassen;* both used the same design as Black Ball's *Coho*—100-car and 500-passenger capacity. The Tsawwassen causeway and terminal were built to accommodate the new ferries on the mainland. Inauguration day for the new two-hour service was June 15, 1960. The following year, the ferry authority purchased Black Ball Line terminals at Departure Bay and Horseshoe Bay, the Sunshine Coast docks, and five vessels. The ferry authority also bought the Gulf Islands Transportation Company along with its four vessels. Black Ball's ferry *Chinook* was renamed the *Saltspring Island Queen* and the *Kahloke* was renamed the *Langdale Queen.*[21]

This was the beginning of the end for CPSS in the ferry business. In 1962, the *Marguerite* and *Patricia* were laid up in Victoria and the *Princess of Nanaimo* and the *Princess Elaine* were both withdrawn from the Nanaimo–Vancouver route. The *Marguerite* served the Seattle–Victoria route from 1975 to 1989. The *Patricia* was chartered by Princess Cruises and operated between Los Angeles and Acapulco. The last remaining vestiges of the former service were the rail and truck ferries operating between Nanaimo and Vancouver.

The B.C. ferry service has expanded considerably since those early days; it is now one of the world's largest ferry systems, carrying more than 21 million passengers and 8 million vehicles annually.

Celebrating the B.C. Centennial

In 1958 Nanaimo celebrated the B.C. centennial with the rest of the province. Princess Margaret paid a visit on June 6 and cut a giant centennial cake, which according to all reports was the largest birthday cake in the world, made by Mike Farano, the chef at the hospital.

The celebrations included the installation of another memorial to the mining industry. A coal-oil lamp with a perpetual flame supplemented the large block of coal already positioned in Dallas Square in 1949 courtesy of the Historical Monuments Board of Canada. Harry Freeman, a former manager of the Jingle Pot Mine, had found the lamp. The old Welsbach Gas Lamp

In 1958 the celebrations for the B.C. centennial included another memorial to the mining industry, a coal-oil lamp with a perpetual flame added to the large block of coal positioned in Dallas Square in 1949.

had lit the streets of Baltimore in 1880, and was extremely rare. Four men helped with the installation: Harry Freeman, Phil Piper, Jack McGregor, and Jack Parker. The Vancouver Island Gas Company donated the lamp.

On the day of the lamp lighting, there was a giant parade complete with horses and carriages. Everyone dressed up in pioneer costumes, and some were on hand to welcome visitors at the Departure Bay ferry dock.

The Italian community contributed by unveiling the Italian Fountain on July 1 at the intersection of Terminal Avenue and Nicol Street. Two Italian Lodges built the fountain and presented it to the city. The fountain committee included Jules Magnano, Tony Blasutig, Ray Capra, Albert Venuti, E. Niccle, and Andy Ercolini.

Gino Sedola, artist and high-school teacher, co-ordinated the design, enlisting the help of local artists David Denbigh and George Norris. The theme for the fountain was a spawning salmon, identifying the city on the sea. It was designed to be a place where old people would sit, children play, and friends meet. Norris and Albert Venuti carved the fish, and Denbigh designed the mosaic work. The mosaic tile came from Mexico. Structural draftsman Jack Ackroyd prepared drawings, and by the spring of 1959, Ray Cagna and his crew began construction.

There were many other highlights that year, among them the RCMP Musical Ride, and Princess Royal Day celebrated on November 27, the date of the arrival of the first mining families from England in 1854. The year ended with a great Christmas tree with gifts for all children up to 9 years of age.

Tragedy at the Nanaimo Zoo

The Nanaimo Zoo was a popular tourist attraction in the Wellington area, north of Nanaimo. The 90-acre zoo was located in the largely rural area, near today's popular Long Lake. Nearby there were several homes and a number of small farms. Owner Paul Hertel imported animals from around the world, turning his 15-year hobby of taming wild animals into a full-scale zoo. The latest acquisition was a baby elephant named Susie. The zoo also had a number of African lions. There were two full-grown female lionesses and one male plus a younger lion, and a llama. Over 30,000 people visited the zoo in 1957.[22] Admission was 50 cents per adult and 25 cents per child. The popular attraction had 200 exhibits, including animals and birds. Visitors enjoyed having their photograph taken beside the animals. One lioness named Fury was particularly popular. Children in the area knew no

In May 1958 a lioness named Fury escaped from the Hertel zoo. In this photo, the Royle family from Nanaimo get acquainted with a large elk at the zoo.

fear of the animals, as they were regular visitors often coming into the back of the zoo grounds.

Originally Hertel wanted to open the zoo in the Alberni area but could not get support from city council even though he argued the zoo could be a major tourist attraction. He began his mini animal kingdom by raising two cougars to adulthood. Gradually he added other animals to his collection; before long he had a small zoo, and more and more visitors started travelling to his farm near Alberni to see the animals. When he proposed moving the zoo to Nanaimo, the SPCA raised objections, suggesting there needed to be improvements made in housing the animals. The SPCA was satisfied after Hertel made alterations to the cages giving the animals more space.

Hertel sometimes let the lions out of their cage; they would walk around him and go back inside when they were told. Therefore, in May 1958, it came as a surprise when the lioness Fury, the tamest of the lions, escaped. The animal had slipped to freedom during the evening feeding despite assistant Jungenkrueger's desperate attempt to stop her by grabbing the 350-pound animal by the tail. He had given her food and then returned with a pail of water. As he poured the water into the trough, Fury forced her way out the door and ran off into the bush. He then alerted Hertel. Hertel and his assistant played a game of hide and seek during the night trying to get the lioness back into her cage. Jungenkrueger had worked for Hertel for five years, feeding and looking after the animals, so was no stranger to them. Hertel called in dogs to help hunt the escaped animal. Fury had escaped before but always returned voluntarily, so the zookeepers were not too worried.

Jungenkrueger was instructed to phone the Vanstone family, which lived about half a mile away and had children, and to warn them the lioness was loose and ask them to warn others in the district. Too late, it was discovered the phone number on the list was the wrong one. About half a mile from the Vanstone's home, Maureen Vanstone, 8, and her sister, Patricia, 6, were on their way down a narrow tree-lined road. Two other children, Lee, 11, and Janet, 7, daughters of Mr. and Mrs. Walter Butcher, were riding bicycles along the same road on their way to meet the Vanstone girls. The children were close enough to greet each other when Fury rose suddenly from the bush. Lee thought at first that it was a dog. When they recognized Fury, the tame lioness whom they had seen so many times at the zoo, they were not alarmed. Maureen called to the lioness, "I see you, Fury, come out of there."[23]

Suddenly the lion leaped towards Maureen. Lee and Janet Butcher dropped their bicycles, and with Patricia Vanstone running behind them, fled in terror to Mrs. Beth Morton's farm nearby. "A lion's got Maureen," they screamed to Mrs. Morton. She phoned Walter Butcher, the children's father, then phoned the Nanaimo RCMP with the news. This was the first time the police had heard about the escaped lion. Butcher grabbed his rifle and ran to the Mortons'. As he rounded a curve in the road, he saw the lion moving away from the road carrying the child's clothing. He fired a shot at it, but it ran off.

Soon the police and ambulance arrived, but it was too late, Maureen was dead. Later the family learned she died of a broken neck and severed jugular, but had not been badly mauled. This news was small comfort for the grieving family. The child was one of five children of Dr. and Mrs. W. Vanstone. Dr. W. Vanstone, a scientist working at the Pacific Biological Station, was in a boat off Newcastle Island when he was notified of the tragedy.

What resulted was described as "a three-hour reign of terror." According to press reports it was the most dramatic hunt in the history of Vancouver Island. An estimated 200 men joined in the hunt. All roads in the vicinity of the zoo were jammed with cars, everyone wanted to help find the lion and put her down. The Nanaimo Fish and Game Club and wildlife officials armed with high-powered rifles joined the RCMP in the search by land, while two airplanes, one from Cassidair and the other belonging to Jim Bonner, searched by air. Jack Beban also offered the services of his plane.

Children were kept indoors as the news of the lion's escape was broadcast. RCMP Corporal Salt spotted the animal near Biggs Farm heading for the ridge north of Long Lake. For three hours they worked their way through the tangled bush before the sound of a fusillade of bullets indicated the death of the lion. Who had fired the end shot? No one knew, but police credited William and Tom Derbyshire, Everett Warneboldt, and Irving and Mervin War with all being in on the kill.

An inquest was held under coroner Dr. W.H. Lewis. No charges were immediately laid in connection with the death, so it came as a surprise to learn on May 6 that Hertel had been arrested for negligence in the slaying of a child by an escaped lion. He was released on bail pending the result of the inquest. The maximum penalty for such a crime was life imprisonment.

Details of the tragedy were revealed at the inquest—the wrong number had been called. Jungenkrueger had mistakenly phoned Mrs. Doris Dunbar of the Somerset Hotel in North Wellington instead of Mrs. Vanstone. Dunbar testified, "He told me a lion was on the loose and to keep the kids in." She confirmed she had received the call but was confused by the conversation. Hertel told the inquest, "I knew the girl so well it was like losing a child of my own." The jury returned an open verdict, adding a rider that the provincial government should have had adequate regulations and controls for the operation of private zoos in B.C. The zoo closed. Today the memory of the popular attraction is intermingled with the tragic death of a child.

A New St. Peter's Church

The Roman Catholic Church had owned the property at Machleary and Fitzwilliam streets since 1876. The unused site on the border of Five Acres and Chinatown gave a commanding view of the city, the harbour, and the mainland mountains. This would be the location of the new St. Peter's Church. Until this time, the congregation worshipped in St. Peter's Church on Wallace Street. This old church had once stood in North Wellington; in 1910 it had been taken apart, board by board, and hauled in wagons and rebuilt on Wallace Street, exactly as it had been in Wellington.

Three priests now served Nanaimo; they were Right Reverend Monsignor A.G. Baker, Pastor Reverend Patrick Ratchford, and Reverend William Mudge.[24] In 1958, the time had come to build a new church. A bank loan was taken out to cover the $350,000 cost.

Tony Radisic was the architect; the contractor, Charles Andrew Classen, oversaw the work being done using mostly volunteer labour. Ken Gogo did the excavating.[25] Ingmar Laurington was the engineer. The first sod was turned in March 1958. Attending the ceremony were Mayor Pete Maffeo, members of the Knights of Columbus, representatives of Catholic organizations, and parishioners. Roman Catholic Bishop James M. Hill, of Victoria, conducted a solemn mass in the old church.

Pouring the cement foundation was a major effort. Once started the foundation had to be poured continuously.[26] About 100 men worked three eight-hour shifts around the clock for two days while the Catholic Women's League supplied coffee and sandwiches for them. Special lighting was brought in to allow the work to continue throughout the night.

Slowly the walls were erected and the church took shape. Marble was imported from Italy for the surface of the high altar. A photo in the *Free Press* of January 12, 1960, shows three men considering ways of manhandling the huge slab of marble into place. The men were T. Zamberoni, Clarence Roberge, and Alec Drolet. The old post office four-faced clock, minus its chimes, found a new home in the bell tower. The painted angels in front of the church were the work of Gerhard and Karl Hartmann. The art style is called "graffito," an Italian word meaning "a little scratch."

Bishop Hill returned to bless the new church at the formal dedication ceremony on Sunday, May 1, 1960. Special guests were MLA Earle Westwood, Mayor Maffeo, and city aldermen. There were representatives from the army, the navy, the air force, and the RCMP, as well as the chief of the Snuneymuxw and the chief of the Nanoose band. Lieutenant-Governor Frank Ross had been invited but sent his regrets. Dr. M.G. Zorkin presided at the dedication banquet that evening.

This had been a big undertaking by the parish. The mortgage burning took place on June 29, 1968. On February 14, 1960, Monsignor A.G. Baker baptized John Gerard Gogo, the son of Ken and Dodie Gogo, the first child baptized in the church.

The Nanaimo Golf Club

Since 1922, the Nanaimo Golf Links had been at the same location; now members looked to expand to an 18-hole golf course. Larry Harris, the general manager at Harmac, brought together a committee to consider the idea. The committee included Harris and club president Stan Dyde, lawyer Don Cunliffe, chartered accountant Bert Pickard, Dan Aldis, who worked with Larry Harris, and Simpsons-Sears manager Rex Covey. Other golfers who gave input were Ewart Maybee, Tom Galloway, and Murray Barbour. All met in Harris's home to consider the future of golf in Nanaimo.

About the same time, Robert and Jean Burns and Dr. William Lindsay, a local chiropractor, established Lynburn Estates Ltd. This land included the Cilaire, Lynburn, and the Vancouver Island Golf Club properties. The real-estate agent for Lynburn Estates was Ernie Butcher, a member of the golf club. He met with the new committee, and the idea took root to have the 18-hole course located on the Lynburn land. Subsequently the club purchased 123 acres for $10,000. The Nanaimo Golf Club was duly established under the Societies Act in 1952.[27]

Well-known Pacific Northwest golfer and B.C. golf course architect A.V. Macan was invited to give advice on the course and clubhouse. After flying over the area with Mike Rivers and Murray Barbour, he had lots of questions, mainly regarding water and soil suitability. The water problem was solved when the club purchased about one-third of an acre of land on which an old pumping shaft was located—in a previous life it had been used in mining operations.

In 1954, the B.C. Vocational Training School began clearing and preparing the first two fairways and practice area, and continued to help in the following years up to 1967; the school used the site as a training ground in preparing the remainder of the 18 holes. Meanwhile, lots in Lynburn Estates were selling at $1,200, the larger lots going for $1,800. After the announcement of the golf course project, the price of small lots rose to $3,600 and that of large lots to $5,500.

Hugh Cliffe, of the Comox Logging Company, then working from Ladysmith, helped remove the stumps. Hugh Ellison and Bill Motherwell installed the irrigating system, and club members did rock picking with help from the young men at the Brannen Lake Correctional School. Mike Rivers, the club pro since 1948, worked tirelessly supervising the construction of the course under the direction of architect Macan. Unfortunately, before the last three holes were completed, Macan died. Rivers served for 42 years in various capacities as pro, manager, and course superintendent.

In 1961, the Nanaimo Golf Club turned over all the assets of the club to a new company, The Vancouver Island Golf Club Ltd. The association was registered as a company, thus having authority to establish the Nanaimo Golf Club, as it is known today.

On November 23, 1961, at a meeting held in the Eagles Hall on Bastion Street, the club decided to sell the old nine-hole course on Wakesiah Avenue. It sold for $67,000; unfortunately, before the deal was finalized a fire destroyed the clubhouse. This was one of the Camp Nanaimo army huts purchased after the war from the Department of National Defence and remodelled to serve as a bar and cocktail lounge for members.[28] At the new course, McArravy and Barley were chosen as the architects for a new clubhouse in January 1961.

The last day of play on the Wakesiah Avenue golf course was May 13, 1962, and opening day on the new course was May 15, 1962. Elmer Bradshaw hit the first ball off No. 1 tee.

Chapter Nineteen

The Sixties

Chinatown Burns

At the end of a hot summer in 1960, Nanaimo's famous Chinatown was destroyed by fire, and 200 people were left homeless. Colin McArthur was fire chief and Albert Dunn the deputy fire chief of the Nicol Street fire hall when on September 30, at 4:47 p.m., the fire alarm call came in from Chinatown. Dunn immediately dispatched the Harewood volunteer fire team; half of Pine Street was still under the jurisdiction of Harewood. The late afternoon was dry and windy. Dunn was ordered by McArthur to drive up the hill to see if his fire hall should also respond to the call. After taking a look at the thick black smoke, he immediately dispatched the entire Nicol Street crew. Other fire departments came from Northfield, Wellington, Cedar, and Ladysmith. Dunn directed the operations at the north end of the fire scene, while Chief McArthur took care of the south end.

Chuck Wong was at his home on Kennedy Street preparing for work at the family's Rendezvous Restaurant, which he owned with his three brothers, Gunner, Henry, and John. He could see Chinatown from his front step. As he walked out to his car he noticed black smoke billowing into the sky from the middle of Pine Street. Wong feared the worst and quickly raced to the scene. He was so anxious he forgot to take the parking brake off his car, so when he arrived at Hecate Street, the wheels of his car were smoking.

Wong ran up the hill and saw residents dragging their possessions, beds, bedding, mattresses, and all sorts of furniture from a building on Pine Street. By this time, the building was totally engulfed in flames, and the fire had started to spread to neighbouring commercial buildings. Most of the mainly wood-frame buildings were touching one another, enabling the fire to spread quickly. He began alerting the neighbourhood, pleading with people to get out. "Chinatown is burning," he shouted. "I could see the power line from one side of the street—it was just like a sparkler coming across the wire. In no time, the telephone pole across the street was in flames."[1]

Fireman Tom MacDonald was on call that day; he could see the smoke from his home in the Woodlands area. He grabbed his gear and raced to the scene of the fire. Wong was still frantically running door to door trying to save residents. The fire was so hot that it began to melt the alloy metal ladder used by the Harewood fire crew. Firemen did what they could to stop the spread of the blaze, but the wind acted against them, creating its own updraft and making it practically impossible to contain. They were also confronted with low water pressure, which made their hoses of little use. Firemen battled the blaze for seven hours, but by then most of Chinatown was gone. McArthur reported there had been no casualties. He said, "We were lucky. It was tough. The wind kept shifting, and we didn't know where the fire would go next."[2]

There were conflicting reports of how the fire started. One version claimed an elderly Chinese man had decided to burn a pile of leaves in his backyard when the fire got away from him, setting an old nearby weathered wooden building ablaze.[3] Louis Fong, former cook of the Tideview Café, said the blaze started in the No. 7 house located on the Harewood side of the street near the Puss-in-Boots Café. It was the Tideview cook, Billy Thom, who first spotted the fire. He and Fong hooked a fire hose up to a hydrant, which stood near the burning building. A boy turned on the water for them after they entered the building, but the ancient hose, rotting with age, burst as soon as the water pressure was applied and little, if any, water reached the fire.[4]

In one room, firemen and volunteers had trouble moving out six elderly men and a child. They just sat around a table refusing to leave. They appeared to be either stunned or in shock; it soon became apparent that two were blind and the others could only walk with difficulty. Stretchers were brought in to remove them.

The Canadian Legion, Branch No. 10, cancelled its rock'n'roll dance—the teenagers were too busy assisting at the fire. They packed out furniture, assisted the elderly, and ran errands. The Legion Hall was used to collect clothing and supplies for the fire victims, who had lost everything.

The community opened its heart to the Chinese victims. Captain Charles Smith of the Salvation Army, Dawson Gordon, head of Nanaimo's Civil Defence organization, and Jim Buckle, head of the Canadian Red Cross, Nanaimo Branch, were on the scene helping. Through Buckle's efforts, 400 blankets arrived from Vancouver by midnight; these were used for bedding down those in need. Camp Nanaimo was put to good use. Major Bob Weir, officer commanding the B.C. Regiment militia unit, even before getting

Nanaimo's famous Chinatown is fondly remembered for its familiar array of wooden buildings with overhanging balconies and wooden sidewalks.

After a long hot summer in 1960, fire destroyed Chinatown.

approval from military headquarters in Vancouver, opened and lit the big hanger ready for salvaged goods and for setting up a clothing centre; he also provided army barracks to house some of the homeless. Dorothy Lucas of the Civil Defence Group registered everyone, and by midnight all had been accounted for.

Forestry industrialist H.R. MacMillan was a passenger on the incoming ferry, the *Princess Patricia*, at 5:30 p.m. The smoke was visible from the ferry and MacMillan was so concerned that he never left the bow. He and Harmac manager Einar Walloe offered any help possible.

Nanaimo opened its heart to the homeless. They were scattered in private homes throughout the city. St. Ann's Convent took some, and 70 elderly Chinese men were housed in the army camp; that night they slept in double-decker bunk beds previously occupied by the military. Civil Defence officers, volunteer nurses, and St. John Ambulance workers escorted them there and made them comfortable.

The following day, crowds of sightseers, curious adults and children, poked around the charred ruins before being ordered from the area by RCMP patrolling the area. Mayor Pete Maffeo wondered if Chinatown would be rebuilt. The problem was that one side of Pine Street was within the city boundaries and owned by the Chinese company shareholders, while the other side was in the Harewood Improvement District and under provincial control.

A Chinese Fire Relief Fund was started, with MacMillan, Bloedel, and Powell River Company leading the way with a cheque for $500 from all the company divisions in Nanaimo, Harmac, Northwest Bay, logging, forestry, and research. Further afield, $3,000 came from the Peking Opera Company, another $3,000 from the Chinese Classical Theatre, and $500 from the Toronto Chinese community. The Wong brothers' Rendezvous Restaurant raised over $1,000 for the fund. News of the fire had made front-page headlines across the country.

There had been four Chinatowns during the evolution of Nanaimo; the fourth extension was from Pine to Machleary streets. After the Second World War, Chinese businessmen bought out Lun Yick Land Company, creating Wah Hing Land Company, a non-profit company with shareholders across Canada.[5] The company operated on a ground rent system, charging $2.50 per month for half a lot or 33 feet, or $5.00 for a full lot. The renter could build then rent space in their building for 50 cents per month per head. Unfortunately, the Wah Hing Land Company did not have enough money to reinvest, so many of the buildings were allowed to deteriorate.

Before the fire, the Chinese community had hoped to replace some of the old residences with new duplexes. There were an estimated 250 residents in Chinatown in 1955. Five years later, 200 remained. Of these, 70 were elderly men who had worked in the mines and who could not afford to live elsewhere, nor could they speak English.

Chinatown had changed considerably over the years. Chinese people, who at one time in Nanaimo's history had been shunned as "Oriental menaces," had assimilated into society and opened their doors to the community. There were four Chinese restaurants operating: the Canton Chop Suey House, Nam King Low Chop Suey House Number 4, The End House, and the Puss 'n Boots. There were also two butcher shops, a grocery, a drug store, and a barber. Chinatown may have been quiet during the day, but it came alive in the evening. The *Vancouver Sun* described the scene: "Juke boxes blare, young people and tourists, both Chinese and White, dance in the narrow aisles between booths and tables of a couple of cafés."[6]

After the fire, the Wah Hing Land Company wound up its affairs and donated property to the Cathay Senior Citizens Housing Society.[7] The society, with the aid of a provincial grant and some local fundraising, built a senior's housing unit; this with additions, is now Hecate Lodge. Sixteen Chinese senior citizens lived out their retirement years in relative comfort. Other portions of Chinatown were sold to Wally Chang.

The fire had destroyed two-thirds of the buildings. In 1962 a few buildings were moved and others were burned. Today there are still a few buildings remaining.

The Wong brothers' Rendezvous Restaurant was a landmark in downtown Nanaimo for many years. It opened in 1956 with its unique Starlight Room. The brothers created a semicircular room with a mural depicting a Chinese night scene set off by a starlit sky. A mirrored wall gave the illusion of openness and enhanced the twinkling stars.[8] The 275-seat popular restaurant had its own formula for success—serve good food for a good price. When the dance halls emptied, the Rendezvous filled up. The restaurant closed in March 2000.

Nanaimo Regional Hospital

After the war Nanaimo and surrounding communities grew to such an extent that it became clear either the hospital had to be enlarged or another hospital had to be built.

Planning for the present Regional Hospital of Nanaimo began with the passing of a money bylaw, followed by negotiations with the provincial authorities and the approval of an architect. The contract for construction was awarded to Smith Brothers and Wilson on September 7, 1960. The hospital planned for 160 acute-care beds. Lieutenant-Governor Frank M. Ross laid the cornerstone, carved by local craftsman S. John Selby, on September 18, 1960.

The Minister of Health Services and Hospital Insurance, the Honorable E.C.F. Martin, officially opened the Nanaimo Regional Hospital on January 6, 1963. More than 6,000 residents toured the facility following the opening ceremonies, setting a B.C. record for the highest attendance at an opening of a hospital in the province. The sculpture "Florence Nightingale—the Angel of Mercy" was part of the landscaped grounds.

The transfer of patients on January 12, 1963, from the Machleary Street hospital to the new Regional Hospital was handled like a civil defence exercise. A year later the fourth floor east wing added 28 more beds, bringing the total to 188. Then in 1967, the sixth floor opened with 37 beds, bringing the complement up to 225. The old hospital was the first home for Malaspina Community College. Later it became Malaspina Gardens, a seniors care facility.

In 1967, the city was well served by 15 general practitioners, 4 gynecologists and obstetricians, 3 surgeons, 2 eye doctors, 1 ear, nose and throat doctor, 1 radiologist, 1 psychiatrist, 1 urologist, 1 internal medicine doctor, 2 pediatricians, 2 orthopedic surgeons, and 13 dentists.[9]

Parks and Recreation Commission

Since the early 1920s the Parks and Recreation Board had been a committee of city council. This changed in 1947, when a commission was appointed to administer the parks, playgrounds, and boulevards of the city. The first three members were Harry Freeman, Archie Lewis, and J. Unsworth. Doug Proctor and Reg Murphy were appointed from the Gyro club since it had been active in the affairs of Parks and Recreation in the past. Harry Freeman was the first chairman, Proctor was vice-chairman, and Arthur Leynard of the city hall staff acted as board secretary. Since the Parks and Recreation Commission was formed, the number of employees has grown from 6 to the present 112.

The major sports facility administered by the city was the three acres that constituted the Central Sports Ground. It had a full-sized baseball diamond and football field, with a grandstand for 1,500. The clubhouse was heated and had modern shower facilities for players, and was also equipped with clubroom, kitchen, toilet facilities, and a good water supply. There was also a bowling green, judged one of the best in the province, situated on what is now known as Piper Park, the present location of the museum. The bowling club paid $1 per year rent. The tennis club also used these facilities, paying the same rate as the bowling club.[10]

There were playgrounds in the city located at Comox Road Park, Deverill Square and the hospital grounds. The playgrounds had children's wading pools and playground apparatus such as swings and slides. Park attendants were on duty when the playgrounds were open.

Bowen Park had yet to be fully developed. At this time it remained in its natural state; the wonderful picnic area, the trails, and the Millstone River attracted many visitors. The park also had a number of cabins for rent and parking space for about 20 trailers.

Georgia Park was considered the "most outstanding" park site, fronting the harbour with a beautiful view of the Strait of Georgia and the snow-capped mountains of the mainland. The park was improved with fencing, lawns, and rose bushes. The main entrance to the small park displayed a Squamish canoe and the totem pole the artist Wilkes James had presented to the city in 1922.

The Civic Arena, Exhibition Park, Grandview Bowl, Robins Park, and Westwood Lake Park were added to the inventory of recreational facilities.

Beban and Bowen Parks

Having purchased the Beban property from the family in 1952, the city began developing a sports and exhibition complex. The Grandview Bowl and Centennial Building were completed in 1958 in time for the B.C. centennial celebration. The completion of the Grandview Bowl introduced the community to a new sport: auto racing. The Cedar Valley Riding Club prepared tracks for horse and chuckwagon races and gymkhanas. Exhibitions that for years had been held in the Civic Arena were moved to Exhibition Park when the Centennial Building was completed.

Bowen Park was the major project of the 1960s; the recreation complex was completed just in time for Canada's centennial celebrations in 1967. The park was named for brothers George and James Bowen, owners of Western Fuel Company, which in 1918 conveyed to the city 125 acres of land between Comox Road and Millstone River to be used as a public park. At that time it was a beautiful wild uncultivated green space, complete with native flowers, towering cedars and Douglas-fir trees, and a cascading river. The property had been used recreationally long before it officially became a park. The city welcomed the official gift and designation as a park.

The park attracted many visitors in the 1920s; some even arrived by car. The Nanaimo Auto Park at Bowen Park was well used in 1925. Over 1,000 cars registered at the Auto Park from April to September; the charge was 50 cents per day. Mr. W.G. Moore was the caretaker.[11]

The Nanaimo Rotary Club had been developing the park for several years prior to 1953. On February 18 that year, the club established the Bowen Park Development Association. The city gave the club approval for the first stage of development. A non-profit society was formed with the purpose of engaging public support from groups and individuals. The Rotarians never intended doing it alone; they needed the support of the community. Stan

On April 19, 1953, over 140 volunteers turned out for the first work bee at the site of Bowen Park, part of a drive to raise money and public awareness for the park. Work bees continued throughout the 1950s.

Dyde chaired the association with Dave Jones as vice-chairman and Harry Cicconi as secretary-treasurer.

The club organized a membership drive that raised a few dollars and also created public awareness about the park and its development. Besides money, there were offers of trucks, bulldozers, and other equipment. On April 19, 1953, over 140 volunteers turned out for the first work bee. Volunteers began clearing an entrance in from Wall Street. The work parties continued, and soon a roadway was cleared and gravelled, the fill donated by Canadian Collieries Ltd. A picnic shelter was constructed with donations from the Associated Commercial Travellers, and a picnic site and parking lot were cleared and landscaped. The Nanaimo Curling Club served coffee, and the Rotary Anns and Soroptimists served sandwiches.[12] The work bees continued throughout the 1950s. In 1962 the Rotary Club turned their developed section of the park and its remaining assets over to the city.[13]

The Nanaimo Rotary Club concluded its active participation in the park development by sponsoring a cairn with a bronze plaque that gave the history of the park, and by placing a Rotary Wheel facing Wall Street, opposite the Nanaimo Curling Rink. The club also donated rose bushes to surround the cairn in memory of fellow club member Bill Horman Sr., who died of a heart attack while working in the park. Another member was memorialized in 1963 with the installation of the Billy Lewis Centenary Rose Garden and sundial. Lewis had been a member for 48 years, having joined a few weeks after the club was chartered. He celebrated his 100th birthday in 1963. Even though the affairs of the association had wound up, the Rotary Club continued to raise money for various projects within the park.

Harry Wipper, manager of the Parks and Recreation Commission, outlined a 10-year master plan for development of the park in 1962. Since then the recreation complex that is well used today took shape. It includes an auditorium, meeting rooms, lounges, workshop rooms, washrooms, and dressing rooms, as well as offices and a storage area.

The Kinsmen Club added to the Bowen Park Recreation Complex by constructing a 25-metre outdoor pool in 1963/64. The pool was built as a winter works program. At first the club hoped to add a roof and have it heated and made for all-year use, but the project was scaled back due to financial difficulties.[14] The Bowen Park Recreation Complex was officially opened on February 8, 1967, by chairman of the Parks and Recreation Commission William (Bill) McGregor, Mayor Pete Maffeo, and Laurie Wallace of the B.C. Centennial Commission.

Vancouver Island Regional Library (VIRL)

A new municipal library opened on June 21, 1961, adding to the improved recreational and cultural aspects of life in Nanaimo. The old municipal library at the corner of Wallace and Fraser streets had been used since 1924, with the Vancouver Island Union Library occupying the lower floor until it moved to the Strickland Street location.

The Nanaimo Library Building Society presented a report to city council on October 18, 1960, outlining all the arguments in favour of a new building. The Wallace Street location had physical limitations, difficult working conditions, and little space for reading rooms, the reference section, or children's needs. Other groups such as the Nanaimo Historical Society, art groups, and the chess club shared the building, and it was also used as an assembly hall. A major argument for a new building was the film library service. Regular film screenings were popular with the public.[15]

A $10,000 donation was made in memory of William Booth Mercer of Nanaimo for a children's wing of the new library. With this money, public subscriptions, and support from the city, the construction of the $60,000 building was able to proceed. The site chosen was 580 Fitzwilliam Street, the northeast corner of Lubbock Square. Architects were McArravy & Barley.

Two hundred people attended the opening on June 21. Guests included Mayor Pete Maffeo and George Darling, the chairman of the VIRL board and the person who spearheaded the drive for a new library. Also present were regional librarian W.R. Taggard and Dr. Helen Stewart, one of the founders of the regional library system, who had pioneered the development of public libraries in B.C. Dr. Stewart had been present when the Nanaimo library was formed in 1920.

The VIRL remained at this location for 36 years; then in 1997 it moved to a new downtown location on Commercial Street.

Chapter Twenty

The Future Secured, History Preserved

The '50s and '60s were decades of tremendous growth in Nanaimo due to the influx of developers and entrepreneurs who saw the potential for growth in the central Island region and began buying up land. By 1961, many wholesale firms had established their main outlets here to service Vancouver Island. All the big stores were located in the downtown area: Simpsons-Sears, Overwaitea Foods, Spencer's, which was purchased by Eaton's, and Safeway. Housing construction boomed as the population moved out of the city. A wide range of government services, both federal and provincial, relocated to Nanaimo due to its central location. Along with this growth, retail and wholesale sectors grew as shopping centres were built.

The name Zorkin has been associated with real-estate projects in Nanaimo for decades. Mladen Zorkin, of Croatia, moved to Nanaimo in 1947 with Joy, his young English bride. Two years later, Zorkin established H.A. Roberts Ltd., a company specializing in commercial development. He looked to the north of the city, along the Island Highway, and in 1952 and 1953 started buying up farmland owned by Mrs. Thompson in the area of Terminal Park. When he had acquired 11 acres, he began clearing the land to build a shopping centre. There were a few skeptics who did not believe a shopping centre would be successful in Nanaimo; after all, even Victoria did not have one. This would be the first on Vancouver Island. There were many obstacles to overcome. At first the Minister of Transportation and Highways, Phil Gaglardi, refused to give permission to allow an access road off the Island Highway, but Zorkin erected his shopping centre anyway. He did get access. Zorkin took the chance of having a food store anchor the shopping centre instead of a department store. His first major tenant was Overwaitea Foods, which would later be the first of the big retailers to move out of the downtown location into the suburbs.

Terminal Park Plaza opened in November 1957. Two years later Safeway signed a 20-year lease and joined its rival Overwaitea. Safeway had been in Nanaimo since November 1932 when it opened in the former Morton's Hardware store.[1]

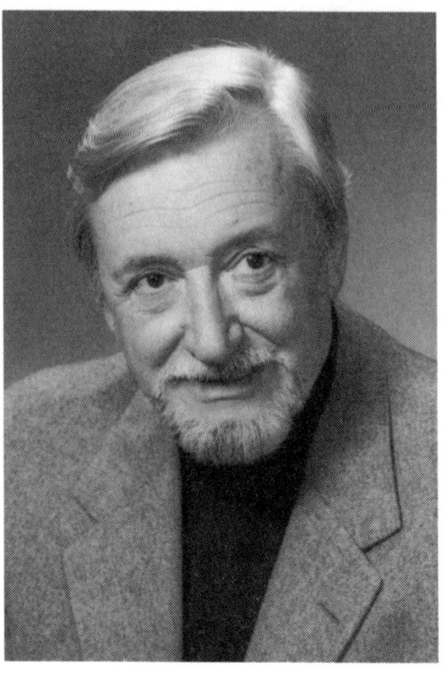

Mladen Zorkin saw the potential for commercial development and built Terminal Park Plaza in 1957, Nanaimo and Vancouver Island's first shopping centre.

Zorkin led the way with other building projects, including the Brechin Point development, for which he donated an acre of land to the city for a public boat launch. Zorkin Road, near the Departure Bay Ferry Terminal, leads to the boat launch site.

Other developers, who saw the success of Terminal Park, began building more shopping centres. Harewood Mall opened in October 1958, then Northbrook Mall in 1965, and Harbour Park Mall on April 27, 1967. Still other malls followed: Country Club on March 12, 1980, Woodgrove on September 30, 1981, Rutherford in 1981, and, more recently, Longwood Centre.

Today there are eight shopping malls—in Nanaimo you can shop till you drop; the city has more retail space per capita than any other city in North America. The malls stretch almost to Parksville, drawing shoppers from many up-Island communities. The last census showed the retail trade here provided jobs for over 5,000 people.

In order for the Harbour Park Mall to proceed, the city had to solve the problem of the downtown parking shortage. In 1964 it filled in a portion of the waterfront inlet and built a causeway across the seaward end to link up with the two major downtown streets. A $410,000 funding bylaw was passed in May to allow the project to proceed. The work was carried out under a winter works program, but the largest contributor to the cost of the development was the CPR. The filled-in portion of the inlet provided 186 parking spaces.

That same year the city's first high-rise, Vancouver Island's tallest building, brought more people into the downtown area. The $1 million, 17-storey "Seacrest," at the corner of Comox and Front streets (entryway from Chapel Street), was built in 1963/64 for F.M. McGregor and Associates of Victoria and George Blely Construction Co. Ltd. of Vancouver. The architect was Wilfred Buttjeo, of Vancouver.[2] The building sold in 1968 to Julius Balshine, a hotel owner from Vancouver, for $1.3 million. Balshine believed the high-rise would "attract retired people from the prairies who would enjoy Nanaimo's good facilities and moderate climate."[3]

In 1960, the Canadian Bank of Commerce moved from its prominent location in the Frontier Building on Church Street to 150 Commercial Street, and in 1963, Frank Ney and his Great National Land & Investment Corporation purchased the old bank building and used it as a real-estate office. The building became known as the Great National Land Building. The City of Nanaimo declared it a heritage building in 1975. The Nanaimo & District Credit Union also moved to a new building on Dunsmuir Street in 1964.

Frank James William Ney succeeded Peter Maffeo as mayor in 1968. Ney's first venture into provincial politics, when he ran as Social Credit candidate against Dave Stupich of the NDP in 1966, was unsuccessful. Ney did not give up and tried again in 1969, and this time he was successful. However, Stupich soundly defeated him in the 1972 election.

Ney was born in London, England, on May 12, 1918. After serving in the RCAF as a pilot during the Second World War, he came to Nanaimo

The Frontier Building, a City-designated heritage structure, is now the Great National Land Building.

in 1946 and began work in real estate with the Nanaimo Realty Company. In 1959, that company purchased Protection Island for $130,000 and subdivided it into 344 lots.

Ney somehow found parcels of land, had other people purchase them, then took care of subdividing, developing, and selling finished homes for a 5 percent commission. Business was so brisk that in 1963 he founded the Great National Land and Investment Corporation as a public company. The company immediately purchased Nanaimo Realty Ltd. By 1965 Great National was catering to every niche in the local market: residential, commercial, industrial, revenue, and waterfront. The most prestigious development was that of Cilaire, designed as an upper-class area, complete with elementary school, access to the beach, and lots of green space.

Nanaimo's long-time colourful mayor, Frank Ney, made everyone smile for over 20 years when he dressed up in his pirate costume and headed the Nanaimo Bathtub Race.

After his election as mayor, Ney began promoting the city, and when it needed increased publicity he provided it in abundance. Many remember him as the colourful mayor of Nanaimo, who for over 20 years made everyone smile when he dressed up in his pirate costume and headed the Nanaimo Bathtub Race. The race, established in 1967, became an annual event between Nanaimo and Vancouver. More recently, as Vancouver's interest declined, the race continues to be a spectacular event starting in Nanaimo Harbour and ending at Departure Bay.

Deane Finlayson was also a developer with vision, and like Zorkin and Ney, he looked at raw land and saw its potential. He was born and educated in Nanaimo. Like Ney, he also had a foray into politics, which led him to become leader of the Conservative Party of B.C. In 1966, Finlayson opened Northbrook Realty Ltd., a real-estate and insurance office in the newly opened Northbrook Mall. He and his wife, Joan, were the first tenants. His company over the years bought up land in the Hammond Bay area, including Piper's Lagoon and Neck Point, and then began developing Morningside Estates. Finlayson was the principal shareholder in Morningside Beach

Properties Ltd.[4] He was also instrumental in the building of Woodgrove Centre through another company, Woodgrove Holdings.

Preserving Nanaimo's History

As Canada approached its centennial in 1967, communities across the country looked for meaningful ways to mark the important milestone in the country's history. Montreal led the way with its very successful World's Fair. In Nanaimo a Centennial Committee was established with Mayor Frank Ney as chairman, and before the year was out, the city had a new museum built on Piper's Park.

Work on establishing the museum began back in 1953 on the 100th birthday of the old HBC's Bastion on Front Street. A group of local people interested in preserving the city's history called a meeting on June 20, 1953, to consider forming a Nanaimo section of the B.C. Historical Association, now known as the Nanaimo Historical Society.[5] Invited guests were Provincial Archivist Willard Ireland and historian Bruce McKelvie. At this meeting, Jack McGregor was elected president, Pat Johnson, secretary, and F. Robinson, treasurer. William Barraclough succeeded McGregor the following year and was president until 1958. His son Edward also served as president in 1986.

The following year William Barraclough and his wife, Ethel, began the task of tracing the descendants of the *Princess Royal* pioneers. On November 27, 1954, a pageant took place celebrating the centennial of that event. The Yellow Point Drama Group, directed by Anne Mossman, re-enacted their

The Nanaimo centennial project in 1967 was its new museum.

arrival at Pioneer Rock, just below the Bastion.[6] Since then, the arrival of the "Black Country" miners and those Scottish miners who were here prior to their arrival has been celebrated annually by the Nanaimo Historical Society and the miners' descendants.

Society members also began tape-recording memoirs of seniors and early pioneers so their history would not be lost. Speakers with knowledge of the history of Nanaimo were invited to monthly meetings, their stories and speeches preserved for the future.

The first physical involvement was to assist in the restoration of the derelict Pioneer Cemetery located at Comox and Wallace. The Hub City Kiwanis Club took on the project of having the site cleared and the headstones placed in the serpentine wall. The former cemetery was converted into a park.

The biggest undertaking of all—the building of a museum—was still ahead. William Barraclough wrote the following in the society's 1964 minute book:

> A museum reflects the history of the past where its treasured objects can be viewed and studied. Our present living can be enriched by the works of art, its writings and natural specimens, together with practical items displayed of cultures that were created out of necessity for human progress by those thoughtful persons who preceded us.[7]

Until this time, items of historical interest had been on display in the old Bastion, where space was limited. With Canada's centennial approaching in 1967, Alderman John G. Parker initiated a meeting on October 7, 1963, of people interested in organizing a museum society. From the 15 people present, Parker was elected chairman and William Barraclough, secretary-treasurer. Other board members included Gino Sedola, Philip J. Piper, and Patricia Johnson; Douglas Greer was legal advisor. By April 1964, the bylaws were approved, and the Nanaimo and District Museum Society was duly registered as a society. William Lewis, now 101 years of age, was granted an Honorary Membership in the society.

Space was secured in the basement of the Credit Union building for historical artefacts until the museum could be built. MacMillan, Bloedel and Pacific Veneer Company donated material for partitions and shelving. The museum collection was growing.

Arthur Leynard chaired the building committee, and the project moved ahead quickly. On March 3, 1965, John Parker advised the society directors that the Centennial Committee was considering the idea of a combined museum, publicity bureau, and Chamber of Commerce Centre, and the suggested site was the lawn bowling green on Piper's Park. Mayor Pete Maffeo expressed his preference for just a museum building.

Meanwhile, architect A.L. Barley presented his plan for a museum and tourist bureau on November 1, 1966. By April the building was well advanced, and by November 15, 1967, the first regular meeting of the museum society was held in the new Nanaimo Centennial Museum located in Piper's Park.

Dr. G. Clifford Carl, the director of the provincial museum in Victoria, officially opened the museum on November 27, 1967. The project had cost $228,000. A commemorative plaque outside the building was unveiled by the chairman of the B.C. Centennial Committee, Deputy Provincial Secretary Laurie Wallace.

Epilogue

Nanaimo, the third-oldest city in B.C., continues to welcome newcomers from across Canada, the U.S., and around the world. The city's economy has diversified significantly since 1967. The forest industry still plays an important role, but technology companies, tourism, and arts and cultural industries have added to the economic mix. These support local businesses that serve local markets such as retail, construction, real estate, and professional services.

The forest industry has always been cyclical. In the 1970s there was a market slump; this, in addition to the modernization of the mills and various labour disputes, put a dent in the economic future of the industry. Employment in logging and scaling operations was reduced.

During the recession of the early 1980s, employment in the forest industry was reduced by 22 percent. Harmac maintained its economic presence. MB built the Island Phoenix sawmill to accommodate the Japanese market. Some smaller mills such as the two Doman Forest Products plants, CIPA Industries, and Coastland Wood Industries continued to operate.

Educational opportunities improved when Malaspina College first opened in 1969 with 680 students in the former hospital building before moving to its new location on 5th Street. Since then the college has received university-college status and has a population of 10,000 full- and part-time students and 1,400 employees, with satellite campuses in Duncan, Powell River, and in the Parksville/Qualicum area. The campus continues to grow, with increased facilities including a new library and new residences.

The province was booming in 1990, and Nanaimo was booming along with it. Newcomers drove the demand for new housing. People moved here to build homes for people moving here. Then, after a decade of growth, forestry and fishing recorded high unemployment. Nanaimo now had a high number of welfare and employment-insurance recipients. In the spring of 2001, however, a call centre located here, providing much-needed employment for young people. Five years ago there were 50 call-centre jobs in Nanaimo; now there are 1,200.

Two ferry terminals in Nanaimo—Departure Bay and Duke Point—now service the mainland. The sheltered harbour has always played an important role in the development of the city. Today the city hosts thousands of boaters, large and small. The Nanaimo Port Authority has invested millions of dollars into waterfront redevelopment, including the waterfront walkway, Swy-a-lana Lagoon park, the fishing dock, a visiting vessel pier, and a new comfort station.

There are two airports: the Nanaimo Airport, south of the city at Cassidy, with regular connections to Vancouver International Airport, and the Nanaimo Seaplane Terminal, operated by the Nanaimo Port Authority. Baxter Air and Harbour Air provide regular service to the mainland.

Currently, the city's biggest initiative is downtown revitalization. A strong downtown is important because it represents all that is good, or bad, about a city. The focus has been on creating more housing and developing the downtown as a centre for arts and culture, with the 800-seat Port Theatre that opened in 1998 as the major attraction. Plans are also underway for a conference centre and hotel complex in the downtown core.

As the city looks to the future, the old Hudson's Bay Company Bastion still stands on Front Street as a silent reminder of Nanaimo's humble past.

Appendix I

Honour Roll of Those Killed in Action, 1939–1945

Alexander, Jim
Allen, J.
Ball, Joseph Dixon
Bohoslowich, Peter W.
Butler, Gordon W.
Butler, John D.
Calverley, W.E.
Carlson, Earl
Clue, Ernest J.
Cooper, D.
Courtney, Fred
Cusson, Paul
Dick, Francis T.
Etherington, Douglas
Farrar, Douglas Gordon
Fiddick, Edwin
Forbes, R.E.
Fryers, Jack
Gates, J.R.
Graham, Wm.
Hacker, John
Hamilton, Alex
Hamilton, Edward
Hann, R.
Hardcastle, Charles M.
Johnston, Victor W.
Jones, Lewis S.
Kilner, Charles M.
Laskovitch, Arthur
Fines, Edgar
McLeod, Neal F.
McMillan, Richard L.
Menzies, James
Mercer, Hugh
Miller, A.M.
Muir, William G.
O'Dwyer, Gerry
Ovington, Roy E.
Patterson, Albert
Petrie, P.
Potter, J.R.
Potter, J.V.
Ramsay, Jack M.
Rothery, T.S.
Sawers, A.T.
Sawers, W.D.
Scott, S.
Smith, Arthur
Spivy, Clifford
Spowart, John R.
Stewart, Thomas M.
Thicke, C.F.
Thomson, J. Edgar
Thomson, Hugh H.M.
Venber, Nicholas
Vipond, George G.
Werts, Frank
West, Charles G.
Wilson, J.P.
Wilson, J.W.

Appendix II

Mayors and Councils Serving Nanaimo, 1920–1967

1920–Mayor Henry McKenzie. Council: T. Hodgson, J. Knight, J.M. McGuckie, Wm. Hart, J. Rowan, J. Barsby.

1921–Mayor Frederick A. Busby. Council: J.E. Planta, A.J. Randle, Wm. Hart, J.M. McGuckie, J. Rowan, J. Barsby.

1922–Mayor Frederick A. Busby. Council: A.J. Randle, A.G. Welch, J.M. McGuckie, J. Barsby, T. Smith, W. Burnip.

1923–Mayor Frederick A. Busby. Council: V.B. Harrison, A.J. Randle, J.M. McGuckie, R.K. Smart, R. McGarrigle, T. Smith.

1924–Mayor Frederick A. Busby. Council: A.J. Randle, D.J. Jenkins, T. Smith, M.A.E. Planta, E.G. Cavalsky, J. Barsby.

1925–Mayor Victor B. Harrison. Council: M.C. Ironside, M.A.E. Planta, D.J. Jenkins, J.K. Hickman, W.J. Ferguson, E.G. Cavalsky.

1926–Mayor Victor B. Harrison. Council: M.A.E. Planta, A.J. Randle, T. Barnard, J.K. Hickman, J. Dixon, W.J. Ferguson.

1927–Mayor Frederick A. Busby. Council: W. Hart, M.C. Ironside, J. Barsby, J. Renney, E.G. Cavalsky, T. Smith.

1928–Mayor Frederick A. Busby. Council: W. Hart, M.C. Ironside, J. Barsby, J. Renney, E.G. Cavalsky, T. Smith.

1929–Mayor Frederick A. Busby. Council: J. Dixon, T. Smith, J. Barsby, J. Renney, M.C. Ironside, W. Hart.

1930–Mayor George A.B. Hall. Council: J. Barsby, E.G. Cavalsky, P.R. Inkster, S. Drake, J. Dixon, J. Green.

1931–Mayor George A.B. Hall. Council: J. Dixon, S. Drake, J. Bennett, E.G. Cavalsky, P.R. Inkster, J. Barsby.

1932–Mayor John Barsby. Council: E.G. Cavalsky, P.R. Inkster, J. Kerr, S. Drake, J. Bennett, J. Dixon.

1933–Mayor John Barsby. Council: E.G. Cavalsky, P.R. Inkster, J. Dixon, J. Kerr, G. Muir, S. Drake.

1934–Mayor John Barsby. Council: E.G. Cavalsky, P.R. Inkster, J. Dixon, J. Kerr, G. Muir, S. Drake.

1935–Mayor John Barsby. Council: E.G. Cavalsky, J. Dixon, S. Drake, P. R. Inkster, J. Kerr, G. Muir.
1936–Mayor John Barsby. Council: J. Dixon, S. Drake, J.G. Hindmarch, P.R. Inkster, J. Kerr, G. Muir.
1937–Mayor John Barsby. Council: S. Drake, W.T. Grieves, J.G. Hindmarch, P.R. Inkster, J. Kerr, G. Muir.
1938–Mayor Victor B. Harrison. Council: S. Drake, W.T. Grieves, J.G. Hindmarch, J. Kerr, D.D. Knox, G. Muir.
1939–Mayor Victor B. Harrison. Council: S. Drake, W.T. Grieves, J.G. Hindmarch, J. Kerr, D.D. Knox, G. Muir.
1940–Mayor Victor B. Harrison. Council: W.T. Grieves, J.G. Hindmarch, J. Kerr, D.D. Knox, G. Muir, C.E. Salter.
1941–Mayor Victor B. Harrison. Council: G. Addison, W.T. Grieves, J.G. Hindmarch, J. Kerr, G. Muir, C.E. Salter.
1942–Mayor Victor B. Harrison. Council: G. Addison, D. Campbell, W.T. Grieves, J. Kerr, G. Muir, C.E. Salter.
1943–Mayor Victor B. Harrison. Council: G. Addison, D. Campbell, W.T. Grieves, J. Kerr, G. Muir, L. Ross.
1944–Mayor Victor B. Harrison. Council: G. Addison, D. Campbell, W.T. Grieves, J. Kerr, G. Muir, L. Ross.
1945–Mayor George Muir. Council: G. Addison, D. Campbell, J. Kerr, L. Ross, E.C. Westwood, C. Wharton.
1946–Mayor George Muir. Council: G. Addison, L. Ross, J. Thompson, E.C. Westwood, C. Wharton, R.T. Wilson.
1947–Mayor George Muir. Council: G. Addison, J.B. McMinn, J. Thompson, E.C. Westwood, C. Wharton, R.T. Wilson.
1948–Mayor George Muir. Council: G. Addison, J.B. McMinn, J. Thompson, E.C. Westwood, C. Wharton, R.T. Wilson.
1949–Mayor George Muir. Council: G. Addison, J.B. McMinn, J. Thompson, E.C. Westwood, C. Wharton, R.T. Wilson.
1950–Mayor Earle C. Westwood. Council: G. Addison, J.B. McMinn, P.J. Piper, J. Thompson, C. Wharton, R.T. Wilson.
1951–Mayor Earle C. Westwood. Council: G. Addison, E. Hall, P.J. Piper, J. Thompson, C. Wharton, R.T. Wilson.
1952–Mayor Earle C. Westwood. Council: G. Addison, E. Hall, P.J. Piper, J. Thompson, C. Wharton, R.T. Wilson.
1953–Mayor George Muir. Council: G. Addison, G. Bryce, R.E. Fawdry, E. Hall, P.J. Piper, J. Thompson.
1954–Mayor George Muir. Council: G. Bryce, D. H. Burns, R.E. Fawdry, E. Hall, G.L. Hall, W. McGregor.
1955–Mayor George Muir. Council: G. Bryce, D.H. Burns, R.E. Fawdry, G.L. Hall, W.C. McGregor, J.G. Williams.

1956–Mayor Earle C. Westwood. Council: G. Bryce, D.H. Burns, J.K. Cook, G.L. Hall, W. McGregor, J.G. Williams.
1957–Mayor Peter Maffeo. Council: E. Blackburn, G. Bryce, D.H. Burns, J.K. Cook, W. McGregor, P.J. Piper.
1958–Mayor Peter Maffeo. Council: E. Blackburn, G. Bryce, D.H. Burns, J.K. Cook, W. McGregor, P.J. Piper.
1959–Mayor Peter Maffeo. Council: G. Bryce, D.H. Burns, J.K. Cook, D.M. Greer, W. McGregor, J.G. Parker.
1960–Mayor Peter Maffeo. Council: G. Bryce, D.H. Burns, J.K. Cook, D.M. Greer, W. McGregor, J.G. Parker.
1961–Mayor Peter Maffeo. Council: G. Bryce, D.H. Burns, J.K. Cook, D.M. Greer, W. McGregor, J.G. Parker.
1962–Mayor Peter Maffeo. Council: G. Bryce, J.K. Cook, D.M. Greer, A.W. MacDonald, W. McGregor, J.G. Parker.
1963–Mayor Peter Maffeo. Council: G. Bryce, J.K. Cook, D.M. Greer, A.W. MacDonald, W. McGregor, J.G. Parker.
1964–Mayor Peter Maffeo. Council: E.E. Barsby, G. Bryce, J.K. Cook, D.M. Greer, A.W. MacDonald, J.G. Parker.
1965–Mayor Peter Maffeo. Council: E.E. Barsby, J.K. Cook, A.W. MacDonald, G. MacKay, Mrs. M. McDougall, J.G. Parker.
1966–Mayor Peter Maffeo. Council: E.E. Barsby, A.W. MacDonald, Mrs. M. McDougall, G. MacKay, P.G. McLoughlin, J.G. Parker.
1967–Mayor Peter Maffeo. Council: K.D. Alexander, E.E. Barsby, Mrs. F.M. McDougall, G.H.A. MacKay, P.G. McLoughlin, J.G. Parker.

Appendix III

Freedom of the City Recipients, 1920–1967

June 24, 1940	Charles E. Salter
April 1941	South Alberta Regiment
February 5, 1951	MLA George S. Pearson
September 10, 1951	Sir Denys Lowson, Lord Mayor of London
November 3, 1958	Mayor John Barsby
November 3, 1958	Mayor Victor B. Harrison
November 3, 1958	Mayor George Muir
November 3, 1958	Mayor/MLA Earle C. Westwood
June 27, 1960	Harold Hackwood, City Clerk
January 8, 1968	Mayor Peter Maffeo

Nanaimo Provincial Representatives, 1920–1967

1920	William Sloan (Liberal)
1928	George Sharratt Pearson (Liberal)
1952	Lorenzo (Larry) Giovando (PC)
1956	Earle Cathers Westwood (SC)
1963	David Daniel Stupich (NDP)

Nanaimo Federal Members, 1920–1967

1917	John McIntosh (Unionist)
1921	Charles Hebert Dickie (Conservative)
1935	James Samuel Taylor (Co-operative Commonwealth Federation)
1940	Alan Chambers (Liberal)
1945	George Pearkes (Progressive Conservative)
1952	Colin Cameron (CCF)
1958	Walter Franklyn Matthews (Progressive Conservative)
1962	Colin Cameron (NDP)
1968	Colin Cameron (NDP) (died in office a month after being re-elected)
1968	Tommy Douglas (NDP)

Appendix IV

Group photo at the Pacific Biological Station in 1929 on the occasion of the official opening of the residence building (page 46).

Front row (sitting) L–R: Mrs. Frederick A. Busby, wife of Mayor of Nanaimo; Mrs. J.L. McHugh, wife of senior fisheries engineer for B.C.; Mrs. W.A. Clemens, wife of station director; Mrs. John Dybhavn; Mrs. Dunnington, mother of Mrs. Berkeley; Mrs. Edith Berkeley, PBS volunteer.

Second row L–R: E.G.Taylor, supervisor of Fisheries, Nanaimo area; Mayor Frederick A. Busby, Nanaimo; Verna Z. Lucas, PBS volunteer; John L. McHugh, senior fisheries engineer for B.C.; Dr. W.A. Clemens, PBS director; Miss Turley; Alfreda Berkeley, PBS volunteer; J.Pease Babcock, commissioner of Fisheries for B.C.; Dr. D.B.Finn, director, fisheries experimental station (Pacific), Prince Rupert; John Dybhavn, member of Biological Board of Canada.

Third row L–R: Cyril Berkeley, PBS volunteer; Dr. John L. Hart, PBS assistant biologist; Miss J.F.L. Hart, PBS volunteer; Mrs. Walter E. Turley; unknown person; Evelyn Keighley, librarian; unknown person.

Fourth row L–R: Frank Palmer, assistant supervisor of Fisheries, Nanaimo area; Walter E. Turley (Turley Bros. built residence building); Jeff Planta, local resident; Mrs. Jeff Planta; Mr. J.J. Turley.

Back row L–R: Magistrate Beevor-Potts; Dave Stephenson, Departure Bay resident; G.H. Wailes, PBS volunteer; Dr. R.E. Foerster, PBS associate biologist; Walter Thompson, Nanaimo postmaster.

Appendix V

Mayor, council, and staff of 1933 (page 103)

Front row L–R: B. Benton, assistant fire chief; John Parkin, fire chief; M. Wardell and J. Anthony, drivers.
Second row L–R: Aldermen S. Drake, George Muir, Peter Inkster; Mayor John Barsby; aldermen E.G. Cavalsky, J. Kerr, J. Dixon.
Third Row L–R: T. James, treasurer; A. G. Welch, police commission; Mrs. H.M. Davidson; E.G. Forward, auditor; Miss Ina Allan; Dr. W. F. Drysdale, Medical Health officer; and magistrate Charles H. Beevor-Potts.
Back Row L–R: W. Shearer, sanitation inspector: R. Dunsmuir, staff; J. Shepherd, works superintendent; A.G.Graham, engineer; Harold Hackwood, clerk.

Endnotes

Abbreviations
NCA–Nanaimo Community Archives
NHS–Nanaimo Historical Society
NRGH–Nanaimo Regional General Hospital

Chapter 1

1. M. Bate, "The Coal Industry of Vancouver Island," p.16. NCA.
2. T. Reksten, *The Illustrated History of British Columbia*, p. 195.
3. *West Coast Advocate*, March 11, 1937.
4. R.G. Harvey, *The Coast Connection*, p. 211.
5. I.V. Williams, L.W.B. Lovick, and B. Gordon, *Service Above Self: 75 Years of Rotary Service to the Nanaimo Community*, p. 49.
6. *Nanaimo Free Press* (October 19, 1921).
7. *Nanaimo Free Press* (February 21, 1921).
8. *Nanaimo Free Press* (February 16, 1921).
9. Office of Corporate Administration fonds, "Police Report November 11, 1925." NCA.
10. Office of Corporate Administration fonds, Series 5: Reports, 1924–27, Folder 16. Letters dated February 15 and March 13, 1926.
11. Buildings file: Willard Service Station, Wallace Street. NCA.
12. Buildings file: Information from Arthur Holstead's daughter, Barbara Pratt. NCA.
13. NHS transcripts 1962–81, Tape No. 29. NCA.
14. *The Daily Colonist*, January 12, 1937.
15. Native Daughters of B.C. Post No. 2, Scrapbook No. 2, p. 40. NCA.
16. *Nanaimo Free Press*, February 15, 1921.
17. *Nanaimo Free Press*, February 16, 1921.
18. *Nanaimo Free Press*, September 28, 1921.
19. *Nanaimo Free Press*, February 19, 1921.
20. NCA Information file: Law enforcement—policing.
21. Office of Corporate Administration fonds, 1928–1932, Unemployment Relief Act Report. NCA.
22. City of Nanaimo Annual Financial Statements. Medical Health Officer report of 1919, 1925. NCA.
23. Ibid., 1922. NCA.
24. NCA Family file—Dr. W.F. Drysdale.
25. NCA Information file: Post Office, *Nanaimo Free Press*, October 1919.
26. Williams and Lovick and Gordon, *Service Above Self*, p. 49.

27. Nanaimo Lawn Bowling Club, personal interview.
28. J. Cass, "The History of Nanaimo's City Parks," 1967. NCA.
29. City of Nanaimo Annual Financial Statement 1920, Parks and Recreation. NCA.
30. Office of Corporate Administration fonds, Parks & Recreation Report, 1923. NCA.
31. L. Lovick, "History of the Rotary Club of Nanaimo No. 689, 1920–1980." NCA.
32. Nanaimo Golf Club, "A Brief History of the Nanaimo Golf Club."
33. Kenneth D. Alexander, "Historical Outline of the Nanaimo Golf Links Ltd, the Nanaimo Golf Club, the Vancouver Island Golf Club Ltd., and the Nanaimo Golf & Country Club."
34. *Nanaimo Free Press*, December 1, 1921.
35. Alexander, p. 1.

Chapter 2

1. City of Nanaimo Annual Financial Statement, Chief of Police report, 1921. NCA.
2. *Nanaimo Free Press*, March 2, 1920.
3. City of Nanaimo Annual Financial Statement. Chief of Police report, 1921. NCA.
4. Viola Johnson-Cull, *Chronicle of Ladysmith and District*, p. 331.
5. E. Newsome, *Pass the Bottle, Rum Tales of the West Coast*, pp. 77–78, 88–89.
6. Phil Jamieson, "History of B.C. Policing." Pamphlet file. NCA.
7. Jan Peterson, *Twin Cities: Alberni-Port Alberni*, p. 223.
8. Royal Canadian Mounted Police (Nanaimo) Collection. NCA.
9. Office of Corporate Administration fonds, Series 4: 1905–1948A, File 57. NCA.
10. Robert Beevor-Potts, personal interview, May 4, 2005.
11. NCA Family file—C.H. Beevor-Potts.
12. Robert Beevor-Potts, personal interview.
13. J. Garner, *Never a Time to Trust*, p. 199.
14. *Nanaimo Daily Free Press*, September 13, 1935.
15. Garner, *Never a Time to Trust*, p. 199.
16. Walter Cordery, "Club's Passion for Wildlife, Outdoors Started in 1905," *The Daily News* (May 6, 2005).
17. Joe Annau's recollection of hunting trip with Jack Murphy and meeting Frank Greenfield.
18. Retailing, Code 19. Article NFP dated 1949, "Ernie Johnson's Store is Magnet for Sportsmen." NCA.

Chapter 3

1. Arthur Leynard, "The Coal Mines of Nanaimo," p. 22.
2. Ministry of Mines Report 1938, G25.
3. "Town goes up for sale," *The Colonist* (March 26, 1936). See also Patricia M. Johnson, *Nanaimo.* Also T.W. Paterson, *Ghost Towns & Mining Camps of British Columbia* pp. 15–17.
4. WFC First Aid Association Minute Book. Clipping of eulogy given by William H. Moore. NCA.

5. St. John Ambulance Association, Nanaimo Branch, pamphlet file. NCA.
6. Ibid., p 8.
7. Minister of Mines Report, 1920, N295.
8. *Nanaimo Free Press*, October 17, 1921.
9. *Nanaimo Free Press*, February 21, 1921.
10. NHS fonds, Series 4: File 10, St. John Ambulance Association speech by Charles Wharton, p. 4.
11. NHS fonds, Charles Wharton, Oral History Interview, 84–7–11: Folder 73. NCA.
12. Lynne Bowen, *Boss Whistle*, p. 91.
13. Charles Wharton speech, p. 3. NCA.
14. Charles Wharton interview. NCA.
15. *Nanaimo Free Press*, June 12, 1937.

Chapter 4

1. *British Columbia: From the Earliest to the Present*, pp. 772–5.
2. British Columbia Fisheries Commission interim report, December 1905.
3. *Nanaimo Herald*, April 17, 1900.
4. *Nanaimo Free Press*, December 6, 1911.
5. *Vancouver Sun*, March 11, 1918.
6. E.B. Norcross, "1918–1928: The Decade of Social Legislation," pp. 13–16.
7. Norcross, p. 16.
8. Norcross. "First Lady of the Legislature."
9. John M. Elson, "Pen Sketches of Canadian Poets," Native Daughters of B.C. Post No. 2 fonds. Scrap Book 1, October 15, 1933, p. 9. NCA.
10. Audrey Alexandra Brown. *A Dryad in Nanaimo*, p. 1.
11. Ibid., p. 56.
12. NCA Family file—Audrey Brown.
13. Kenneth Johnstone, *The Aquatic Explorers*, p. 112.
14. Ibid., pp. 130–1.
15. Ibid., p. 153.
16. Ibid., p. 152.
17. Ibid., p. 229.

Chapter 5

1. NCA Family file—Dr. W. Nicholson.
2. *Nanaimo Free Press*, August 18, 1919.
3. *Nanaimo Free Press*, February 6, 1920.
4. Ibid., February 6, 1920.
5. NCA Family file—Dr. W. Nicholson.
6. Norcross ed., *Nanaimo Retrospective, The First Century*, pp. 49–53.
7. Office of Corporate Administration fonds, 1924–27, Folder 17. NCA.
8. Hotels–Malaspina Hotel. NCA.
9. Ibid.
10. Marie Leduc, "The Glory Days."
11. Ibid., August 1, 1927.
12. *Nanaimo Free Press*, July 21, 1927.
13. Plant, *Spies & Buys* (Centennial Edition, 1958).
14. Upper Island Musical Festival official program, April 1937. NCA.

15. *Spies & Buys* (December 1953), p. 3.
16. Ibid.
17. *Nanaimo Daily Free Press* (February 1, 1962).
18. NCA Information file: Hotels—Malaspina Hotel.
19. NRGH fonds, Board Minutes, October 17, 1924. NCA.
20. Pamela Mar, *The Light of Many Candles*, p. 20.
21. Nanaimo Regional Hospital Society fonds, "Nanaimo's New Hospital." NCA.
22. Mar, p. 22.
23. NRGH fonds, Minutes, July 9, 1925. NCA.
24. Office of Corporate Administration fonds, Series 4: Correspondence, 1905–1948A. Letter dated January 26, 1925. NCA.
25. Native Daughters of B.C. Post No. 2, Scrap Book No. 1. NCA.
26. NCA Family file—John Hilbert.
27. Mark Bate fonds, NCA.
28. *Nanaimo Free Press*, September 20, 1927.
29. Mark Bate fonds, NCA.
30. P. Nicholls, *From The Black Country to Nanaimo 1854*, Volume 2.
31. Office of Corporate Administration fonds, 1924–27, Folder 16, January 9, 1926. NCA.
32. NCA Family file—E. Hiram Gough.

Chapter 6

1. G. Duffell, *The History of Pauline Haarer School*. NCA.
2. *Nanaimo Daily Free Press*, April 15, 1946.
3. Ibid.
4. *Nanaimo Daily Free Press*, September 13, 1945.
5. Nanaimo Independent Preparatory School, Booklet, "Our Nanaimo: 1867–1967." NCA.
6. Duffell, NCA.
7. J. Lewis-Harrison, *The People of Gabriola*, p. 179.
8. NCA Family file—Pauline Haarer.
9. Duffell, p. 16.
10. *Nanaimo Daily Free Press*, Jubilee Edition, 1924. "Nanaimo has most excellent Business College."
11. Native Daughters of B.C. Post No. 2, Scrapbook 1937, p. 22. NCA.
12. *Nanaimo Daily Free Press*, March 15, 1962.
13. *Nanaimo Free Press*, Golden Jubilee Edition, 1874–1924, p. 27.
14. *Nanaimo Free Press*, Golden Jubilee Edition, 1874–1924, p. 18.
15. Ibid., p. 27.

Chapter 7

1. John P. Nickel, 125th Anniversary brochure, p. 9.
2. *Nanaimo Free Press*, July 21, 1930.
3. *Nanaimo Free Press*, July 19, 1930, p. 1.
4. Office of Corporate Administration fonds, 1928–1932, Folder 14, Report dated February 17, 1930, from Fire Warden's Committee. NCA.
5. Albert E. Hendy, p. 29. NCA.
6. Ibid.

7. R.E. Avery, "The Nanaimo Fire." NCA.
8. Ibid., pp. 85–6.
9. Office of Corporate Administration fonds, Series 5: 1937, Reports. NCA.
10. *The Daily Colonist*, January 12, 1937.
11. Albert Dunn, personal interview, May 5, 2005.
12. E.O.S. Scholefield, "British Columbia from the Earliest Times to the Present," p. 1093.
13. Nicholls, *From The Black Country to Nanaimo*, Volume 4.
14. *Nanaimo Daily Free Press*, August 24, 1935.
15. City of Nanaimo Annual Financial Statements 1920–1967. NCA.
16. Albert Dunn speech to NHS, January 10, 2002. All information in this section comes from this source unless otherwise stated.
17. R. MacIsaac, D. Clark, and C. Lillard, *The Devil of Decourcy Island: The Brother XII*, p. 19.
18. J. Oliphant, *Brother Twelve*, p. 170.
19. Ibid.
20. W.E. Barraclough, "Brother XII tale draws crowd." NCA.
21. NHS fonds, Series 2: Tape Recordings 14A & 14B. NCA.
22. Ibid.
23. Oliphant, *Brother Twelve*, p. 167.
24. MacIsaac, Clark, and Lillard, p. 58.
25. NHS fonds, Series 2: NCA.

Chapter 8

1. S.W. Jackman, *Portraits of the Premiers*, p. 196.
2. Jean Barman, *The West Beyond the West*, p. 358.
3. Electoral History of B.C. 1871–1986, Seventeenth General Election.
4. S.W. Jackman, p. 213.
5. George Bowering, *Bowering's B.C.: A Swashbuckling History*, p. 270.
6. Ibid., p. 270.
7. M. Helgeson, ed., *Footprints: Pioneer Families of the Metchosin District Southern Vancouver Island 1851–1900*, pp. 174–5.
8. H.J.M. Johnston, ed., *The Pacific Province: A History of British Columbia*, p. 259.
9. Jackman, p. 248.
10. T.H. McLeod and I. McLeod, *Tommy Douglas, The Road to Jerusalem*, pp. 233, 274, 277.
11. Charles Lillard and Lynn Welburn, *Discover Nanaimo*, pp. 108–9.

Chapter 9

1. Leynard, "The Coal Mines of Nanaimo," p. 22.
2. Bowen, p. 203. Citing Jack Ostle tape. Coal Tyee Society Interviews in Malaspina University College Library.
3. Office of Corporate Administration fonds, Reports 1928–1932, "Unemployment Relief." NCA.
4. Bowen, p. 203. Coal Tyee Society Interviews: William Crawshaw and Albert Tickle.
5. Leynard, pp. 8, 9.
6. Office of Corporate Administration fonds, 1928–1932, Folder 13. NCA.

7. Ibid., 1928–1932, Folder 17, 1930, Resolution dated December 1, 1930. NCA.
8. Ibid., Box 3, Series 5: Reports 1928–1932. NCA.
9. Pierre Berton, *The Great Depression, 1929–1939*, p. 135.
10. Ibid., p. 86.
11. Reksten, *The Illustrated History of British Columbia*, p. 298.
12. City of Nanaimo Engineering & Public Works fonds, A. Douglas Kerr, "South Fork Dam," March 19, 1932. Presentation to the Association of Professional Engineers of B.C. NCA.
13. Office of Corporate Administration fonds 1928–32, Reports, Folder 14. NCA.
14. Ibid., Folder 17. South Forks. NCA.
15. Ibid., Folder 13. Report dated November 24, 1930. NCA.
16. Norcross, ed., *Nanaimo Retrospective*, p. 134.
17. R. Mackie, "The Newcastle Island Resort Pavilion 1931–1941," paper prepared for the Heritage Conservation Branch, Victoria, B.C. April 1983, p. 11. NCA.
18. Office of Corporate Administration fonds, Series 6: 1925–52 B, Files 52–77, Files 4–6. Letter dated March 31, 1930, from city clerk to CPR C.D. Neroutsos, manager of B.C. Coast Service. NCA.
19. *Nanaimo Free Press,* May 1, 1931.
20. *Nanaimo Free Press,* June 20, 1931.
21. R. D. Turner, *Those Beautiful Coastal Liners*, p. 96.
22. *Vancouver Sun*, June 14, 1935, p. 24.
23. NCA Information file: Recreational activities, Clipping: *Nanaimo Daily Free Press*, Jubilee Edition, 1948.
24. Mackie, p. 85.
25. *Nanaimo Daily Free Press*, June 20, 1931.
26. *Nanaimo Daily Free Press*, February 16, 1934. "Beban to build export Lumber mill in Nanaimo."
27. NCA Family file—Frank & Hannah Beban.
28. Ibid., Letter to the editor from Kathleen Brown stating her father, James Green, built the house in the early 1930s.
29. Garner, *Never Chop Your Rope*, p. 157.
30. NCA Family file—Beban. Interview with Jean Addison and Dave Lindson, March 5, 1997.

Chapter 10

1. Norcross, ed., *Nanaimo Retrospective*, p. 127.
2. NCA Family file—Dr. G.A.B. Hall.
3. NCA Family file—D. L. Giovando. Gus Thomson, "Nanaimo Doctors: Saving Lives for Century," *Nanaimo Daily Free Press* [n.d.]
4. NHS transcripts 1962–81, Tape 31. NCA.
5. NCA Family file—Gertrude Hall.
6. NCA Family file—Dr. Oswald Grey Ingham.
7. Williams, Lovick, and Gordon, *Service Above Self*, p. 91.
8. Bowen, "Miner's son made it in medicine."
9. Native Daughters Scrapbook 1949, "Salk vaccine in B.C. a striking success," Sept. 30, 1955. NCA.

10. Office of Corporate Administration fonds, Series 4: Correspondence 1925–1952B, File 203. Letters dated January 28, 1933, November 29, 1939, December 6, 1940. NCA.
11. Johnston, ed., *The Pacific Province*, p. 301.

Chapter 11

1. Office of Corporate Administration fonds, Series 5: Reports, 1937, Folder 31. Report from Finance and Legislative Committees dated December 6, 1937. NCA.
2. Ibid., p. 2.
3. Corporate Administration fonds, Engineering Department 1992–005 C: Bastion Street Bridge. NCA.
4. *Nanaimo Free Press*, April 30, 1937.
5. *Nanaimo Free Press*, April 27, 1937.
6. Native Daughters Scrapbook 1937, p. 23. NCA.
7. *Nanaimo Free Press*, April 22, 1937.
8. *Nanaimo Free Press*, July 4, 1939.
9. Letter from finance committee dated December 7, 1937 recommends the purchase for $6,000. Office of Corporate Administration fonds, Series 5: Reports. NCA.
10. *Nanaimo Daily Free Press*, December 31, 1937.
11. Building file, 48 Arena Street. Article of May 17, 1990, "Gyro idea now landmark." NCA.
12. *Nanaimo Free Press*, May 15, 1940.
13. *The Daily Colonist*, Sunday, May 19, 1940.
14. Stu Keate "Nanaimo is Booming," "Sport shots."[Author's archives.]
15. Ibid.
16. Williams, Lovick and Gordon, *Service Above Self*, p. 56.
17. *Nanaimo Daily Free Press*, May 15, 1940.
18. Nanaimo Curling Club Scrapbook.
19. *Nanaimo Free Press*, January 9, 1875. Article: "Citizens filled time with curling."
20. Nanaimo Curling Club Scrapbook, Elmore Philpott's article dated February 12, 1952. Newspaper unknown.
21. Nanaimo Curling Club Ladies Scrapbook.

Chapter 12

1. Office of Corporate Administration fonds, Series 4: Correspondence, 1905–1948A, Files 45–66. Letter of November 1, 1938. NCA.
2. Office of Corporate Administration fonds, Series 4: 1925–52. Letter dated March 2, 1937. NCA.
3. Ibid., Series 5: Reports 1948–51. Council report of December 11, 1950.
4. Ibid., Files 28–51. Letter dated January 10, 1951 from Mayor E.C. Westwood to MP R.W. Mayhew. NCA.
5. Ibid., January 11, 1951, MP George R. Pearkes to Mayor Westwood.
6. Ibid., January 15, 1951, MP R.W. Mayhew to Mayor Westwood.
7. Ibid., February 22, 1951, MP George R. Pearkes to Mayor Westwood.
8. Ibid., April 3, 1951, Mayor Westwood to A.A. Anderson, Dept. of Public Works.

9. Office of Corporate Administration fonds, Series 4: 1925–52, Correspondence. Letter dated June 18, 1951, Pearkes to Mayor Westwood. NCA.
10. *Nanaimo Free Press*, May 6, 1942.
11. Office of Corporate Administration fonds, Series 4: 1905–1948A, Correspondence unfiled, Folder 13. Letter of May 13, 1942. NCA.
12. Ibid., File 49: Dominion Government. NCA.
13. Ibid., Correspondence re: Hirst Estate. NCA.
14. Water transportation–Ferries file. Undated article *Nanaimo Daily Free Press*, 1949, "A New Open Door." NCA.
15. Corporate Administration fonds, Series 6: 1925–52 B Files 52–77. File 4–6. Letter dated June 4, 1949. NCA.
16. Turner, *Those Beautiful Coastal Liners*, pp. 126–7.
17. Ibid., p. 27.
18. NCA Family file—Captain Bill Higgs. Article from *Nanaimo Daily Free Press*, 1948 Jubilee edition.
19. Lewis-Harrison, *The People of Gabriola*, p. 212.
20. Ibid., also NCA Information file: Transportation—Marine. "Nanaimo Towing Co. Facilities of Great Port Value."
21. B.P. Williams, "Gabriola Ferry *Eena*, 1955–64," *Shale* (March 2001), p. 15. All information about the *Eena* comes from this source. Used with permission.
22. Nanaimo Museum Research file: Water transportation—Ferries. NCA.
23. Lewis-Harrison, p. 217.

Chapter 13

1. R. Collishaw and R.V. Dodds, *Air Command, A Fighter Pilot's Story*, p. 236.
2. Ibid., p. 254.
3. NCA Family file—Raymond Collishaw.
4. Office of Corporate Administration fonds, Series 4: Correspondence, 1905–1948A File 6-5 Dominion Government. Letter dated June 15, 1938. NCA.
5. NCA Information file: Transportation—air.
6. G. Gibson and C. Renison. *Bull of the Woods, the Gordon Gibson Story*, p. 148.
7. Reginald H. Roy, *For Most Conspicuous Bravery*, p. 177.
8. Office of Corporate Administration fonds, Series 4: Correspondence, 1905–1948A File 45–66, Dominion Government. NCA.
9. Ibid., letter dated October 25, 1940. NCA.
10. *The Daily Colonist*, Victoria, October 2, 1940, "Troops occupy Nanaimo Camp."
11. *Nanaimo Free Press*, October 2, 1940. "Men on active service take up camp here."
12. Office of Corporate Administration fonds, Series 4: 1925–1952B, files 28–51. Dominion Government.
13. Pamphlet file, "A History of the Salvation Army in Nanaimo, 1888–1994." NCA.
14. Cordery. "Big bands were a big part of city's night life." *The Star* (July 28, 2004): A11.

15. Connie Filmer Scrapbook: Camp Nanaimo and the Second World War. NCA.
16. Ibid.
17. NCA Family file—Peter Maffeo.
18. Office of Corporate Administration fonds, Series 4: Correspondence, File 60, Air-Raid Precautions (A). Final report on civil defence Nanaimo and District by Pete Maffeo, controller of Civil Defence, Nanaimo and District. NCA.
19. *Nanaimo Free Press*, February 24, 1942.
20. Peter Maffeo's final report.
21. Garner, *Never a Time to Trust*, pp. 78–85.
22. *Nanaimo Free Press*, May 4, 1942.
23. Office of Corporate Administration fonds, Series 4: Sub-series 3, 1905–1948A, Files 89–102. NCA.
24. Ibid., Files 45–66. Letter of November 19, 1940 to K.W. Taylor, secretary of Wartime Prices and Trade Board. Rental control regulations applied not only to the city, but also the district. NCA.
25. Ian le Cheminant, "Our House," *Nanaimo Magazine* (May 1994).
26. Office of Corporate Administration fonds, Series 4: Files 1905–1948A. Files 45–66: Letter of April 9, 1941 to MP R.W. Mayhew, regarding serious housing situation. Letter also notes that housing is needed for shipbuilders. NCA.
27. Ibid., Files 45–66. Dominion Government file. Letter from Department of Pensions and National Health December 10, 1942. NCA.
28. Ibid., January 12, 1943. NCA.
29. Ibid., Sub-series 3. 1925–1952A File 49 Dominion Government. Letter of August 20, 1946. NCA.
30. G. Frith, "History of Hospitals in Nanaimo," an abridged edition. Nanaimo Regional Hospital Society fonds. NCA.
31. Office of Corporate Administration fonds, Series 4: Correspondence, 1905–1948A Files 45–66. Letter dated August 6, 1940 to Prime Minister Mackenzie King. NCA.
32. Duffell, "The History of Pauline Haarer School," p. 4.
33. Johnston, ed., *The Pacific Province*, pp. 321–22.
34. S. Allinson, "A Petticoat Army," *Times-Colonist* (April 8, 2001): D12.
35. *West Coast Advocate*, June 20, 1940.
36. *Nanaimo Daily Free Press*, July 21, 1944.
37. R. Malthouse, Long History of Shipbuilding," NCA Information file: Shipbuilding. NFP article.
38. Office of Corporate Administration fonds, Series 4: Correspondence, 1905–1948A. Dominion Government file. Letter re: shipbuilding dated April 9, 1941. NCA.
39. *Nanaimo Free Press*, May 25, 1944.
40. Office of Corporate Administration fonds, Series 4: Correspondence, 1905–1948A File 49 Dominion Government. Letter dated March 19, 1943, from Minister of National Defence for Naval Services to Mayor, NCA.
41. *Nanaimo Free Press* (January 7, 1942).
42. *Nanaimo Free Press* (July 21, 1944).
43. Cordery, "Nanaimo Remembers. Forrester Saved Lives of Five Fellow Sailors," *The Daily News* (March 4, 2005).

Chapter 14

1. Filmer collection, *Nanaimo Daily Free Press* (n.d.). NCA.
2. Filmer collection. "Jap Balloon now in city: 'Fangs' drawn," [n.d.] [n.p.] See also Catherine Smith, "When Japan bombed our Pacific Coast," *Islander* (March 17, 1985).
3. Catherine Lang, *O-Bon in Chimunesu*, p. 18.
4. *Nanaimo Free Press* (January 14, 1942).
5. Roy Ito. *We went to War.*
6. Office of Corporate Administration fonds, Series 5: Reports 1942–1947. Mayor's report of March 12, 1942. NCA.
7. Lang, p. 116.
8. *Nanaimo Free Press* (May 7, 1945).
9. *Nanaimo Free Press* (May 9, 1945).
10. *Nanaimo Free Press* (August 16, 1945).
11. *Nanaimo Free Press* (August 15, 1945).
12. *Nanaimo Free Press* (September 13, 1945).

Chapter 15

1. Office of Corporate Administration. Series 4: Correspondence, Sub-series 3. File 90, Camp Nanaimo. Letters of request to the War Assets Corporation. NCA.
2. Peterson, *Journeys*, pp. 261, 265.
3. NCA Information file: Indian Hospital. Article by Rex Malthouse, "Indian Hospital closing ends era, opens another," from Native Daughter's Scrapbook, p75.
4. Ibid., Nicholls research. Nanaimo Indian Hospital 1950–1957.
5. C. Brown, ed. *The Illustrated History of Canada*, pp. 460–2.
6. R.H. Roy, *For Most Conspicuous Bravery*, p, 235.
7. Canada Parliament, House of Commons, Debates (June 23, 1948), pp. 5761–62.
8. NCA Information file: Military Services, armed forces, army camp.
9. *Nanaimo Daily Free Press* (December 9, 1992).
10. T.S. Murty and P.B. Crean, "A Reconstruction of the Tsunami of June 1946 in the Strait of Georgia." [Author's archives.]
11. *Nanaimo Daily Free Press* (June 24, 1946 and June 25, 1946).
12. Families Code 22 Box 11 file 50. Dr. Wilfred Nicholson on Paul Robson visit. NCA.
13. *Nanaimo Daily Free Press* (February 14, 1947).
14. Office of Corporate Administration fonds, Series 4: Correspondence, Sub-series 3. 1925–1952 NCA.
15. G. Castle, "Hotel Built During Parksville's Heyday as Rail Centre."
16. NCA Information file: Communication Services—Broadcasting. *Nanaimo Daily Free Press*, December 10, 1958. "Radio CHUB in Nanaimo Goes to 10,000 Watts. See also *The Vancouver Sun*, May 25, 1949. "Nanaimo's Voice Heard on Radio."
17. *Nanaimo Daily Free Press* (August 19, 1948). See also the *Daily Colonist* (August 19, 1948).
18. NCA Information file—Parks.
19. *Nanaimo Free Press* (September 13, 1945).

20. Turner, *Those Beautiful Coastal Liners*, p. 130.
21. *Spies & Buys* (June 1953), p. 4.
22. Office of Corporate Administration, Series 4: Correspondence, Sub-series 3. File 49 Dominion Government. Letter dated September 14, 1950. NCA.
23. Ibid., letter of February 5, 1951.
24. NCA Information file: Air transportation. Article dated October 18, 1951 "Mt. Benson Crash Second Worst in Canadian History."
25. *Nanaimo Daily Free Press* (October 18, 1951). "Civil Defence Lends Air; 19 Bodies Down."
26. Peterson, *Twin Cities*, p. 304.
27. NCA Information file—Transportation.
28. NCA Information file—Air transportation.

Chapter 16

1. *Nanaimo Free Press* (May 15, 1940).
2. NCA Family file—Shelby Saunders. Obituary, *Nanaimo Free Press* (May 1, 1965).
3. Garner, *Never Chop Your Rope,* p. 124.
4. Johnson-Cull and Mawson, *Chronicle of Ladysmith and District*, p. 250. Information about Comox Logging comes from this source.
5. R.S. Mackie, *Island Timber*, p. 263.
6. Plant, ed., *Spies & Buys* (Centennial Edition). NCA.
7. NCA Family file—Sam Madill. Various newspaper articles have been used in this section: "Logging Machinery built in Nanaimo," [n.d.] also *Nanaimo Free Press Jubilee Edition*, "Sam Madill is Fine Example of Local Progress," also *Nanaimo Daily Free Press* (August 31, 1957), "Enterprise, Hard Work Built Engineering Firm."
8. Garner, *Never Chop Your Rope*, pp. 156–162.
9. *Harmac Division News* (June 7, 1985), "Harmac is 35 years Old This Month." Courtesy Joe Annau.
10. *Nanaimo Daily Free Press* (August 11, 1950).
11. Joe Annau personal interview, May 4, 2005.
12. Ken Drushka, *HR: A Biography of H.R. MacMillan*, p. 287.
13. *Nanaimo Daily Free Press* (July 6, 1950).
14. Annau interview.
15. *Harmac Division News* (June 7, 1985).
16. Nanaimo Museum Research collection, MacMillan-Bloedel: Harmac & Lumber Industry. NCA.
17. *Harmac Conveyor* Vol. 1, No. 9 (October 1976). Courtesy Joe Annau.
18. "Harmac Pulp Operations, Nanaimo," p. 4.
19. Ibid., p. 4.
20. Garner, *Never Chop Your Rope*, p. 84. The story of the whistle farm comes from this source.
21. Ibid., p. 91.
22. Nanaimo District Museum, Whistle Farm exhibit, 2005.

Chapter 17

1. NCA Information file: Boundaries—City Boundary Extensions.
2. Census of Canada, Ottawa: Statistics Canada.

3. Native Daughters Scrapbook, p. 156. Obit. (January 10, 1967). NCA.
4. Victor Harrison file. Code 11. Box 1 Civic File No. 4. NCA.
5. NCA Family file—Joseph Westwood (Earle C. Westwood).
6. NHS fonds, Sound Recordings: Tape 9. Transcript: Folder 56, Peter Maffeo. NCA.
7. NHS fonds, Tape 9. Peter Maffeo interview with William Barraclough, November 29, 1963. NCA.
8. NCA Family file—George Addison. Also George Addison fonds.
9. George Bryce fonds, NCA.
10. Helgeson, *Footprints*, p. 177. Also William McGregor obit. Died April 11, 1991.
11. Nicholls, Volume 5: The Malpass Descendants.

Chapter 18

1. Olive Annau (née Ormond), personal interview, May 5, 2005.
2. The social norms depicted in this section come from a variety of sources but mainly from Dorothy Plant's *Spies & Buys* magazine of 1951 and 1952.
3. W.A.C. Bennett, Kelowna Museum.
4. Bowering, p. 302; Jackman, p. 260.
5. *Electoral History of B.C. 1871–1986.*
6. "Mayor Westwood's Elevation to Cabinet Rank a Tribute Both to Himself and His Home City," *Nanaimo Daily Free Press* (September 29, 1956), p. 4.
7. Plant, *Spies & Buys* (1958 Centennial Edition).
8. Kelowna Museum brochure, "W.A.C. Bennett's Political Cartoons."
9. City of Nanaimo Corporate Administration Fonds. City Hall Scrapbook 1949–51. NCA.
10. City of Nanaimo, City Clerk's office. The "Arms" of Nanaimo. NCA.
11. City of Nanaimo Corporate Administration Fonds, City Hall Scrapbook 1949–51. NCA.
12. Office of Corporate Administration fonds, Series 4: 1925-52B. File 87. Royal Visit. NCA.
13. NCA Building file: Government Building, Block 56.
14. NCA Information file: Postal Services.
15. *Nanaimo Daily Free Press* (February 27, 1960), "Black Ball Sets New Standards of Service."
16. Plant, *Spies & Buys* Vol. 2, No. 6 (October 1952).
17. Plant, *Spies & Buys* (Centennial edition), "Blackball celebrates a century and a half."
18. *Nanaimo Daily Free Press* (February 27, 1960).
19. B.C. Ferries brochure, "Celebrating Forty Years of Bringing People Together, 1960–2000."
20. Ibid.
21. K. Muenter, "Twenty-Five Years Later."
22. C.P. Lyons, *Milestones on Vancouver Island*, p. 170.
23. The story has been told from a number of press accounts: *Times-Colonist* (May 4, 1958), *Nanaimo Daily Free Press* (May 3, 1958), *Times-Colonist* (May 6, 1958).
24. NCA Pamphlet file: Dodie Gogo, St. Peter's Church 1960–2000, quoting

The Torch (March, 1958). Information in this section is from this source unless otherwise stated.

25. *Nanaimo Daily Free Press* (July 21, 1958).
26. *Nanaimo Daily Free Press* (September 10, 1958).
27. Alexander, "Historical Outline of the Nanaimo Golf Links Ltd." Courtesy Nanaimo Golf Club.
28. Office of Corporate Administration fonds. Series 4: Correspondence, Camp Nanaimo. NCA.

Chapter 19

1. Litt, "The Razing of Chinatown."
2. *Nanaimo Daily Free Press* (October 1, 1960).
3. *Nanaimo Daily Free Press* (June 8, 1993).
4. *Nanaimo Daily Free Press* (October 1, 1960), "Chinatown Goes Up in Fire."
5. Savory, "Nanaimo's Chinese Community."
6. *Vancouver Sun Magazine Supplement* (January 29, 1955).
7. *Nanaimo Daily Free Press* (September 30, 1960).
8. D. Bellaart, "The final Rendezvous."
9. Nanaimo Independent Preparatory School brochure.
10. *Nanaimo Daily Free Press*, Jubilee Anniversary Edition 1948. "Parks Board has Accomplished Lot Within Two Years."
11. Office of Corporate Administration fonds, Reports, 1924–27, Folder 12. NCA.
12. Williams, Lovick, and Gordon, *Service Above Self*, pp. 57–9.
13. NCA Information file: Parks, Bowen Park.
14. *Nanaimo Daily Free Press* (December 10, 1963).
15. NCA Information file: Library. *The Key*, 1996 edition. VIRL 50th Anniversary.

Chapter 20

1. *Nanaimo Daily Free Press* (November 24, 1932).
2. NCA Building file: Chapel Street. No. 1 (25). NFP February 7, 1963, article, "Nanaimo getting first high-rise."
3. *Nanaimo Daily Free Press* (August 2, 1968).
4. D. Dash, *Chief Straight Tongue: The Story of Deane Finlayson*, p. 127.
5. NHS fonds, Series 1: folder 4. Notice of meeting.
6. NCA Information file: Organizations, NHS.
7. Barraclough, "A Brief History of the Centennial Museum."

Bibliography

Books, Articles, and Pamphlets

Alexander, Kenneth D. "Historical Outline of the Nanaimo Golf Links Ltd, the Nanaimo Golf Club, the Vancouver Island Golf Club Ltd., and the Nanaimo Golf & Country Club." [n.p.]

Allinson, Sidney. "A Petticoat Army." Victoria *Times Colonist (*April 8, 2001): D12.

Anon. "Harmac Pulp Operations Nanaimo." 50th Anniversary Publication. Pope & Talbot, 2000.

Armstrong, Ron. "Root Canal for Old Rip." Victoria *Times Colonist* (August 23, 1998).

Avery, R.E. "The Nanaimo Fire." *The Caduceus* 11, 3 (October 1930).

Barman, Jean. *The West Beyond the West: A History of British Columbia.* Toronto: University of Toronto Press, 1991.

Barraclough, William. "A Brief History of the Centennial Museum." Paper. [NCA.]

———. "Brother XII Tale Draws Crowd." Article. [NCA.]

Bate, Mark. "The Coal Industry of Vancouver Island." Brochure. [NCA.]

———. Speech after being presented with a fine oil painting. [Mark Bate fonds, NCA]

Bellaart, Darrell. "The Final Rendezvous." *Nanaimo New Bulletin (*March 13, 2000).

Berton, Pierre. *The Great Depression, 1929–1939.* Toronto: McClelland and Stewart, 1990.

Bowen, Lynne. *Boss Whistle: The Coal Miners of Vancouver Island Remember.* Nanaimo, B.C.: Rocky Point Books and Nanaimo and District Museum Society, 2002.

———. "Miner's Son Made It in Medicine." Victoria *Times Colonist* (June 27, 2004): C11.

Bowering, George. *Bowering's B.C.: A Swashbuckling History.* Toronto: Penguin Books Canada, 1996.

British Columbia Ferry Services. "Celebrating Forty Years of Bringing People Together, 1960–2000." Brochure.

Brown, Craig., ed. *The Illustrated History of Canada.* Toronto: Lester & Orpen Dennys, 1987.

Cass, John. "The History of Nanaimo's City Parks." Paper. (1967). [NCA.]

Castle, Geoffrey. "Hotel Built During Parksville's Heyday as Rail Centre." Victoria *Times Colonist* (January 25, 1992).

Census of Canada. Ottawa: Statistics Canada.

Collishaw, Raymond, and R.V. Dodds. *Air Command, A Fighter Pilot's Story.* London: William Kimler, 1973.
Cordery, Walter. "Big Bands Were a Big Part of City's Night Life." *Harbour City Star* [Nanaimo] (July 28, 2004).
———. "Nanaimo Remembers. Forrester Saved Lives of Five Fellow Sailors." *The Daily News* [Nanaimo] (March 4, 2005).
Dash, Donna. *Chief Straight Tongue: The Story of Deane Finlayson.* Nanaimo, B.C.: Donna Dash, 2004.
Drushka, Ken. *HR: A Biography of H.R. MacMillan.* Madeira Park, B.C.: Harbour Publishing, 1995.
Duffell, George, "The History of Pauline Haarer School." Paper. [NCA.].
Elsen, W.H. *Water over the Wheel.* Chemainus: Schutz Industries, 1981.
Frith, Gordon, "History of Hospitals in Nanaimo: an Abridged Edition." Paper. [NCA.].
Garner, Joe. *Never a Time to Trust: a Story of British Columbia, Her Pioneers, Predators and Problems.* Nanaimo, B.C.: Cinnabar Press, 1984.
———. *Never Chop Your Rope: a Story of British Columbia Logging and the People Who Logged.* Nanaimo, B.C.: Cinnabar Press, 1988.
Gibson, Gordon, and Carol Renison. *Bull of the Woods: the Gordon Gibson Story.* Vancouver: Douglas & McIntyre, 1980.
Gogo, Dodie. "St. Peter's Church 1960–2000." *The Torch* (March, 1958). [NCA.]
Goodwin, Doug. Religious Study paper, UBC, 1976. [NCA.]
Hannon, Leslie F. Canada at War: the Record of a Fighting People. *The Canadian Illustrated Library.* Toronto: McClelland and Stewart, 1967.
Harvey. R.G. *The Coast Connection.* Lantzville, B.C.: Oolichan Books, 1994.
Helgeson, Marion, ed. *Footprints: Pioneer Families of the Metchosin District Southern Vancouver Island 1851-1900.* Metchosin, B.C.: Metchosin School Museum Society, 1983.
Hendy, Albert E. A Brief History Since Its Foundation: St. Paul's Church 1859–1952. [NCA.].
Ito, Roy. *We went to War. The Story of the Japanese Canadians Who Served During the First and Second World Wars.* Stittsville, Ont.: Canada's Wings, 1984.
Jackman, S.W. *Portraits of the Premiers: An Informal History of British Columbia.* Sidney, B.C.: Gray's Publishing, 1969.
Jamieson, Phil. "History of B.C. Policing." Pamphlet. [NCA.]
Johnson, Patricia M. *Nanaimo.* Nanaimo, B.C.: City of Nanaimo, 1974.
Johnson-Cull, Viola, and E. Norcross. *Chronicle of Ladysmith and District.* Ladysmith, B.C.: Ladysmith New Horizons Historical Society, 1980.
Johnston, Hugh J.M., ed. *The Pacific Province: A History of British Columbia.* Vancouver: Douglas & McIntyre, 1996.
Johnstone, Kenneth. *The Aquatic Explorers: a History of the Fisheries Research Board of Canada.* Toronto: University of Toronto Press and Fisheries Board of Canada, 1977.
Kerr, A. Douglas. "South Fork Dam." [n.p.] (March 19, 1932). [NCA.]
Kimura, Kishizo. "The Natural Products Marketing Act Applied Upon Dry Herring and Dry Salmon Industries." [n.p.] [NCA.]
Lang, Catherine, *O-Bon in Chimunesu: A Community Remembered,* Vancouver: Arsenal Pulp Press, 1996.

Leduc, Marie. "The Glory Days." *Nanaimo Daily Free Press* (September 13, 1996).
Lewis-Harrison, June. *The People of Gabriola*. Cloverdale, B.C.: D.W. Friesen, 1982.
Leynard, Arthur. "The Coal Mines of Nanaimo." [n.p.] 1982. [NCA.]
Lillard, Charles and Lynn Welburn. *Discover Nanaimo.* Nanaimo, B.C.: Greater Nanaimo Chamber of Commerce, 1992.
Litt, Catherine. "The Razing of Chinatown." *Nanaimo News Bulletin* (September 28, 2000).
Lower, A.R.M. *Colony to Nation: A History of Canada*. Toronto: Longman's, 1946.
Lyons, C.P. *Milestones on Vancouver Island.* Vancouver: Evergreen Press, 1958.
Mar, Pamela. *The Light of Many Candles: One Hundred Years of Caring Service.* Nanaimo Auxiliary to NRGH, 2000.
McGirr, Flora. Paper. Junior Red Cross. {NCA]
MacIsaac, Ron and Don Clark, and Charles Lillard. *The Devil of Decourcy Island, The Brother XII.* Victoria: Press Porcepic, 1989.
MacKay, Donald. *Empire of Wood: The MacMillan Bloedel Story*. Vancouver: Douglas & McIntyre, 1982.
Mackie. Richard S. *Island Timber: A Social History of the Comox Logging Company Vancouver Island.* Victoria. Sono Nis Press, 2000.
Mackie, Richard. "The Newcastle Island Resort Pavilion 1931-1941." Victoria, B.C.: Heritage Conservation Branch, 1983. [NCA.]
McLeod, Thomas H. and Ian McLeod. *Tommy Douglas: The Road to Jerusalem.* Edmonton: Hurtig Publishers, 1987.
Muenter, Klaus. "Twenty-Five Years Later: Ferry Service Enjoys Tidalwave of Support." *Nanaimo Daily Free Press* (July 4, 1985).
Murty, T.S. and P.B. Cream. "A Reconstruction of the Tsunami of June 1946 in the Strait of Georgia." *Tsunami Workshop Abstracts*. Victoria: Institute of Ocean Science, 1985.
Nanaimo Community Heritage Commission. *Columns, Cornices, & Coal.* The City of Nanaimo, 1999.
Nanaimo Golf Club. "A Brief History of the Nanaimo Golf Club."
Nanaimo Independent Preparatory School Brochure. "Our Nanaimo 1867–1967." [NCA.]
Newsome, Eric. *Pass the Bottle: Rum Tales of the West Coast*. Victoria: Orca Book Publishers, 1995.
Nickel, John P. "St. Andrew's Presbyterian Church, 125th Anniversary Brochure," 1865–1990. [NCA.]
Nicholls, Peggy. *From The Black Country to Nanaimo 1854* 1 to 5. Nanaimo: Nanaimo Historical Society and Peggy Nicholls, 1991 to 1995.
Norcross, E. Blanche. "1918–1928: The Decade of Social Legislation." *British Columbia Historical News* (B.C.H.N) 17, 1: 13–16
———. "First Lady of the Legislature." *Times Colonist* [n.d.].
———, ed. *Nanaimo Retrospective: The First Century.* Nanaimo: Nanaimo Historical Society, 1979.
Norris, George. "Canadian Italians Build a Fountain."[NCA.]
Ohs, Darrell. "Years of Salt and Herring." Victoria *Times Colonist* (March 23, 2003): D11.

Oliphant, John. *Brother Twelve: The Incredible Story of Canada's False Prophet and His Doomed Cult of Gold, Sex, and Black Magic.* Toronto: McClelland and Stewart, 1991.

Ormsby, Margaret A. *British Columbia: A History*. Toronto: The Macmillan Company of Canada Limited, 1958.

Paterson, T.W. *Ghost Towns & Mining Camps of British Columbia.* Langley, B.C.: Stagecoach Publishing, 1979.

Peterson, Jan. *Journeys Down the Alberni Canal to Barkley Sound.* Lantzville, B.C.: Oolichan Books, 1999.

———. *Twin Cities: Alberni-Port Alberni*. Lantzville, B.C.: Oolichan Books, 1994.

Province of British Columbia. *Electoral History of British Columbia 1871–1986.* Victoria, B.C.: Legislative Library, 1988.

Reksten, Terry. *The Illustrated History of British Columbia*. Vancouver: Douglas & McIntyre, 2001.

Rose, Rollie. "History of the Airport Goes Back to 1942 and the Second World War." *Nanaimo Skies* [n.d.].

Roy, Reginald H. *For Most Conspicuous Bravery, A Biography of Major-General George R. Pearkes, VC through Two World Wars.* Vancouver: University of B.C., 1977.

Savory, Kathleen, M. "Nanaimo's Chinese Community."[NCA.]

Salvation Army in Nanaimo. "A History 1888–1994." [NCA.]

Scholefield, E.O.S. "British Columbia—From the Earliest Times to the Present." *Biographical* Vol III. Vancouver. The S.V. Clarke Publishing Company, 1914.

Smith, Catherine. "When Japan Bombed Our Pacific Coast." *Times Colonist* (March 17, 1985).

Thomson, Gus. "Nanaimo Doctors: Saving Lives for Century." *Nanaimo Daily Free Press* [n.d.] [NCA.]

Turner, Robert D. *Those Beautiful Coastal Liners*. Victoria: Sono Nis Press, 2001.

White, Howard, ed. *Raincoast Chronicles Five*. Madeira Park, B.C.: Harbour Publishing, 1976.

Williams, B. Parker. "Gabriola Ferry *Eena* 1955-64." *Shale* (March 2001).

Williams, Ian V. and Len W.B. Lovick and Bruce Gordon. *Service Above Self: 75 Years of Rotary Service to the Nanaimo Community*. Nanaimo Rotary Club: 1943.

Newspapers, Periodicals, and Magazines

British Columbia Historical News, Cranbrook, B.C.

Harmac Conveyor, Nanaimo, B.C.

Harmac Division News, Nanaimo, B.C.

Harmac News, Nanaimo, B.C.

Harbour City Star, Nanaimo, B.C.

Nanaimo Daily Free Press

Nanaimo Free Press

Nanaimo Herald

Nanaimo Magazine

Nanaimo News Bulletin
Nanaimo Skies
Nanaimo Times
Port Alberni News
Shale, Gabriola Island Historical and Museum Society, Gabriola B.C.
Spies & Buys, Nanaimo, B.C.
The Caduceus, Canadian Bank of Commerce newsletter, Toronto, Ont.
The Christian Guardian
The Colonist, Victoria, B.C.
The Daily Colonist, Victoria, B.C.
The Daily News, Nanaimo, B.C.
The Province, Vancouver, B.C.
The Star, Nanaimo, B.C.
Vancouver Sun
Times Colonist, Victoria, B.C.
West Coast Advocate, Port Alberni, B.C.

Audiotapes, Letters, Interviews, Minute Books, Journals, Notes, and Research

Addison, Jean. Interview with Dave Lindson. March 5, 1997. [NCA.]
Annau, Joe. Personal interview. May 2005.
Olive Annau (née Ormand). Personal interview. May 5, 2005.
Beevor-Potts, Robert. Personal interview. May 4, 2005.
Barraclough, William. Interview with Peter Maffeo. November 29, 1963. [NCA.]
Coal Tyee Society. Interviews in Malaspina University College Library.
Dunn, Albert. Personal interview. May 5, 2005.
Isaacson, S.V. Research data on Canadian Collieries. [NCA.]
Kelowna Museum Brochure: "W.A.C. Bennett's Political Cartoons."
Kelowna Museum. W.A.C. Bennett holdings.
Nanaimo City Hall. Scrapbook 1949–51. [NCA.]
Nanaimo Curling Club. Scrapbook.
Nanaimo Historical Society. Tape Recordings. Series 2. [NCA.]
Nanaimo Historical Society. Transcripts 1962–81. Tape No. 29. [NCA.]
Nanaimo District Museum. "Water transportation—Ferries." [NCA.]
———. "The Whistle Farm: The Bob Swanson Story."
Nanaimo Regional General Hospital. Minutes. [NCA.]
Native Daughters of B.C. Post No. 2. Scrapbooks. [NCA.]
Native Sons of B.C. Minute Book 1915–1964. [NCA.]
Nicholls, Peggy. "Nanaimo Indian Hospital 1950–1957." [NCA.]
Western Fuel Company First Aid Association Minute Book. [NCA.]
Wharton, Charles. Oral History Interview, 84-7-11 [NCA.]

Government Records

British Columbia Fisheries Commission, Interim report, December 1905.
Canada Parliament. House of Commons Debates. June 23, 1948.
All City of Nanaimo files are located in Nanaimo Community Archives [NCA].
Building file, Chapel Street. No. 1 (25)
City of Nanaimo Annual Financial Statements 1920–1967.
Office of Corporate Administration fonds. Series 4. 1905–1948.
Office of Corporate Administration fonds. Reports 1924–1927.
Office of Corporate Administration fonds. 1928–1932.
Office of Corporate Administration fonds. Series 4, 1925–1952.
Office of Corporate Administration fonds. Series 5. 1942–1947.
Office of Corporate Administration fonds. Series 5, 1948–1951.
City of Nanaimo Corporate Administration Fonds. City Hall Scrapbook 1949–1951.
City of Nanaimo Engineering & Public Works fonds.
City Clerk's Office Correspondence 1905–1948.
Chief of Police Report of 1921.
Medical Health Officer Report of 1919, 1922, 1925.
Ministry of Mines Reports 1913–1940.

Index

Addison, George, 104, 168
airports: Nanaimo (Cassidy), 12, 119-21, 131, 137, 140, 150-52, 154, 163, 205; Raymond Collishaw Terminal, 119; air services, 150-52, 154, 163; Seaplane Terminal, 205
Annau, Joe, 157-59
Anthony, Jim, 71-72, 212
Athletic Club, 19, 47
automobiles, 12-13, 102

banks: Canadian Bank of Commerce, 69-71: Bank of Montreal, 75, 199; Royal Bank of Canada, 27, 84
Barley, Alfred, 77-78
Barraclough: William, Ethel (wife), Edward (son), 78, 167, 201-2
Barsby, John, 57, 60, 103-4, 164-66
Bastion, 15, 94, 202, 205
Bastion Street Bridge, 103, 120, 145, 177
Bate, Mark, Sarah (first wife), Hannah (second wife, née Harrison), 55, 57-58
BC Ferry Corporation, 180
Beban: Frank, Hannah (wife, née Hodgson), 94-96, 154, 194; Jack (son), 95, 150, 184
Beban Mine, 36, 87
Beevor-Potts, Charles Hebert, Lionel (son), 25, 75-76, 211-12
Bennett, W.A.C., 82, 84, 88, 172-74, 179-80
Berkeley, Cyril J., Edith (wife), 45-47, 211
Bird, E.H., 21, 52
Black Ball Line Ferries, 114, 178-80
Boat Harbour, 32, 74
Booth, Ernest Banks, 177
Bowen, George, James (brothers), 20
Bowen Park, 109, 169, 194-96
Boy Scouts, Nanaimo St. George's Troop, 64
Bradshaw, Elmer, 129-30, 187
Brechin School, 59-60, 96, 126, 163, 198
Brother XII, Aquarian Foundation, 25, 74-78, 165
Brown, Audrey Alexandra, 41-43
Browne, Dr. Carman, 36, 97, 99-100
Brown, Dr. George B., 21, 54
Bryce, George, 167-69, 178, 208-9
Busby, Frederick A., 52, 55, 57-58, 104, 164, 207, 211
Burns, Haig, 167, 178, 208-9
Burns, Robert, Jean (wife), 170, 186
Butcher, Walter family, 183-84

Cameron, Colin, 83-84, 210
Cameron, Dr. Maxwell, report, 59-60
Camp Nanaimo, 60, 107-8, 122, 132, 136, 177, 189; Diefenbunker, 141, 144; hospital, 123; Tent City, 123; sale of buildings, 141, 187
Canadian Collieries, 9, 21, 29, 32, 84, 122, 138, 148-49, 155, 168, 195
Canadian Pacific: Railway (CPR), 17, 49, 90; Navigation Company, 168; Steamship Service, 110, 114, 178
Canadian Red Cross, 126, 128, 140, 166-67, 189
Carter, Norman, 18, 61

Cassidy, 9, 30, 120, 155
Cassidy Airport. *See* airports
Cavalsky: Edward George, Laura (wife), 51, 57, 91, 168, 207-8, 212
Cedar, 9, 32, 59-60, 68, 125, 148, 163, 188
Cedar-by-the-Sea, 74
Central Sports Ground, 20, 30, 96, 193
Chambers, Alan, 82, 142, 210
Chase River, 14, 34, 59-60, 127, 163
Chemainus, 111; evacuation of Japanese from, 134-35, 154, 161
Chinatown fire, 189-92
Chinese, 22-23, 31, 64, 73, 92, 95, 154, 161
CHUB radio, 147-48, 170
churches: Anglican, 68-70, 105, 177; Congregational, 66; Methodist, 17, 57, 64; St. Andrew's Presbyterian, 19, 64; St. Andrew's United Church, 116, 136, 164, 168; St. Peter's Roman Catholic Church, 51, 83, 116, 178, 185-86; Church Union 66-68
Civic Arena, 105-6, 120, 129, 136, 142, 156, 166, 175, 194
civil defence: 125-26, 143-44, 151, 167, 179, 189, 191; Air Raid Precautions (ARP), 125-26, 136; homing pigeons, 126; sirens, 126, 129, 136-37
Clemens, Dr. and Mrs. Wilbert Amie, 42, 44-45, 211
Coburn, John W. 21, 52, 55, 153-54
Collishaw, Raymond, 118-19
Comox Logging Company, 30, 120-21, 154-55, 186
Co-operative Commonwealth Federation (CCF), 79-84, 142-43, 173
Conservative Party, 38, 79, 81, 142-43, 165, 172-73, 200
Corfield, Captain M.A., 115
Corfield, Norman T., 52
Cumberland, 34, 73, 94, 97
Cunliffe, Don, 113, 186
Cunliffe, Frank, 52, 75, 77, 142

Department of Indian Affairs Hospital, 141
Departure Bay: 17, 38, 42, 45, 59, 65, 100, 163, 171-72, 181, 200, 211; Ferry Terminal, 114, 178-80, 198, 205
Depression, the Great: 9, 21, 27, 30, 32, 34, 36, 45, 49, 59, 62, 70, 73, 77, 81-82, 90-94; effect on city, 102-3, 164; effect on coal industry, 86-88, make-work projects, 80, 88-89, 103; stock-market crash, 77, 86; unemployment, 18, 80, 87-89, 94, 102-3, 105, 164, 204; work camps, 88
Dewar, Jim, 27-28, 126
Dickie, Charles Hebert, Eliza (wife), 82, 210
Dixon, Joseph, 91, 168, 207-8, 212
Douglas, Tommy, 83, 174, 210
Drake: Samuel, Ethel (wife), 91, 102-3, 169, 207-8, 212
Drysdale, Dr. W.F., 18-19, 36, 89, 97, 212
Dunn, Albert, 71-73, 188
Dunsmore, Andrew, 17-18, 104, 164
Dunsmuir: Robert, James, Alex, 39, 94

earthquake (1946), 144-45
East Wellington, 161, 163
Eby, Oliver, 21, 52
Esquimalt & Nanaimo Railway, 11, 27, 49, 87, 91, 161
Extension, 9, 30, 36, 60, 94, 154

Filmer, Connie, 124-25
Finlayson, Deane, Joan (wife), 200
First World War: 12, 21, 29, 63-64, 128; veterans, 22, 26, 58, 98, 114, 118, 121, 125, 137, 153, 166
Fletcher, George A., 12; G.A. Fletcher Music Co. Ltd., 16, 74-75, 104, 108, 171
Foerster, Dr. Russell Earle, 44, 48, 146, 211
forestry: 9, 82, 88, 94, 110, 153, 191, 204; logging, 95, 110, 134, 153-57; sawmills, 95, 110, 129, 157
Franklyn Street Gymnasium, 20, 105, 166

Gabriola Island, 9, 53, 60-61, 64, 94, 154, 163, 174
Gabriola Island Ferry Company, 114-17
Gibney, Ed., 171
Gibson, Gordon, 120-21
Giovando, Dr. Larry, 36, 84, 95, 97-98, 108, 173, 178, 210
Gogo: Ken, Dodie (wife), John Gerard (son), 185-86
Gough, Samuel, Hiram (son), 58
Granby: Consolidated Mining, Smelting and Power Company, 30, 97, 168; village, 17, 30
Greenfield, Frank, Min (wife), 26-28, 126, 151
Gyro Club: 12, 20, 26, 99, 105, 166, 193; playground, 65; Victory Day celebration, 138

Haarer, Pauline, 60-62
Hackwood, Harold, 58, 112, 210, 212
Hall: Dr. George A.B., Alan and Earl (sons); 34, 36, 55-56, 87-88, 91, 97-98, 164, 207
Hall Clinic, 97-98, 164
Hall, Gertrude ("Happy," wife of Alan), 98-99
Hanna, Frank A., 52, 152
Harewood, 34, 59-60, 68, 84, 126, 163, 188-89, 191, 198
Harmac Pulp Mill: 9, 112, 160, 163, 186, 191, 204; opening, 157; expansion, 158; mill managers, 159
Harrison: Eli, Eunice (wife), 63; Victor Birch (son): law firm, 57, 75-79, 165; mayor, 105, 120, 122, 129, 130, 164, 166, 207-8, 210
Hawthornthwaite, James Hurst, 22, 38, 57
Hertel, Paul, 182-84
Hertel Zoo. *See* Nanaimo Zoo
Higgs, William (Bill), 114-15, 180
Hilbert, John, 55, 57
Hindmarch, J.G., 102-4, 208
Hodgson, Thomas, 57-58, 207
Hogle, Dr. J.H., 12, 35, 63, 99
Holstead, Arthur ("Sparks"), Robina (wife), 14-15
Horne: Adam Grant, 19; Adam H. (son), 19, 177
hotels, 13, 21, 32, 72, 75, 91, 134, 155, 168, 184. *See also* Malaspina Hotel
H.R. MacMillan Export Company, 159
Hudson's Bay Company (HBC), 9, 201
Hunt, John, 20, 64

Imperial Order Daughters of the Empire (IODE), 49-51
Ingham, Dr. Oswald Grey, 33-35, 97, 99
Inkster, Peter R., 91, 102-3, 154, 161, 207-8, 212
Ironside, M. Charles, 57, 91, 94, 207
IXL Stables/Garage and Storage, 69, 74

Japanese: 82, 90, 121, 132-33, 135, 137, 154, 204; internment of, 133; confiscation of fishing boats, 134
Johnson, Ernie, 28
Johnson, Patricia, 201-2

Kerr, John, 168, 207-8, 212
Kinsmen Club, 105, 137, 196
Kiwanis Club, 12, 105, 168, 202

Ladysmith, 9, 17, 24, 30, 34, 52, 56, 64, 84, 97, 111, 115, 129, 134, 142, 150, 155, 157, 165, 171, 173, 175, 186, 188
Lantz, Frank H., 31
Lantzville: 9, 17, 31-32, 59-60, 157; colliery, 31; Hotel, 32
Leighton: Arthur, Alice (wife), 21, 100
Lewis, William, 195, 202
Leynard, Arthur, 174, 193, 202
Liberal Party, Liberal-Conservative Coalition, 38-41, 79, 80-82, 142-43, 172-73, 186
Lister, Rev. David, 66-68

MacMillan, H. R., 157-58, 191
Madill, Sam, Norman and Charles (sons), S. Madill Limited, 95, 151, 156
Maffeo: Peter, Vera (wife), 20, 105, 147, 166-68, 203, 209-10; Davenport Ice and Ice Cream Plant, 52; mayor, 99, 117, 148, 164, 167, 185, 191, 196, 199; civil defence, 125-26, 138
Malaspina Community College/ University, 204
Malaspina Hotel, 43, 51-54, 106-7, 147, 166-67, 170, 177
Manson, Doug, 15, 35
Manson, Dr. A.E., 36, 97
Manson, William, 57-58
Matthews, Walter Franklyn, 83, 210
Mayo Lumber Company, 155-56
McArthur, Colin, 72, 188-89
McGregor: Jack C., Catherine (wife), 69, 94, 181, 201; William (Bill) Charles (son) and Angelina (wife, née Clovis), 167, 169, 178, 196, 208-9
McKelvie, Bruce A., 75-76, 140, 201
McKenzie, Henry, 50, 207
McLellan, Alex and Robert Jr. (brothers) 83
McLellan, Donald, 104
McPhee, Dr. T.J., 36, 52, 56, 99
medical epidemics: 19-20, 34, 50, 54; tuberculosis, 95, 100-1, 141; poliomyelitis, 100-1
mining industry: 29-33, 110, 119, 138, 149-50, 180; Big Strike (1912-14), 20, 36; coal production, 29
Mrs. McCree's Nursing Home, 98, 104
Mount Benson: 9, 98
Muir, George, 113, 136, 147, 164-66, 174, 178, 207-8, 210, 212
Murray, J.W., 66-67
music: jazz, 13, 15-17; bands, 17, 171; choirs, 17, 19, 99, 137, 164; Doug Manson's Orchestra, 15, 35; Jensen's Orchestra, 17, 35; Louis Armstrong, 128; Paul Robeson, 146-47, 167; Pimlott's Orchestra, 17, 93, 106, 137; Stu Storrie's Band, 124. *See also* Silver Cornet Band

Nanaimo Board of Trade, 52, 91, 116, 150
Nanaimo Chamber of Commerce, 113, 125, 154, 166, 179, 202
Nanaimo: amalgamation, 163; population, 9, 22, 54, 163-64, 197; Colliery Dams, 18; Harmac supply, 157, 159; South Fork Dam, 88-90; garbage, 18-19; new city hall, 174-76; coat-of arms, 174; water chlorination, 127; water services, 18, 58, 89-90, 102, 143, 165
Nanaimo Clippers, 106-7, 148
Nanaimo Commonwealth Holding Society (NCHS), 83-85
Nanaimo Curling Club, 108-9, 195
Nanaimo District Museum/Centennial Museum, 168, 193, 201-3
Nanaimo Fire Department: 57-58, 63, 68-69, 89, 125; amalgamation, 163; chiefs, 69, 71-74, 212; fires: (1930), 69-70; (1937), 71, 154, 187; Chinatown, 188-89
Nanaimo Fish and Game Club, 27, 165, 184
Nanaimo Golf Club, 141, 186-87
Nanaimo Harbour Commission/Port Authority: 113, 205; Hirst Wharf, 112; National Assembly Wharf, 110-12
Nanaimo Historical Society, 196, 201-2
Nanaimo Hospital: Franklyn Street, 34, 39, 49, 63, 71, 79, 98, 127, 180; building new hospital, 54-57, 164, 204; Regional Hospital, 192-93, insurance 82, 101
Nanaimo Lawn Bowling Club, 20
Nanaimo Public Library, 20, 49-51; Vancouver Island Regional Library, 196
Nanaimo School Board, 58, 104-5, 141, 151
Nanaimo Yacht Club, 20, 94, 100, 154, 166
Nanaimo Zoo (Hertel zoo), 182-84

Nanoose, 9, 31, 154, 161, 185
Native Sons of B.C. Post No. 3, 51, 58, 166
New Democratic Party (NDP), 83, 85, 199, 210. *See also* Co-operative Commonwealth Federation
Newcastle Island, 9, 27, 94, 137, 164, 177
Newcastle Island Pleasure Resort, 90-93
Newcastle Shipbuilding Co. Ltd., 129-31
New Ladysmith Lumber Company, 21, 52, 153-54
Ney, Frank, 85, 199-201
Northfield, 17, 31, 94, 163, 169, 188
North Wellington, 57, 184-85

Ormond, Robert H., 21, 52, 170

Pacific Biological Station, 38, 42, 44-48, 184, 211
Parker, John G., 168, 181, 202, 209
Parkin, John, 69, 71-73, 212
Parks and Recreation: Board, 19-20; Commission, 169, 193, 196
parks: Beban, 96; Bowen, 20, 109, 169, 194-96; Exhibition, 194; Grandview Bowl, 194; Westwood Lake, 194; Georgia, 194; Haliburton Street Gyro Park, 10, 65; Georgia, 194; Millstream, 20; Piper, 193, 201, 203; Robins, 35, 109, 194; Westwood Lake, 194
Parksville, 18, 34, 65, 147-48, 163, 198, 204
Pearkes, George R.: Lieutenant-Governor, 144, war service, 122; Pacific Command, 121-22, 125, 132; politics, 82, 111-12, 142-44, 147, 150, 210
Pearson, George S., Emeline (wife), 18, 21, 55, 73, 210; MLA, 62, 79, 80-81, 84, 147-48, 173; business (Malcolm-Pearson), 80; bridge, 178
Petroglyph Provincial Park, 148-49
Piper, Philip J., 194, 167, 177, 181, 202, 208-9
plane crashes: Mount Benson (1951), 151; Mount Whymper (1944), 126
Planta, Albert E., 57-58, 65, 207
police: 13, 16-17, 22-23, 25, 58, 75, 134-35, 185; magistrates, 25; Provincial Police, 25, 134; RCMP, 24-25, 134
Port Alberni, 12, 18, 28, 47, 109, 134-35, 145-47, 162, 170-71, 173, 175, 183
post office: 13, 64, 127; letter carriers, 19, 178; new post office, 176-78; postmasters, 19, 177-78, 211; Big Frank, 11, 185
Protection Island: 9, 11, 116, 163; Victory blaze, 138; purchase, 200
Pygmy Pavilion, 92-93, 124, 129, 137, 153, 177

Qualicum, 18, 35, 134, 163, 173, 204
Queen Charlotte Airline, 150-51

radio, 12-14, 104, 115, 152. *See also* CHUB
Randle, Joseph, 51, 207
ravine, the, 16, 18-19, 103
Regional District of Nanaimo, 99, 163
Ricker, Dr. William (Bill) Edwin, 46, 48
Rotary Club of Nanaimo No. 589, 12, 17-18, 20-21, 100, 108, 165-66, 179, 194-95
Royal Canadian Legion, 26, 104, 154

Salvation Army, 123-24, 137, 151, 189
Saunders, Shelby M., 92, 126, 153, 177
School District No. 68, 59-62
schools, 19, 20, 59-60, 62
Second World War: 21, 36, 54, 59, 84, 93, 100, 118, 120-35, 152, 156, 165, 176, 191; civil defence, 125-27; shortages, 93, 127; V-E Day, 136; V-J Day, 137; women in the workforce, 128; war brides, 140; *See also* Camp Nanaimo

Sedola, Gino, 181, 202
Shaw, John, 55, 57-58; school, 20, 59-60, 104
Shirras, John, 13, 22-23, 135
ships: *Charmer*, 24, 91-92; HMCS *Nanaimo*, 130; SS *Quadra*, 24; *Princess*: *Adelaide*, 135: *Elaine*, 91-92, 104, 114, 180; *Elizabeth*, 92, 114; *Joan*, 91-92, 114, 122; *Marguerite*, 114, 180; *of Nanaimo*, 114, 180; *Victoria*, 92
shopping centres, 75, 198-99
Silver Cornet Band, 55, 57-58, 136-38; Nanaimo Concert Band, 171, 175
Sloan: William, Flora McGregor (first wife), Catherine McDougall (second wife), 34, 37-38, 44, 55-58, 65, 79-80, 120; Gordon, (son), Nancy Porter Nicol (wife of Gordon), 81, 153
Smith, Mary Ellen, Ralph (husband), 38-39; maiden speech as MLA, 39; social reforms, 40-41
Snuneymuxw, 20-21, 73, 149, 155, 185
Social Credit Party, 85, 173, 179, 199
South Wellington, 33, 60-61, 84, 97, 169
Spencer's Department Store, 75, 108, 137, 197
Sprott-Shaw Business College, 62
St. Ann's Convent, 42-43, 62-63, 191
St. George's On-The-Hill Boys' School, 62-64, 126
St. John Ambulance Association, 33-34, 36, 83, 99-100, 125, 191
Stupich, David, 83-85, 117, 173, 199, 210
Swanson, Bob, 160-62

Taylor, James Samuel, 82, 210
Taylor, Reverend George, 38, 44-45, 48
theatres: Bijou/Strand, 70, 73-74; Capitol, 70, 95, 104, 129, 171; Cassidy and Starlite drive-ins, 171; Port, 205
Thomas, Larry, 147-48
Thompson: John, Sr., 113, 154; Noel and John Jr., 154, 208; Thompson Lumber Co. Ltd. 113, 154
Thompson, Walter, 12, 177, 211
Tully, Dr. John Patrick, 47-48
Turley Brothers, 70, 105; Walter E., 211

Unemployment Insurance, 140, 178
Unemployment Relief Act, 18, 87, 89
United Mine Workers of America (UMWA), 36, 142, 169
Upper Island Musical Festival, 17, 53, 164

Vancouver Coal Mining and Land Company (Vancouver Coal Company), 9, 33, 72, 112
Vancouver Island Regional Library. *See* Nanaimo Public Library
Van Houten, A. C., 52, 95
Victorian Order of Nurses, 169

Walloe, Einar, 159, 191
Wardill, Stan, 15, 25
Weeks, Thos. H., Weeks Motors Ltd., 13, 52, 69
Wellington, 9, 31, 60, 64, 125-26, 160, 182, 188
Western Fuel Company (WFC), 9, 11, 20-21, 29-30, 33, 35, 64, 90, 94, 98, 122, 194
Westwood, Earle, Dorothy (wife, née Planta), 85, 87, 111, 117, 157, 164-66, 173-75, 185, 194, 208-10
Wharton, Charles, 34-36, 125, 208
Williams, Parker, 38, 116
Williams, Dr. Seiriol, Ena (wife), 34-35, 100
Wilson, Edward Arthur. *See* Brother XII
Wipper, Harry, 196
Wong, Chuck, 188-89, 191-92

Yarrow, George, 33, 34

Zorkin, Dr. Mladen G., Joy (wife), 185, 197-98, 200

Photo Credits

Minister of Mines Report, 1925: p. 31

Nanaimo Community Archives: pp. 17 (1996-004-AP43), 53 (1993-051-M-PC1), 56 (1996-034-AP320), 89 (1995-021-A-PC22), 97 (1992-026-A-P84, Englefield Studio), 106 (1996-024-A-P46, Kin Jung Lee), 113 (1997-003-A-PC6), 138 (1992-026-A-P42), 160 (1998-014-A-P6), 171 (2000-012-A-PC2), 172 (1992-026-A-P21, Englefield Studio), 176 (City Hall Scrapbook), 181 (2000-010-A-PC1), 190 bottom (2001-014-A-P10, June and Dick Leahy), 198 (1992-026-A-P83), 199 (1992-026-A-P143, Englefield Studio), 200 (A-0503-1998-009-C-P58, with permission from A. Catto & Peirson), 201 (A0503-1998-009-C-P71, Englefield Studio)

Nanaimo District Museum: pp. 14 (C3-223), 32 (Q1-16), 35 (03-51), 63 (C1-30), 76 (I3-46), 91 (Q-3-14), 93 (N2-70, Lovick Studio), 103, (J-17), 107 (G1-105), 123 (M-34), 124 (L1-62), 130 (Q3-142), 167 (J1-10), 190 top

Pacific Biological Station: p. 46

Jill Stannard: p. 61

Service Above Self, Rotary Club. With permission: pp. 80, 195

B.J. Pettit: p. 119

George Lawlor: p. 148

Royle family: p. 182

Black Diamond City
Nanaimo—The Victorian Era
1-894384-51-2 $18.95

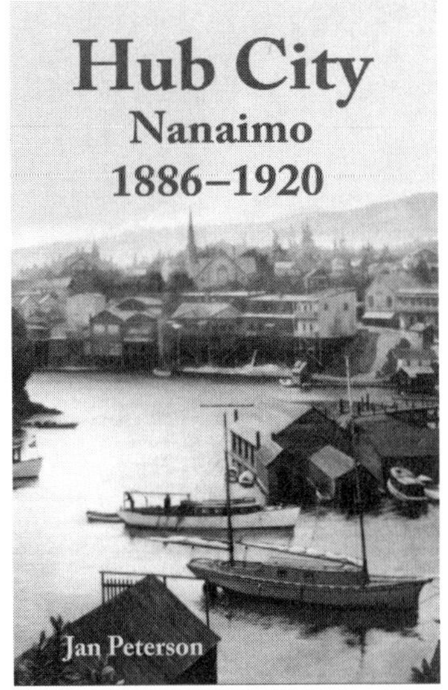

Hub City
Nanaimo—1886-1920
1-894384-66-0 $19.95

Brimming with well-documented facts and illustrated with archival photographs, Jan Peterson's trilogy on the history of Nanaimo, British Columbia, is required reading for anyone interested in the rich history of this Vancouver Island city.

Black Diamond City: Nanaimo—The Victorian Era chronicles the evolution of Nanaimo from its First Nations history and coal industry to its becoming a diversified Victorian-era community.

Hub City: Nanaimo—1886–1920 continues the story, tracing the city's development from the arrival of the Esquimalt & Nanaimo Railway to the end of the First World War.

Visit www.heritagehouse.ca for more great titles from Heritage House.

Jan Peterson was born in Scotland; she immigrated with her family to Kingston, Ontario, in 1957. In 1972 she moved to the Alberni Valley with her husband, Ray, and their three children. She is recognized for her many years of involvement in the arts and in community service, for her skill as an artist, and for her interest in history. Jan retired to Nanaimo in 1996, where she continues to research and write. She is the author of seven books: *The Albernis: 1860–1922*; *Twin Cities: Alberni–Port Alberni*; *Cathedral Grove: MacMillan Park*; *Journeys down the Alberni Canal to Barkley Sound*; *Black Diamond City: Nanaimo—The Victorian Era*; *Hub City: Nanaimo 1886–1920*; *Listen tae yer Granny: Scottish Folklore, Proverbs, Rhymes and Reminiscences.*